Internet and World Wide Web Simplified™

IDG's 3-D Visual™ Series

IDG Books Worldwide, Inc.
An International Data Group Company
Foster City, CA • Indianapolis • Braintree, MA • Chicago • Dallas

Internet and World Wide Web Simplified™

Published by
IDG Books Worldwide, Inc.
An International Data Group Company
919 E. Hillsdale Blvd., Suite 400
Foster City, CA 94404
(415) 655-3000

Library of Congress Catalog Card No.: 95-076876
ISBN: 1-56884-658-4
Printed in the United States of America
10 9 8 7 6 5 4 3 2

Distributed in the United States by IDG Books Worldwide, Inc.

Distributed by Computer and Technical Books in Miami, Florida, for South America and the Caribbean; by Longman Singapore in Singapore, Malaysia, Thailand, and Korea; by Toppan Co. Ltd. in Japan; by IDG Communications HK in Hong Kong; by WoodsLane Pty. Ltd. in Australia and New Zealand; and by Transworld Publishers Ltd. in the U.K. and Europe.

For general information on IDG Books in the U.S., including information on discounts and premiums, contact IDG Books at 800-762-2974 or 317-895-5200.

For U.S. Corporate Sales and quantity discounts, contact maranGraphics at 800-469-6616, ext. 206.

For information on international sales of IDG Books, contact Helen Saraceni at 415-655-3021, Fax number 415-655-3295.

For information on translations, contact Marc Jeffrey Mikulich, Director of Rights and Licensing, at IDG Books Worldwide. Fax Number 415-655-3295.

For sales inquiries and special prices for bulk quantities, write to the address above or call IDG Books Worldwide at 415-655-3000.

For information on using IDG Books in the classroom, or ordering examination copies, contact Jim Kelly at 800-434-2086.

U.S. Corporate Sales	**U.S. Trade Sales**
Contact maranGraphics at (800) 469-6616, ext. 206 or Fax (905) 890-9434.	Contact IDG Books at (800) 434-3422 or (415) 655-3000.

Trademark Acknowledgments

The animated characters are the copyright of maranGraphics, Inc.

IDG Books Worldwide, Inc., is a subsidiary of International Data Group. The officers are Patrick J. McGovern, Founder and Board Chairman; Walter Boyd, President. International Data Group's publications include: ARGENTINA'S Computerworld Argentina, Infoworld Argentina; AUSTRALIA'S Computerworld Australia, Australian PC World, Australian Macworld, Network World, Mobile Business Australia, Reseller, IDG Sources; AUSTRIA'S Computerwelt Oesterreich, PC Test; BRAZIL'S Computerworld, Gamepro, Game Power, Mundo IBM, Mundo Unix, PC World, Super Game; BELGIUM'S Data News (CW) BULGARIA'S Computerworld Bulgaria, Ediworld, PC & Mac World Bulgaria, Network World Bulgaria; CANADA'S CIO Canada, Computerworld Canada, Graduate Computerworld, InfoCanada, Network World Canada; CHILE'S Computerworld Chile, Informatica; COLOMBIA'S Computerworld Colombia, PC World; CZECH REPUBLIC'S Computerworld, Elektronika, PC World; DENMARK'S Communications World, Computerworld Danmark, Macintosh Produktkatalog, Macworld Danmark, PC World Danmark, PC World Produktguide, Tech World, Windows World; ECUADOR'S PC World Ecuador; EGYPT'S Computerworld (CW) Middle East, PC World Middle East; FINLAND'S MikroPC, Tietoviikko, Tietoverkko; FRANCE'S Distributique, GOLDEN MAC, InfoPC, Languages & Systems, Le Guide du Monde Informatique, Le Monde Informatique, Telecoms & Reseaux; GERMANY'S Computerwoche, Computerwoche Focus, Computerwoche Extra, Computerwoche Karriere, Information Management, Macwelt, Netzwelt, PC Welt, PC Woche, Publish, Unit; GREECE'S Infoworld, PC Games; HUNGARY'S Computerworld SZT, PC World; HONG KONG'S Computerworld Hong Kong, PC World Hong Kong; INDIA'S Computers & Communications; IRELAND'S ComputerScope; ISRAEL'S Computerworld Israel, PC World Israel; ITALY'S Computerworld Italia, Lotus Magazine, Macworld Italia, Networking Italia, PC Shopping, PC World Italia; JAPAN'S Computerworld Today, Information Systems World, Macworld Japan, Nikkei Personal Computing, SunWorld Japan, Windows World; KENYA'S East African Computer News; KOREA'S Computerworld Korea, Macworld Korea, PC World Korea; MEXICO'S Compu Edicion, Compu Manufactura, Computacion/Punto de Venta, Computerworld Mexico, MacWorld, Mundo Unix, PC World, Windows; THE NETHERLANDS' Computer! Totaal, Computable (CW), LAN Magazine, MacWorld, Totaal "Windows"; NEW ZEALAND'S Computer Listings, Computerworld New Zealand, New Zealand PC World, Network World; NIGERIA'S PC World Africa; NORWAY'S Computerworld Norge, C/World, Lotusworld Norge, Macworld Norge, Networld, PC World Ekspress, PC World Norge, PC World's Produktguide, Publish& Multimedia World, Student Data, Unix World, Windowsworld; IDG Direct Response; PAKISTAN'S PC World Pakistan; PANAMA'S PC World Panama; PERU'S Computerworld Peru, PC World; PEOPLE'S REPUBLIC OF CHINA'S China Computerworld, China Infoworld, Electronics Today/Multimedia World, Electronics International, Electronic Product World, China Network World, PC and Communications Magazine, PC World China, Software World Magazine, Telecom Product World; IDG HIGH TECH BEIJING'S New Product World; IDG SHENZHEN'S Computer News Digest; PHILIPPINES' Computerworld Philippines, PC Digest (PCW); POLAND'S Computerworld Poland, PC World/Komputer; PORTUGAL'S Cerebro/PC World, Correio Informatico/Computerworld, Informatica & Comunicacoes Catalogo, MacIn, Nacional de Produtos; ROMANIA'S Computerworld, PC World; RUSSIA'S Computerworld-Moscow, Mir - PC, Sety; SINGAPORE'S Computerworld Southeast Asia, PC World Singapore; SLOVENIA'S Monitor Magazine; SOUTH AFRICA'S Computer Mail (CIO),Computing S.A.,Network World S.A., Software World; SPAIN'S Advanced Systems, Amiga World, Computerworld Espana, Communicaciones World, Macworld Espana, NeXTWORLD, Super Juegos Magazine (GamePro), PC World Espana, Publish; SWEDEN'S Attack, ComputerSweden, Corporate Computing, Natverk & Kommunikation, Macworld, Mikrodatorn, PC World, Publishing & Design (CAP), Datalngenjoren, Maxi Data,Windows World; SWITZERLAND'S Computerworld Schweiz, Macworld Schweiz, PC Tip; TAIWAN'S Computerworld Taiwan, PC World Taiwan; THAILAND'S Thai Computerworld; TURKEY'S Computerworld Monitor, Macworld Turkiye, PC World Turkiye; UKRAINE'S Computerworld; UNITED KINGDOM'S Computing /Computerworld, Connexion/Network World, Lotus Magazine, Macworld, Open Computing/Sunworld; UNITED STATES' Advanced Systems, AmigaWorld, Cable in the Classroom, CD Review, CIO, Computerworld, Digital Video, DOS Resource Guide, Electronic Entertainment Magazine, Federal Computer Week, Federal Integrator, GamePro, IDG Books, Infoworld, Infoworld Direct, Laser Event, Macworld, Multimedia World, Network World, PC Letter, PC World, PlayRight, Power PC World, Publish, SWATPro, Video Event; VENEZUELA'S Computerworld Venezuela, PC World; VIETNAM'S PC World Vietnam

Screen Shot Acknowledgments

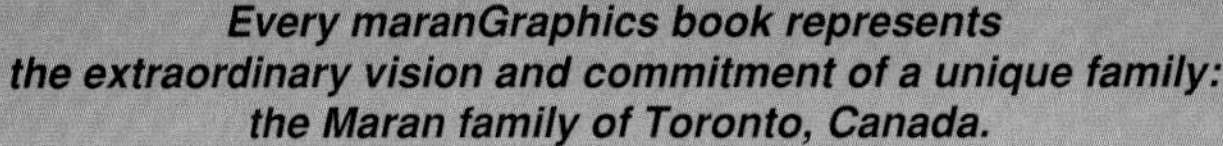

Every maranGraphics book represents the extraordinary vision and commitment of a unique family: the Maran family of Toronto, Canada.

Back Row (from left to right): *Sherry Maran, Rob Maran, Richard Maran, Maxine Maran, Jill Maran.*
Front Row (from left to right): *Judy Maran, Ruth Maran.*

Richard Maran is the company founder and its inspirational leader. He developed maranGraphics' proprietary communication technology called "visual grammar." This book is built on that technology—empowering readers with the easiest and quickest way to learn about computers.

Ruth Maran is the Author and Architect—a role Richard established that now bears Ruth's distinctive touch. She creates the words and visual structure that are the basis for the books.

Judy Maran is Senior Editor. She works with Ruth, Richard, and the highly talented maranGraphics illustrators, designers, and editors to transform Ruth's material into its final form.

Rob Maran is the Technical and Production Specialist. He makes sure the state-of-the-art technology used to create these books always performs as it should.

Sherry Maran manages the Reception, Order Desk, and any number of areas that require immediate attention and a helping hand.

Jill Maran is a jack-of-all-trades and dynamo who fills in anywhere she's needed anytime she's back from university.

Maxine Maran is the Business Manager and family sage. She maintains order in the business and family—and keeps everything running smoothly.

Oh, and three other family members are seated on the sofa. These graphic disk characters help make it fun and easy to learn about computers. They're part of the extended maranGraphics family.

Credits

Author & Architect:
Ruth Maran

Author of Web Section and Internet Consultant:
Neil Mohan

Newsgroup Section
Author: Gene Spafford
Editor: David C. Lawrence

Editors:
Judy Maran
Kelleigh Wing

Proofreaders:
Brad Hilderley
Paul Lofthouse

Layout Designer:
Christie Van Duin

Illustrators:
Tamara Poliquin
Chris K.C. Leung
Russell Marini
Andrew Trowbridge
Dave Ross
David de Haas

Indexer:
Mark Kmetzko

Post Production:
Robert Maran

Acknowledgments

Special thanks to Mark Siegel, Anthony Perry and Magic Online Services International.

Thanks to the dedicated staff of maranGraphics, including Brad Hilderley, Chris K.C. Leung, Paul Lofthouse, Alison MacAlpine, Jill Maran, Judy Maran, Maxine Maran, Robert Maran, Sherry Maran, Russ Marini, Greg Midensky, Tamara Poliquin, Andrew Trowbridge, Christie Van Duin, Kelleigh Wing, and Lorena Zupancic.

Finally, to Richard Maran who originated the easy-to-use graphic format of this guide. Thank you for your inspiration and guidance.

TABLE OF CONTENTS

CHAPTER 1

GETTING STARTED

CHAPTER 2

THE WORLD WIDE WEB

CHAPTER 3

ELECTRONIC MAIL

CHAPTER 4

NEWSGROUPS AND CHAT

TABLE OF CONTENTS

CHAPTER 5

FTP AND GOPHER

CHAPTER 6

ONLINE SECURITY AND SHOPPING

Once upon a time, in a land far,

INTRODUCTION TO THE INTERNET

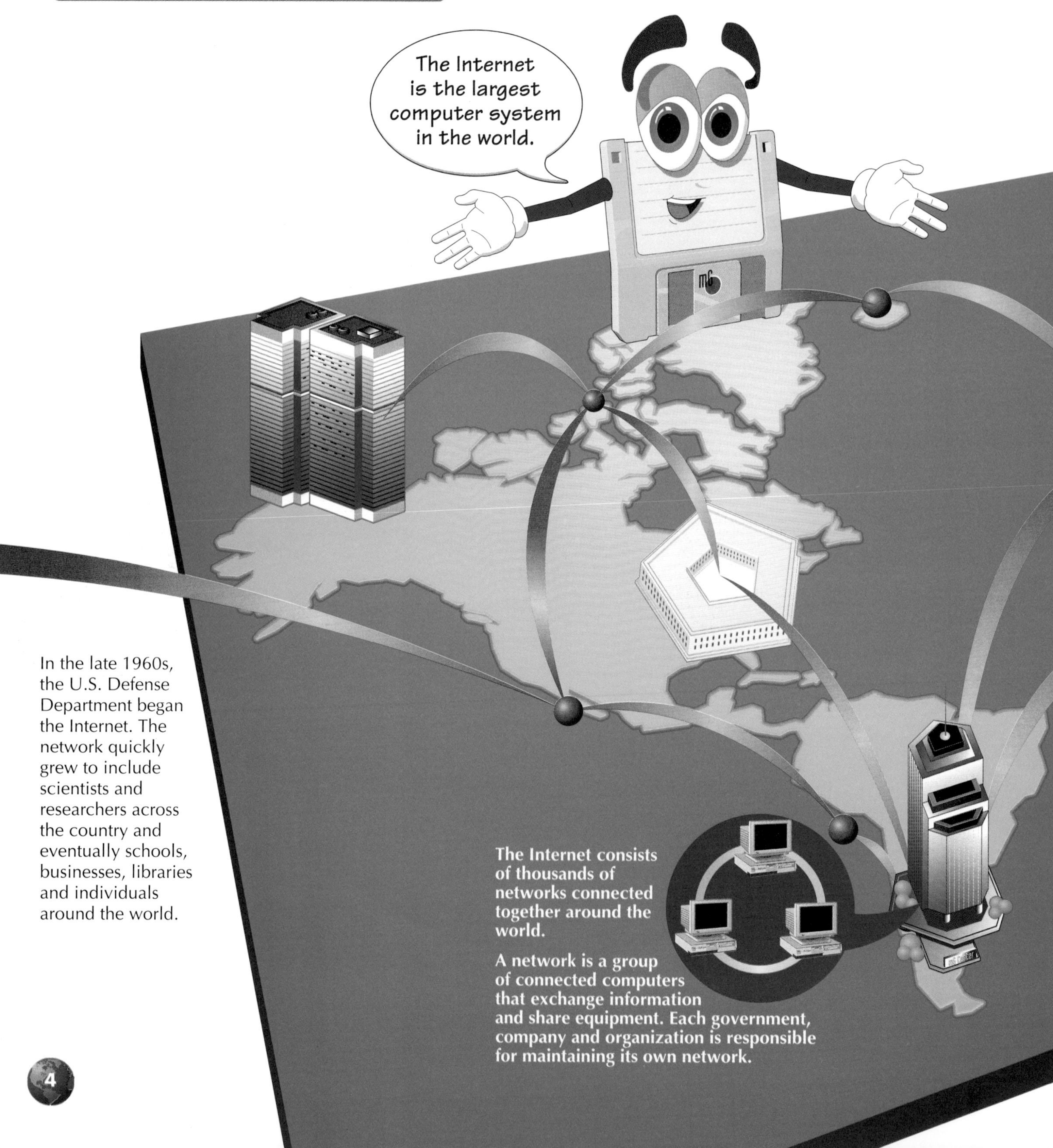

The Internet is the largest computer system in the world.
mG

In the late 1960s, the U.S. Defense Department began the Internet. The network quickly grew to include scientists and researchers across the country and eventually schools, businesses, libraries and individuals around the world.

The Internet consists of thousands of networks connected together around the world.

A network is a group of connected computers that exchange information and share equipment. Each government, company and organization is responsible for maintaining its own network.

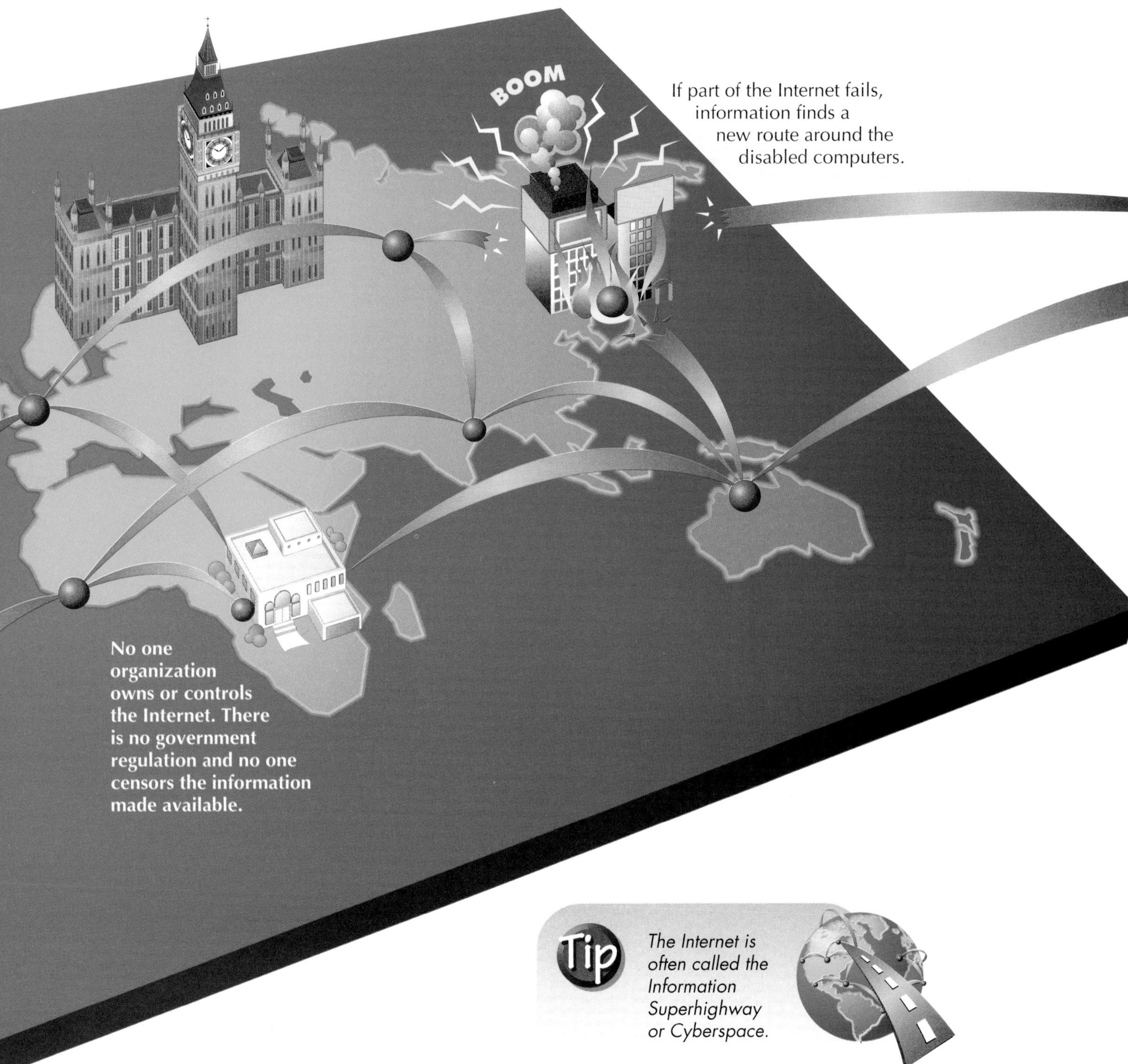

If part of the Internet fails, information finds a new route around the disabled computers.

No one organization owns or controls the Internet. There is no government regulation and no one censors the information made available.

Tip *The Internet is often called the Information Superhighway or Cyberspace.*

WHAT THE INTERNET OFFERS

The Internet offers many fun and exciting features.

ELECTRONIC MAIL

The Internet lets you exchange messages with people around the world. This can include friends, colleagues, family members, customers and even people you meet on the Internet. Electronic mail is fast, easy, inexpensive and saves paper. Exchanging electronic mail is the most popular feature on the Internet.

INFORMATION

You can get information on any subject imaginable. You can review newspapers, magazines, academic papers, government documents, television show transcripts, famous speeches, recipes, job listings, works by Shakespeare, airline schedules and much more.

PROGRAMS

Thousands of free programs are available on the Internet. These programs include word processors, spreadsheets, games and much more.

ENTERTAINMENT

Hundreds of simple games are available for free on the Internet. You can play backgammon, chess, poker, football and much more. The Internet also lets you review current movies, hear over 1,000 television theme songs, read the scripts of every Monty Python movie ever made and have interactive conversations with people around the world–even celebrities.

DISCUSSION GROUPS

The Internet lets you meet people around the world with similar interests. You can ask questions, discuss problems and read interesting stories. There are thousands of discussion groups on topics such as environment, food, humor, music, pets, photography, politics, religion, sports and television.

ONLINE SHOPPING

You can order goods and services on the Internet without ever leaving your desk. You can buy items such as flowers, books, used cars, computer programs, stocks, music CDs and pizza.

EQUIPMENT NEEDED

PROGRAMS

You need special programs to use the Internet. Most service providers give you the programs free of charge.

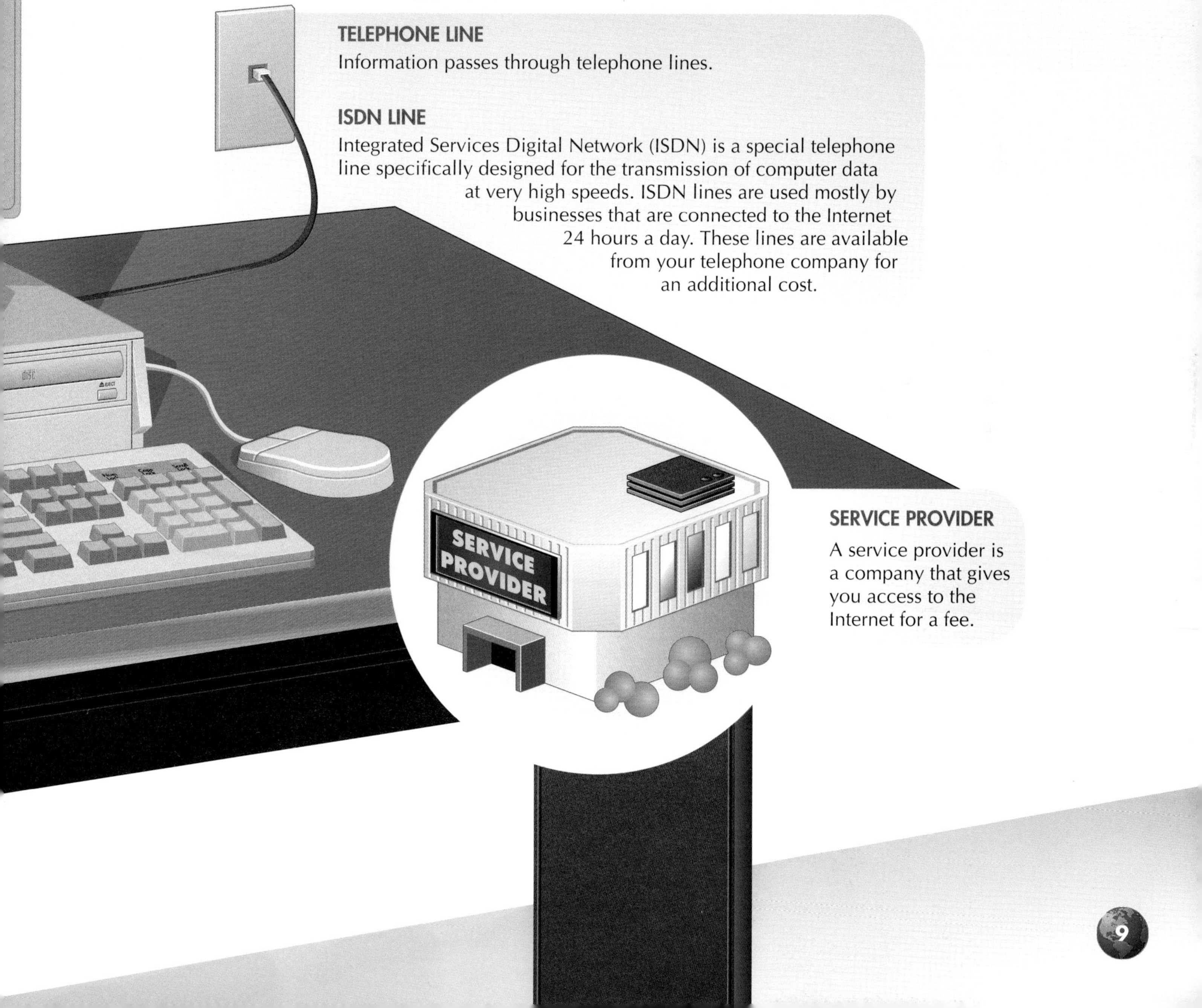

TELEPHONE LINE

Information passes through telephone lines.

ISDN LINE

Integrated Services Digital Network (ISDN) is a special telephone line specifically designed for the transmission of computer data at very high speeds. ISDN lines are used mostly by businesses that are connected to the Internet 24 hours a day. These lines are available from your telephone company for an additional cost.

SERVICE PROVIDER

SERVICE PROVIDER

A service provider is a company that gives you access to the Internet for a fee.

MODEMS

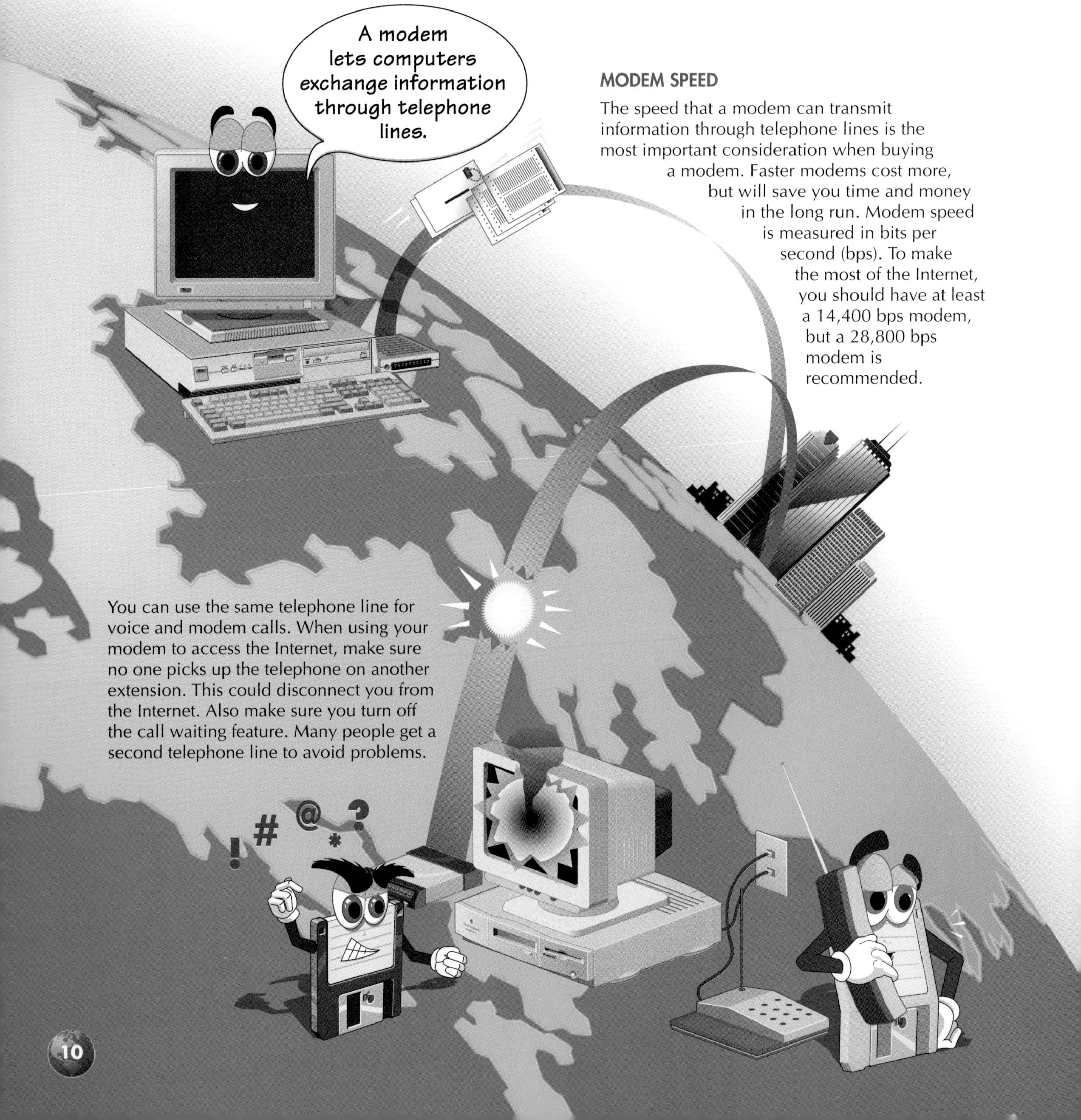

A modem lets computers exchange information through telephone lines.

MODEM SPEED

The speed that a modem can transmit information through telephone lines is the most important consideration when buying a modem. Faster modems cost more, but will save you time and money in the long run. Modem speed is measured in bits per second (bps). To make the most of the Internet, you should have at least a 14,400 bps modem, but a 28,800 bps modem is recommended.

You can use the same telephone line for voice and modem calls. When using your modem to access the Internet, make sure no one picks up the telephone on another extension. This could disconnect you from the Internet. Also make sure you turn off the call waiting feature. Many people get a second telephone line to avoid problems.

EXTERNAL AND INTERNAL MODEMS

EXTERNAL MODEM

An external modem is a small box that plugs into the back of a computer. An external modem takes up room on your desk, but you can use it with more than one computer.

INTERNAL MODEM

An internal modem is a special card that slides into a computer. It is less expensive than an external modem, but is more difficult to set up.

FAX MODEMS

Make sure you buy a modem with fax capabilities. A fax modem lets you send faxes from your computer to a fax machine or to another computer.

WHO PAYS FOR THE INTERNET?

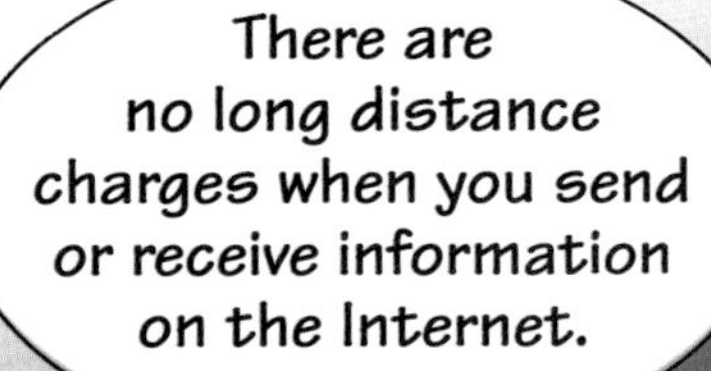

There are no long distance charges when you send or receive information on the Internet.

Once you pay for your connection to the Internet, you can exchange information free of charge.

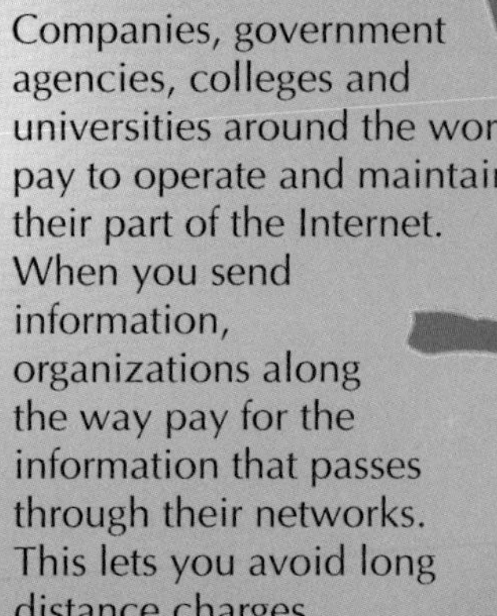

Companies, government agencies, colleges and universities around the world pay to operate and maintain their part of the Internet. When you send information, organizations along the way pay for the information that passes through their networks. This lets you avoid long distance charges.

WHO OFFERS FREE INFORMATION?

GOVERNMENTS

Governments offer information such as federal budgets and NASA reports to educate the public.

COLLEGES AND UNIVERSITIES

Colleges and universities make information such as journals and software available to the public.

COMPANIES

Companies offer free information to promote a good reputation and to interest you in their products. For example, Ford offers information about its cars and trucks on the Internet.

INDIVIDUALS

Individuals around the world offer information to give something back to the community. For example, one individual offers over one thousand television theme songs that you can access and hear for free on the Internet.

HOW INFORMATION TRANSFERS

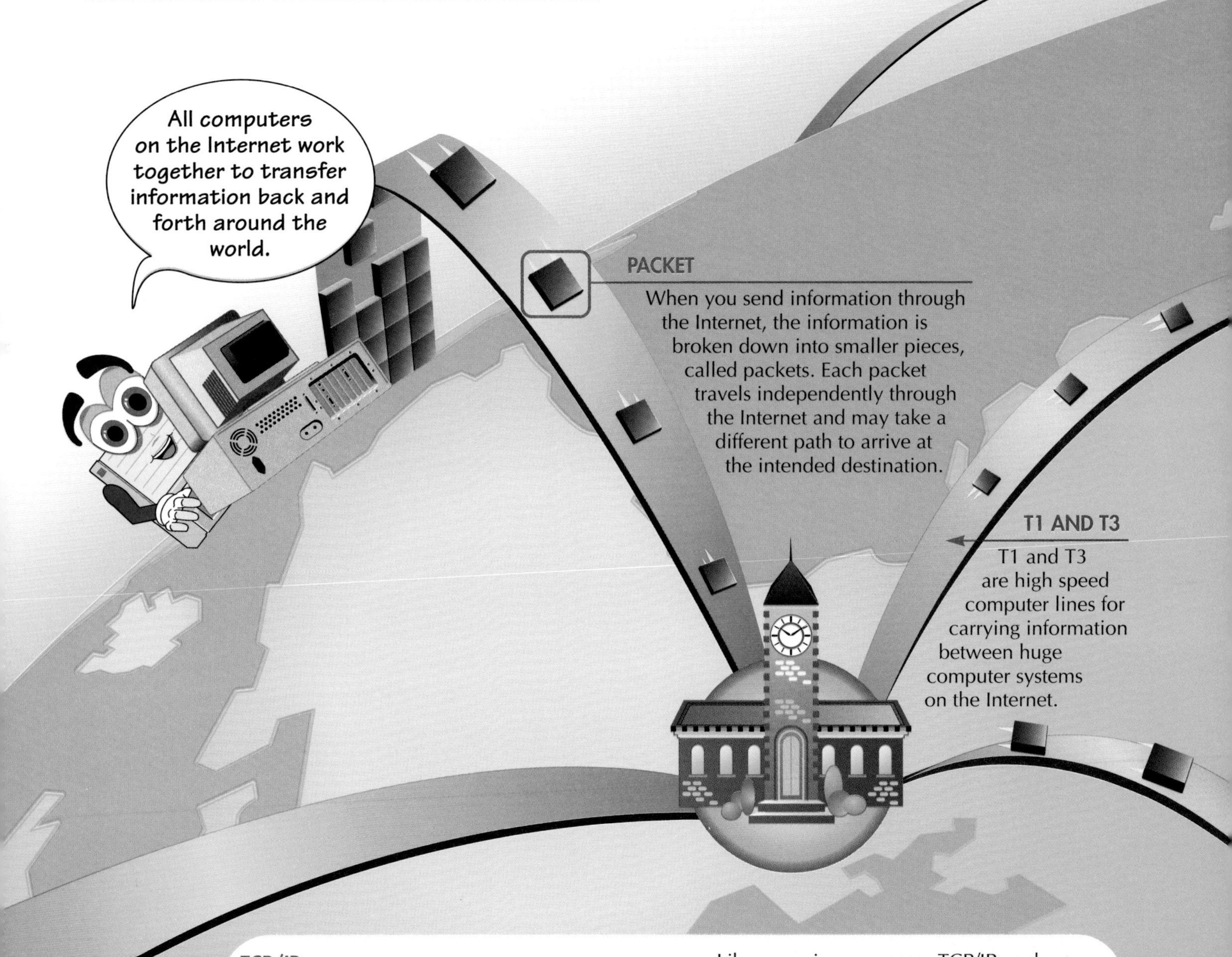

All computers on the Internet work together to transfer information back and forth around the world.

PACKET

When you send information through the Internet, the information is broken down into smaller pieces, called packets. Each packet travels independently through the Internet and may take a different path to arrive at the intended destination.

T1 AND T3

T1 and T3 are high speed computer lines for carrying information between huge computer systems on the Internet.

TCP/IP

Computers on the Internet communicate using a common language called TCP/IP, which stands for Transmission Control Protocol/ Internet Protocol.

Like a moving company, TCP/IP packages and addresses information and then ensures that the information arrives safely at the intended destination.

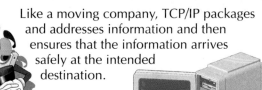

ROUTER

Routers are specialized computers that regulate the traffic on the Internet. A packet may pass through many routers before reaching its intended destination.

Like a good travel agent, a router picks the most efficient route, based on the traffic and the number of stopovers.

HOST

A host is any computer that is directly connected to the Internet.

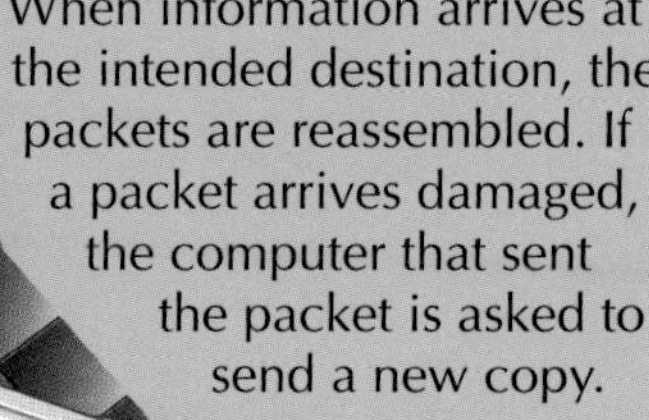

When information arrives at the intended destination, the packets are reassembled. If a packet arrives damaged, the computer that sent the packet is asked to send a new copy.

HOW TO CONNECT TO THE INTERNET

BULLETIN BOARD SYSTEM (BBS)

A bulletin board system (BBS) is usually a small computer system managed by one person or a local interest group.

Most BBSs let you use their services free of charge, but some charge a yearly fee.

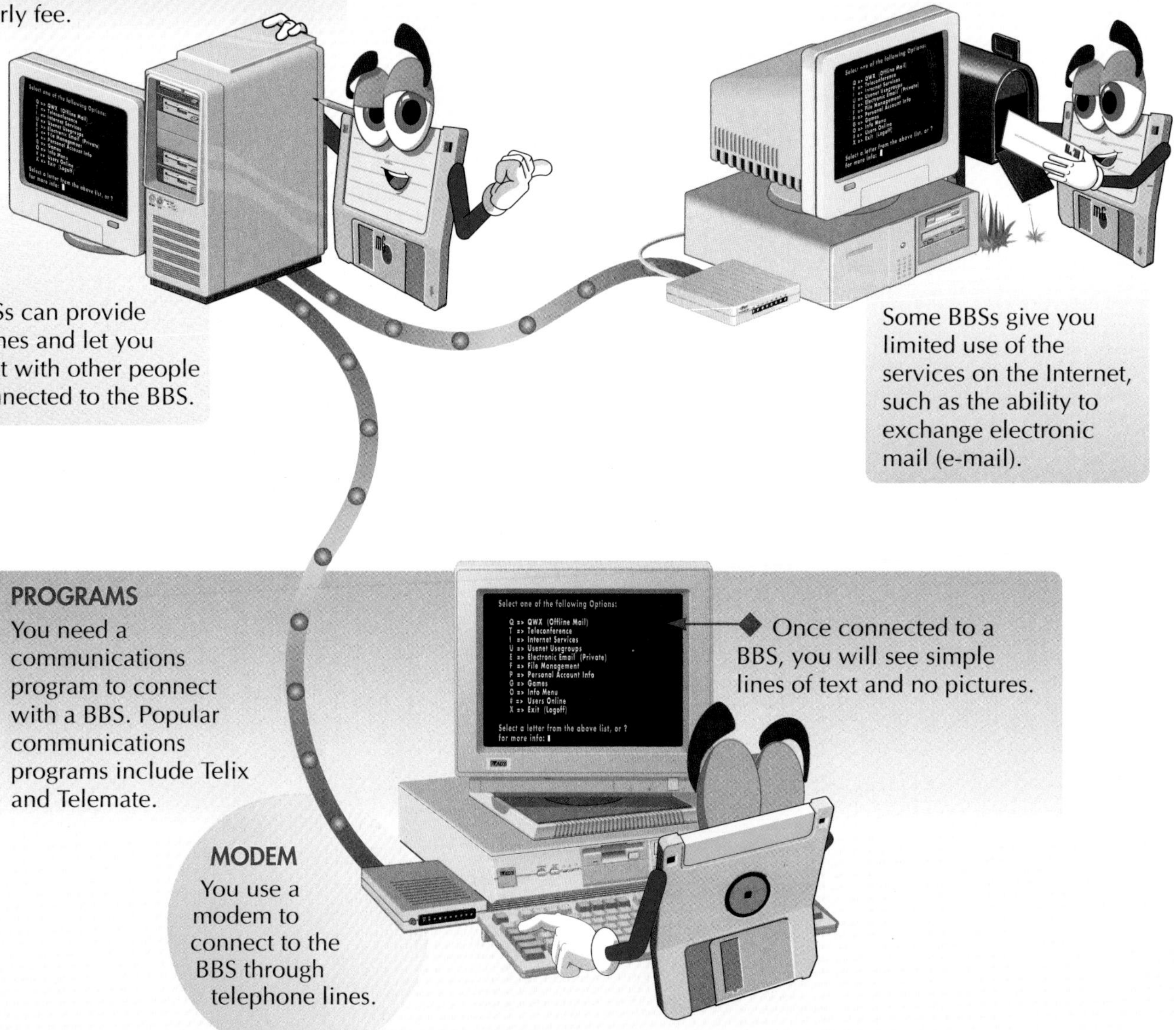

BBSs can provide games and let you chat with other people connected to the BBS.

Some BBSs give you limited use of the services on the Internet, such as the ability to exchange electronic mail (e-mail).

PROGRAMS

You need a communications program to connect with a BBS. Popular communications programs include Telix and Telemate.

◆ Once connected to a BBS, you will see simple lines of text and no pictures.

MODEM

You use a modem to connect to the BBS through telephone lines.

FREENET

A freenet is a bulletin board system (BBS) that provides free community information, such as current events and school calendars. Most freenets offer basic access to the Internet, such as the ability to exchange electronic mail (e-mail).

Freenets are supported by volunteers and local donations.

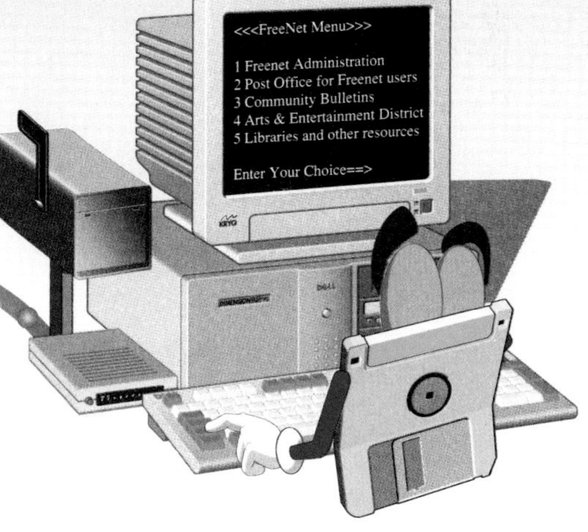

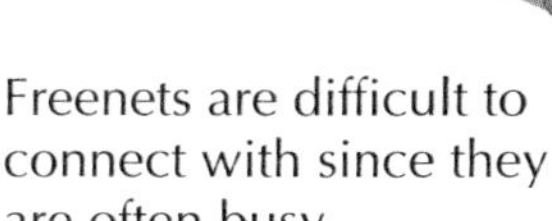

Freenets are difficult to connect with since they are often busy.

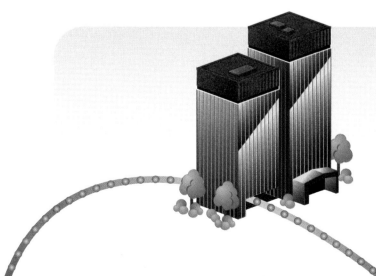

DIRECT CONNECTION

Universities, government agencies and large companies usually connect their computers directly to the Internet. This direct connection allows for very fast transmission of information and provides access to the Internet 24 hours a day.

HOW TO CONNECT TO THE INTERNET

COMMERCIAL ONLINE SERVICES

A commercial online service can give you access to the Internet for a fee.

Well-known commercial online services include America Online, CompuServe, The Microsoft Network and Prodigy.

A commercial online service also offers its own information, such as daily news, weather reports and encyclopedias. The information is well-organized and easy to find, unlike information on the Internet.

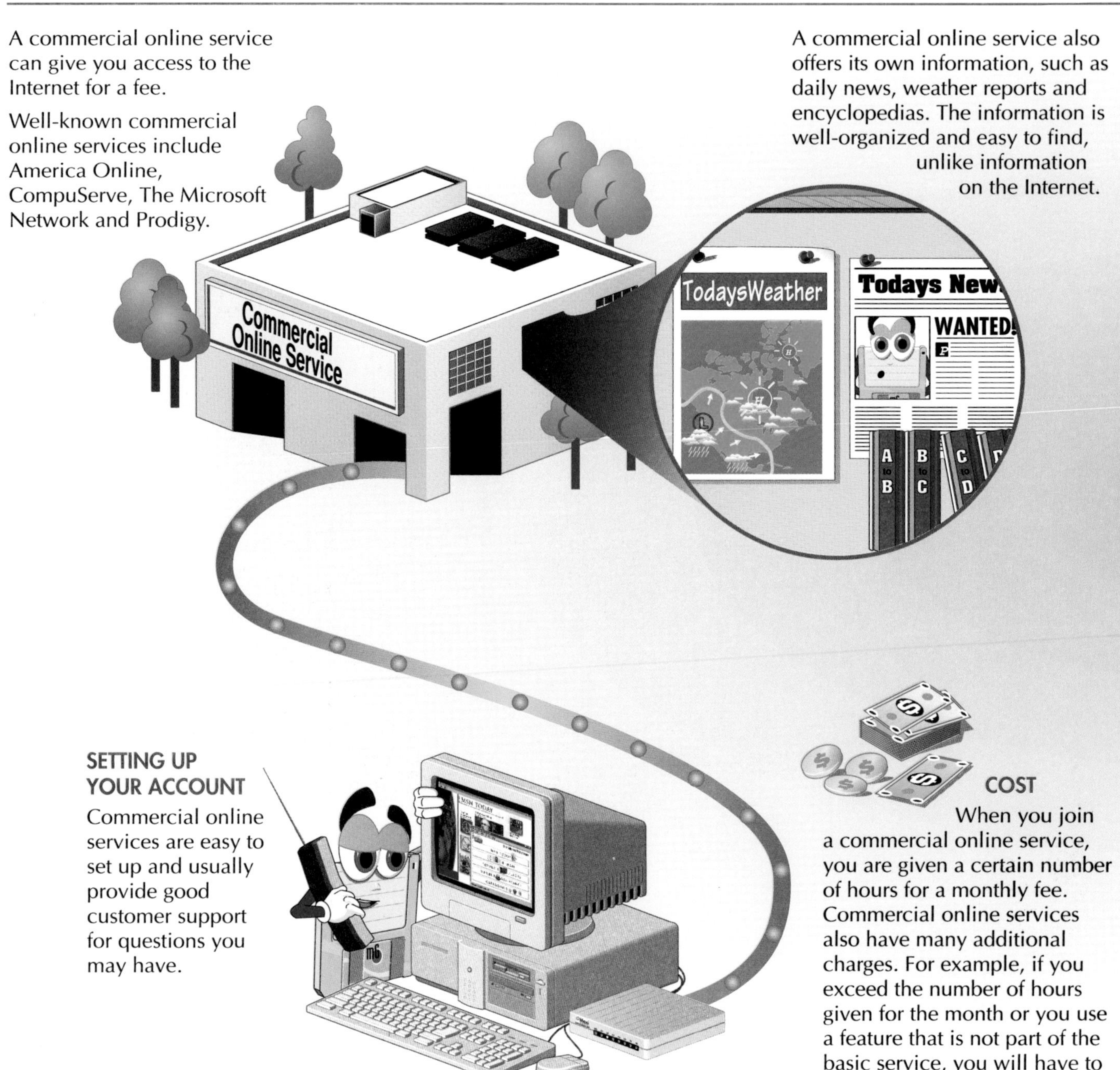

SETTING UP YOUR ACCOUNT

Commercial online services are easy to set up and usually provide good customer support for questions you may have.

COST

When you join a commercial online service, you are given a certain number of hours for a monthly fee. Commercial online services also have many additional charges. For example, if you exceed the number of hours given for the month or you use a feature that is not part of the basic service, you will have to pay extra.

America Online

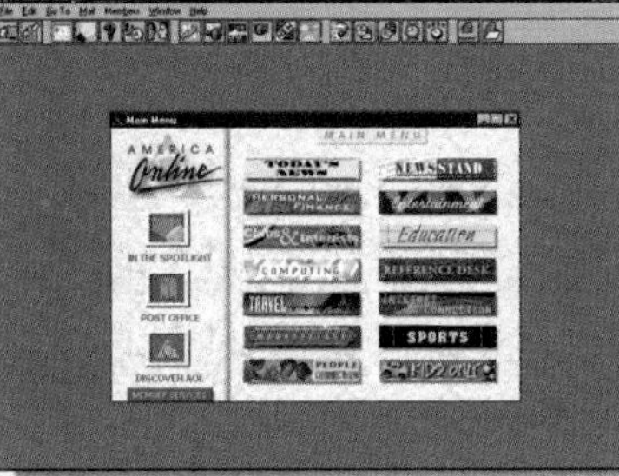

Prodigy

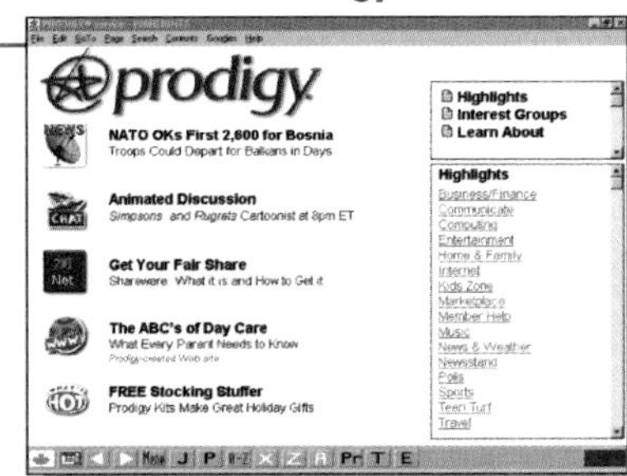

PROGRAMS

Commercial online services provide the programs you will need to use the service and access the Internet.

The Microsoft Network

CompuServe

MODEM

You use a modem to connect to a commercial online service through telephone lines. Choose a service with a local telephone number to avoid long distance charges.

If you plan on using the Internet regularly, connect through an Internet service provider, not a commercial online service. This will save you money.

Note: For information on Internet service providers, refer to page 20.

HOW TO CONNECT TO THE INTERNET

INTERNET SERVICE PROVIDERS

An Internet Service Provider (ISP) is a company that gives you access to the Internet for a fee.

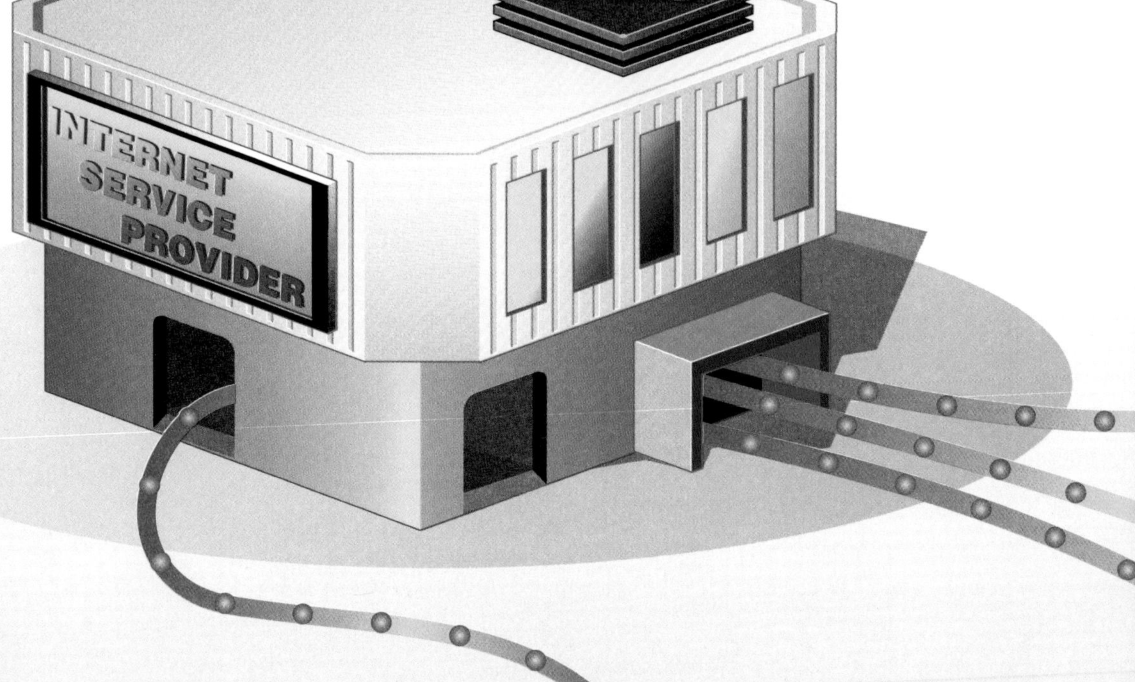

SETTING UP YOUR ACCOUNT

Connecting to the Internet through a service provider can be difficult to set up. Most providers offer assistance over the telephone to help you get connected.

Most providers charge a fee for setting up your account. This fee is usually between $10 and $40.

MODEM

You use a modem to connect to a service provider through telephone lines. Choose a provider with a local telephone number to avoid long distance charges.

You need at least a 14,400 bps modem, but a 28,800 bps modem is recommended.

WAYS TO CONNECT

There are three main ways you can connect to an Internet service provider. Some providers let you choose the type of connection you can use.

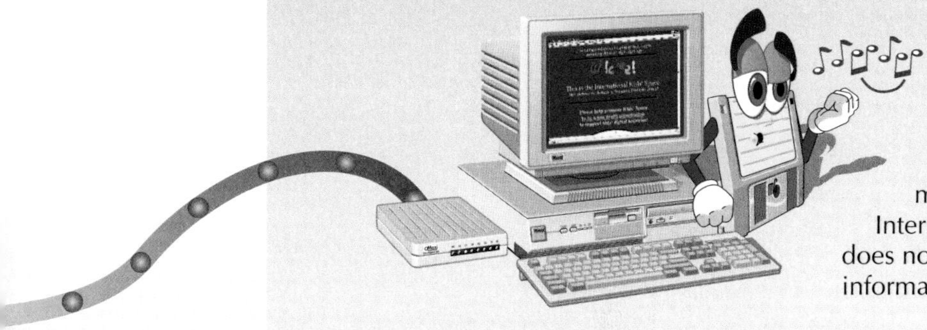

SLIP

Serial Line Internet Protocol. The oldest and most popular method of connecting to an Internet service provider. SLIP does not check to make sure that information arrives error free.

CSLIP

Compressed SLIP. The same as SLIP except the information is squeezed together to speed the transfer of data.

PPP

Point-to-Point Protocol. A newer method that is more reliable than SLIP since it checks that information arrives error free. PPP is also faster and provides better security.

HOW TO CONNECT TO THE INTERNET

INTERNET SERVICE PROVIDERS

PROGRAMS

Most Internet service providers supply you with the programs you will need to use the Internet. You can also buy the programs at computer stores.

You will need three types of programs.

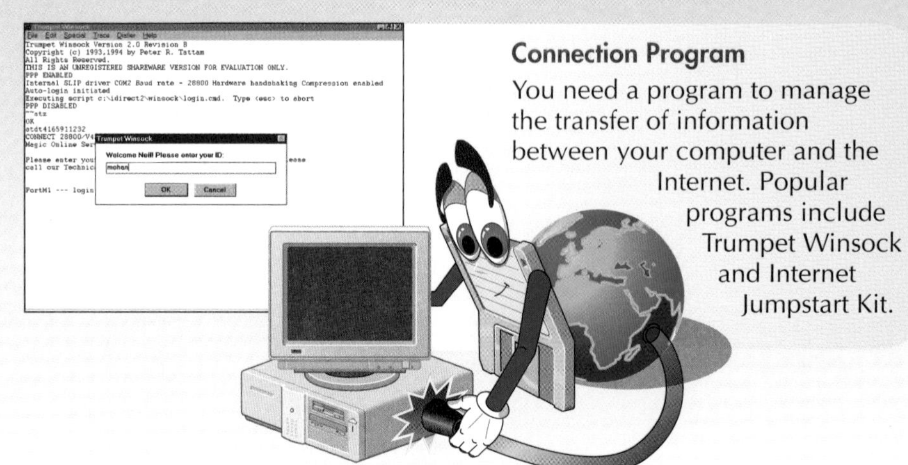

Connection Program

You need a program to manage the transfer of information between your computer and the Internet. Popular programs include Trumpet Winsock and Internet Jumpstart Kit.

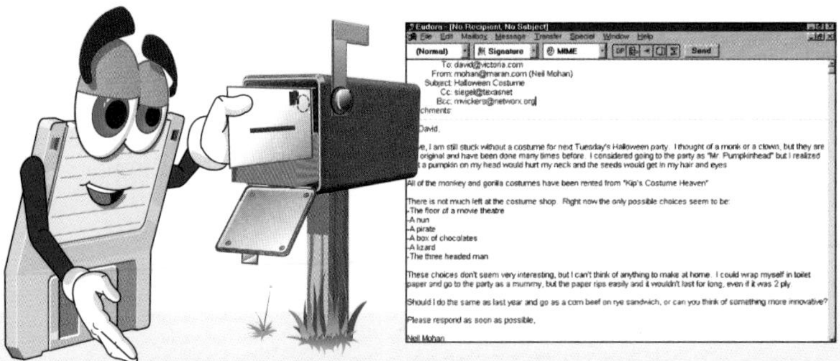

E-Mail Program

You need a program to send and receive electronic mail (e-mail) over the Internet. Eudora is currently the most popular program.

Browser

You need a program to view and explore information on the Internet. Netscape is currently the most popular program.

COST

Cost is an important consideration when choosing an Internet service provider.

Service providers give you a certain number of hours per day or month. Generally, 2 hours a day or 40 hours a month is enough for most people.

Service providers usually charge between $10 and $30 per month or a few hundred dollars per year.

If you exceed the total number of hours, you are usually charged for every extra hour you are on the Internet. The charge can range from 25¢ to $3 an hour.

Some large providers let you use the Internet free of charge during off-peak hours, such as 11 p.m. to 8 a.m.

DYNAMIC AND STATIC ADDRESSING

The location of your account on the Internet can change (dynamic) or remain the same at all times (static). Dynamic accounts are less expensive and ideal for most people, while static accounts are recommended for advanced users and companies.

USER-TO-LINE RATIO

Ask the service provider how likely you are to get a busy signal when you try to connect. The user-to-line ratio tells you how many people there are for every telephone line. A good ratio is 15 to 1. If there are more than 15 people for each telephone line, you may get a busy signal when you try to connect.

SERVICE PROVIDER LISTING

Here are some service providers that can give you access to the Internet. You can also find service providers in phone books, local newspapers and magazines.

AUSTRALIA

Melbourne, Australia

Internet Interface Systems	(03) 9.525.0922
NetSpace	(03) 9889.1122

Sydney, Australia

Geko	(02) 439.1999
Magnadata	(02) 264.7326

CANADA

Calgary, Alberta

Canada Connect	(403) 777-2025
InterNode	(403) 296-1190

Halifax, Nova Scotia

Atlantic Connect	(902) 429-0222
ISIS	(902) 429-4747

Montreal, Quebec

CAMontreal	(514) 288-2581
Infobahn Online	(514) 481-2585

Ottawa, Ontario

Cyberus Online	(613) 233-1215
Internet Connectivity	(613) 828-6221

Regina, Saskatchewan

SASKNet	1-800-644-9205
Unibase Telecom Ltd	(306) 789-9007

Toronto, Ontario

Internet Direct	(416) 233-7150
Magic Online Services	(416) 591-6490

Vancouver, British Columbia

Internet Direct	(604) 691-1600
ProNET	(604) 688-9282

Winnipeg, Manitoba

Escape	(204) 925-4290
Magic Online Services	(204) 949-7777

IRELAND

Cork Online Services	(021) 277124
Ireland Online	(01) 855.1739

JAPAN

Global Online Japan	(03) 5330.9380
Twics Internet	(03) 3351.5977

SINGAPORE

Pacific Internet	872.1455
Sing NET	730.8079

SOUTH AFRICA

Internet Africa	(21) 683.4370
Internet Solutions	(12) 841.2530

UNITED KINGDOM

Atlas Internet	(0171) 312.0400
Demon Systems	(0181) 349.0063
EasyNet	(0171) 209.0990
ZyNet	(1392) 426160

UNITED STATES

Albany, New York

AlbanyNet	(518) 465-0873
NetHeaven	(518) 885-1295

Albuquerque, New Mexico

CyberPort	(505) 324-6400
Route 66	(505) 343-1060

Anchorage, Alaska

Corcom	(907) 563-1191
MicroNET	(907) 279-0051

Atlanta, Georgia

Intergate	(404) 429-9599
Internet Atlanta	(404) 410-9000

Baltimore, Maryland

Clark Net	(410) 254-3900
CharmNet	(410) 558-3900

Birmingham, Alabama

Internet Connect	(205) 722-0199
interQuest	(205) 464-8280

Boston, Massachusetts

Cyber Access	(617) 396-0491
Xensei	(617) 376-6342

Buffalo, New York

Access Global	(716) 694-5029
Moran Communications Group	(716) 639-1254

Charleston, South Carolina

Netside Network	(803) 732-7757
SC SuperNet	(803) 748-1207

Chicago, Illinois

NetWave	1-800-961-WAVE
Tezcat Communications	(312) 850-0181

Cincinnati, Ohio

Internet Cincinnati	(513) 887-8877
ONEnet Communications	(513) 326-6000

Cleveland, Ohio

ExchangeNET	(216) 615-9400
Multiverse	(216) 344-3080

Dallas,Texas

Dallas Internet	(214) 881-9595
I-Link	(512) 388-2393

Denver, Colorado

Envisionet	(303) 770-2408
Indra's Net	(303) 546-9151

Des Moines, Iowa

Des Moines Internet	(515) 270-9191
eCITY	(515) 277-1990

Detroit, Michigan

MichNET	(313) 764-9430
Msen	(313) 998-4562

Hartford, Connecticut

imagine.com	(203) 527-9245
Miracle Communications	(203) 523-5677

Honolulu, Hawaii

Hawaii Online	(808) 533-6981
HulaNet	(808) 524-7717

Houston, Texas

Digital Mainstream	(713) 364-1819
Nettap	(713) 482-3903

UNITED STATES (CONTINUED)

Indianapolis, Indiana

IndyNet (317) 251-5208
Net Direct (317) 251-5252

Jackson, Mississippi

Internet Doorway (601) 952-1570
TEC Link 1-800-701-3472

Jersey City, New Jersey

Eclipse (908) 412-0700
NovaSys (201) 887-8189

Kansas City, Missouri

SKYNet (816) 421-2626
Socket Services (314) 499-9131

Las Vegas, Nevada

Access Nevada (702) 294-0480
InterMind (702) 878-6111

Little Rock, Arkansas

Axess Providers (501) 225-6901
Internet Partners (501) 785-0300

Los Angeles, California

LA Internet (310) 442-4670
LightSide (818) 858-9261

Louisville, Kentucky

IgLou Internet (502) 966-3848
The Point (812) 246-7187

Memphis, Tennessee

Edge Net (615) 726-8700
Telalink (615) 321-9100

Miami, Florida

CyberGate (305) 428-4283
World Network (305) 535-3090

Milwaukee, Wisconsin

Axis Net (414) 290-AXIS
Internet Connect (414) 476-ICON

Minneapolis, Minnesota

Minnesota MicroNet (612) 882-7711
Minnesota Online (612) 225-1110

Missoula, Montana

Internet Connect (406) 721-4952
Netrix (406) 257-INET

New Orleans, Louisiana

AccessCom (504) 887-0022
Communique (504) 527-6200

New York City, New York

Interport (212) 989-1128
Pipeline (212) 267-3636

Newark, New Jersey

Internet Online Services (201) 928-1000
New Jersey Internet (201) 697-3338

Norfolk, Virginia

InfiNET 1-800-849-7214
UUNet (703) 206-5600

Oklahoma City, Oklahoma

InterConnect Online (405) 949-1800
Internet Oklahoma (405) 721-1580

Omaha, Nebraska

Nebraska Onramp (402) 339-NEON
Probe Technology (402) 593-9800

Philadelphia, Pennsylvania

Net Access (215) 576-8669
VoiceNET (215) 674-9290

Phoenix, Arizona

Internet Direct 1-800-879-3624
PrimeNet (602) 395-1010

Pittsburgh, Pennsylvania

CityNET (412) 481-5406
Pittsburgh Online (412) 681-6130

Portland, Maine

InternetMaine (207) 780-0416
MaineStreet (207) 657-5078

Portland, Oregon

Teleport (503) 223-0076
Transport Logic (503) 243-1940

Providence, Rhode Island

CompUtopia	(401) 732-5588
Log On America	(401) 453-6100

Raleigh-Durham, North Carolina

Interpath	1-800-849-6305
Vnet	1-800-377-3282

Riverton, Wyoming

NETConnect	(801) 865-7032
Wyoming Internet	(307) 332-3030

Sacramento, California

NSNet	(916) 856-1530
Sacramento Network Access	(916) 565-4500

Salt Lake City, Utah

AROSnet	(801) 532-AROS
Internet Alliance	(801) 964-8490

San Antonio, Texas

Internet Direct	(210) 308-9800
Texas Net	(210) 272-8111

San Diego, California

ConnectNET	(619) 450-0254
ElectriCiti	(619) 338-9000

San Francisco, California

CRL Network Services	(415) 837-5300
San Francisco Online	(415) 861-7712

San Jose, California

a2I Communications	(408) 293-8078
AbleCOM	(408) 441-6000

Seattle, Washington

Northwest Nexus	1-800-539-3505
Seanet	(206) 343-7828

St. Paul, Minnesota

WaveFront	(612) 638-9594
Winternet	(612) 941-9177

Tampa Bay, Florida

Florida Online	1-800-676-2599
SuperNet	1-800-746-0777

Tucson, Arizona

Internet Direct	(602) 274-0100
RTD Systems	(602) 318-0696

Washington, D.C.

CrossLink	(703) 642-1120
Internet Interstate	(301) 652-4468

Wichita, Kansas

FutureNet	(316) 652-0070
SouthWind	(316) 263-7963

Wilmington, Delaware

DCANET	(302) 654-1019
Internet Delaware	(302) 737-1001

NORTH AMERICAN PROVIDERS

There are also providers that service both Canada and the United States.

America Online	1-800-827-6364
CompuServe	1-800-848-8990
Delphi	1-800-695-4005
Microsoft Network	1-800-386-5550
NETCOM	1-800-353-6600
Portal Information Network	1-800-433-6444
Prodigy	1-800-PRODIGY
PSINET	1-800-827-7482

In this chapter you will learn about the World Wide Web and the vast amount of information it offers.

CHAPTER 2

THE WORLD WIDE WEB

 Introduction to the World Wide Web

 Web Browser

 Hypertext

 Explore the Web

URL

 Graphics

 Sound and Video

 Virtual Worlds

 Yahoo

 Lycos

 WebCrawler

INTRODUCTION TO THE WORLD WIDE WEB

You need a high-speed modem to use the World Wide Web. You should have at least a 14,400 bps modem.

Note: For information on modems, refer to page 10.

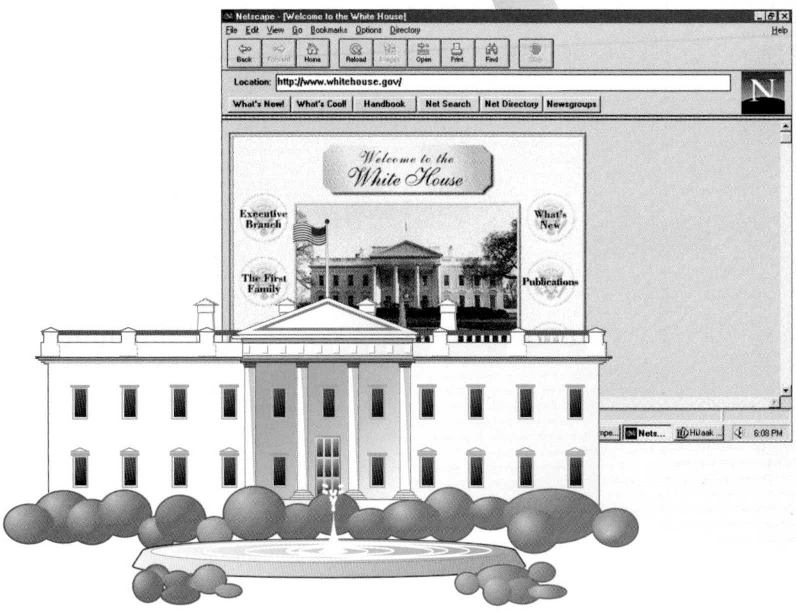

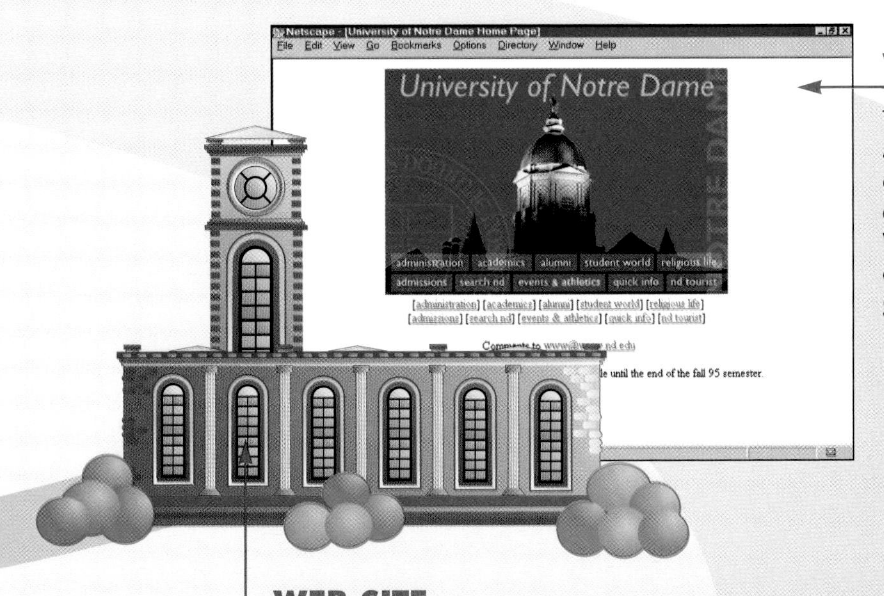

WEB PAGE

The World Wide Web consists of a huge collection of documents, called Web pages, that are stored on computers around the world. Web pages provide a vast amount of information and can include graphics, sound and even movies.

WEB SITE

A Web site is a university, government agency or company that stores Web pages you can view.

The World Wide Web is also called WWW or W3.

WEB BROWSER

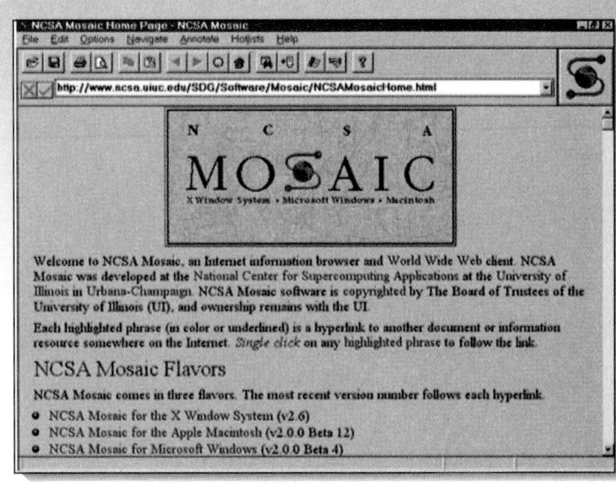

NCSA MOSAIC

NCSA Mosaic™ was the first graphical Web browser.

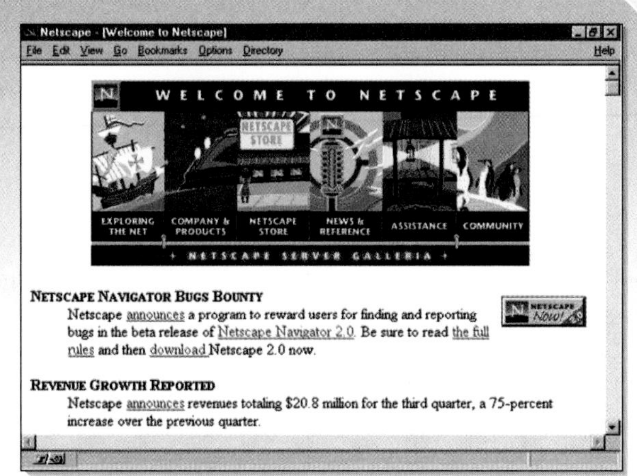

NETSCAPE NAVIGATOR

Netscape Navigator is currently the most popular Web browser.

HYPERTEXT

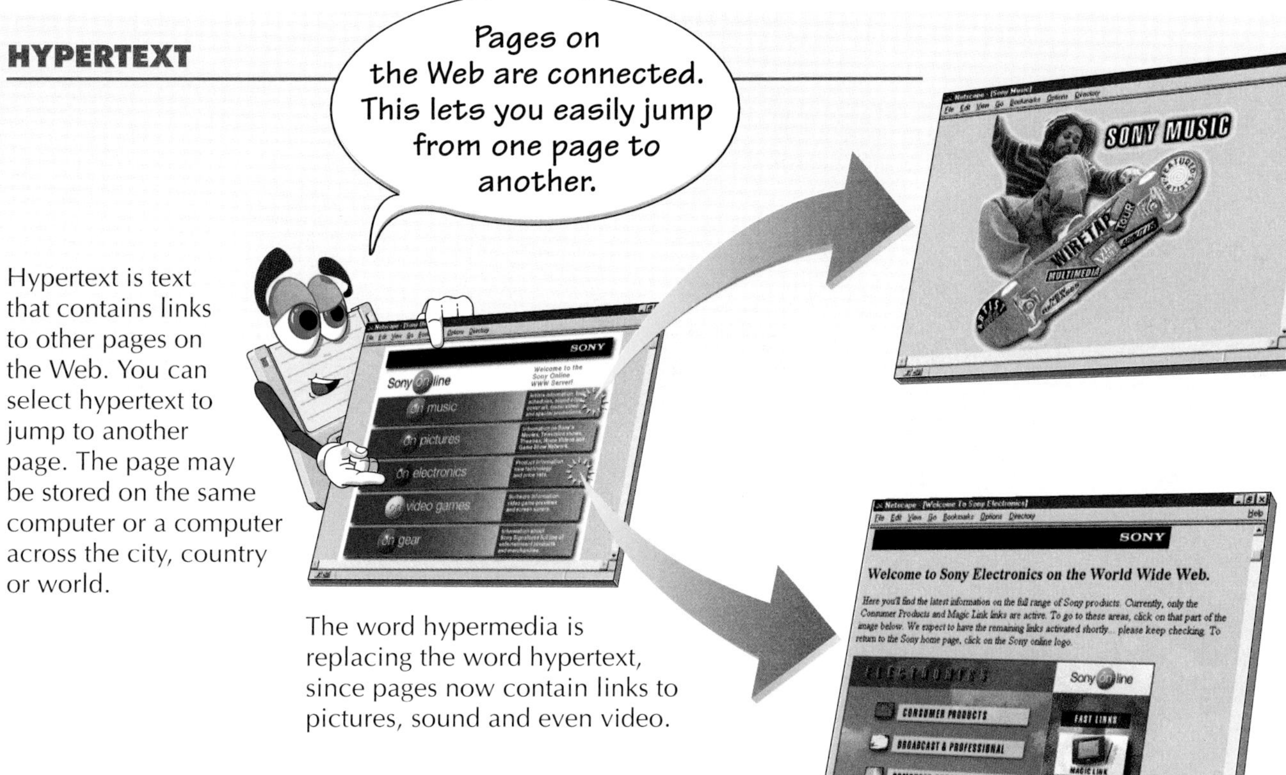

Pages on the Web are connected. This lets you easily jump from one page to another.
SONY MUSIC
SONY
Welcome to Sony Electronics on the World Wide Web.

Hypertext is text that contains links to other pages on the Web. You can select hypertext to jump to another page. The page may be stored on the same computer or a computer across the city, country or world.

The word hypermedia is replacing the word hypertext, since pages now contain links to pictures, sound and even video.

HTML

HyperText Markup Language (HTML) is a programming language used to create pages on the Web. HTML creates links between Web pages and defines how text and graphics will appear on a page.

EXPLORE THE WEB

EXPLORE THE WEB

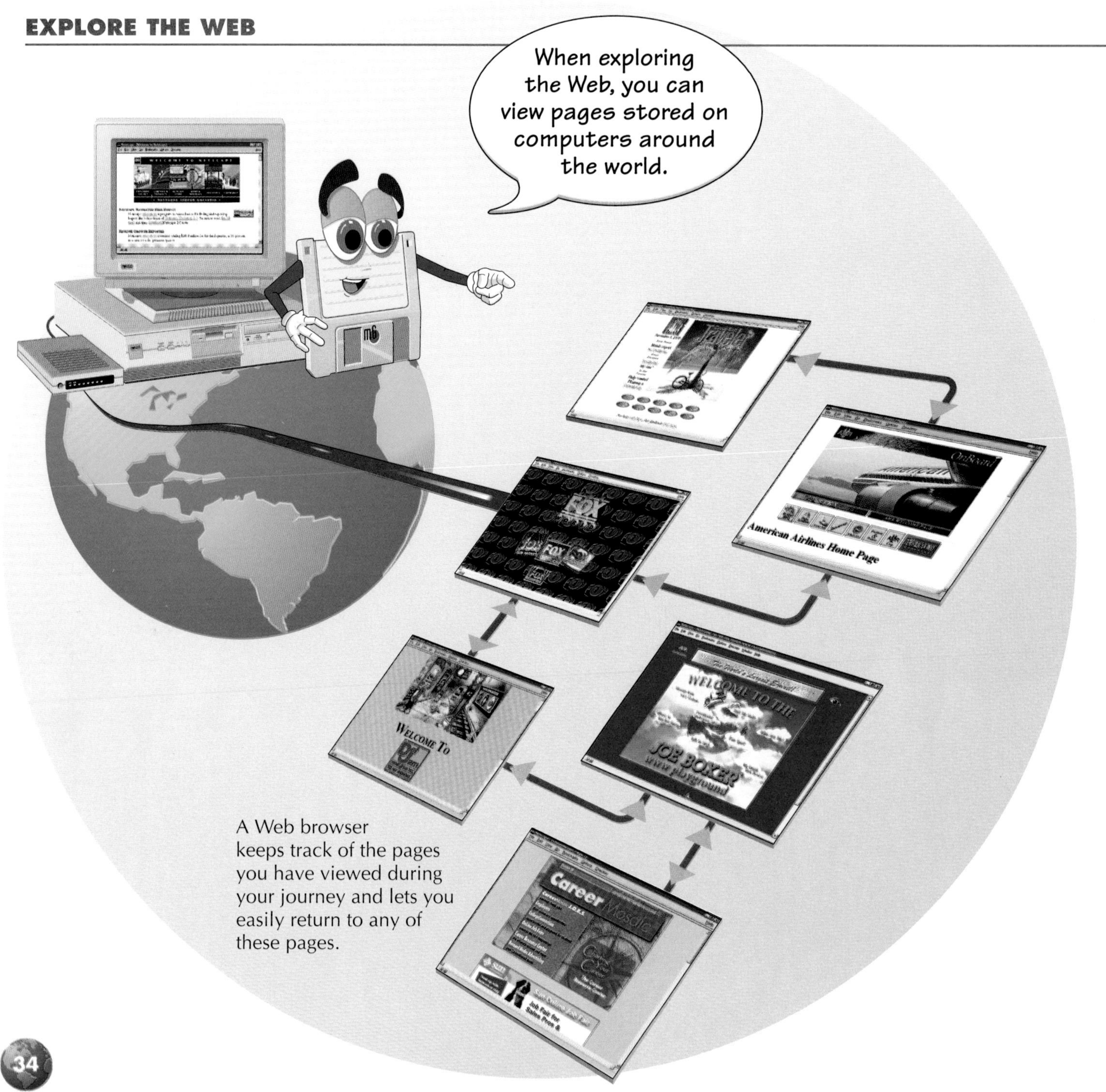
When exploring the Web, you can view pages stored on computers around the world.
American Airlines Home Page
WELCOME TO THE
JOE BOXER
Career Mosaic

A Web browser keeps track of the pages you have viewed during your journey and lets you easily return to any of these pages.

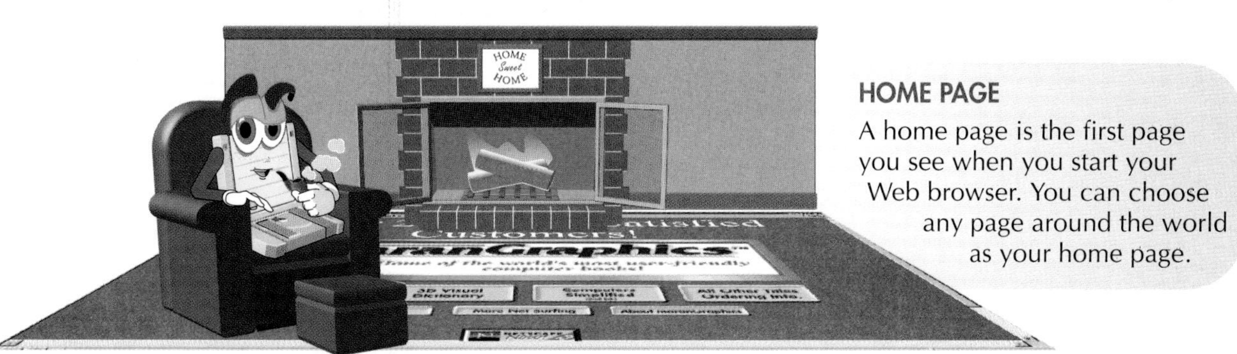

HOME PAGE

A home page is the first page you see when you start your Web browser. You can choose any page around the world as your home page.

THE HISTORY LIST

The history list displays a list of all the pages you have viewed since the last time you started your Web browser. The history list lets you instantly go to any of the pages listed.

BOOKMARKS

You can keep a list of all your favorite Web pages. This lets you quickly return to these pages at any time.

Each Web browser has a different name for this feature.

- Netscape calls this feature **bookmarks**.
- NCSA Mosaic calls this feature **hotlists**.
- Microsoft's Internet Explorer calls this feature **favorites**.

URL

Each page on the Web has a unique address, called the Uniform Resource Locator (URL).
This way!
Pink Floyd

You can instantly display a Web page that you have heard or read about by entering its URL. This page can be stored anywhere around the world.

The use of upper and lower case letters must be exact.

A URL consists of several parts.

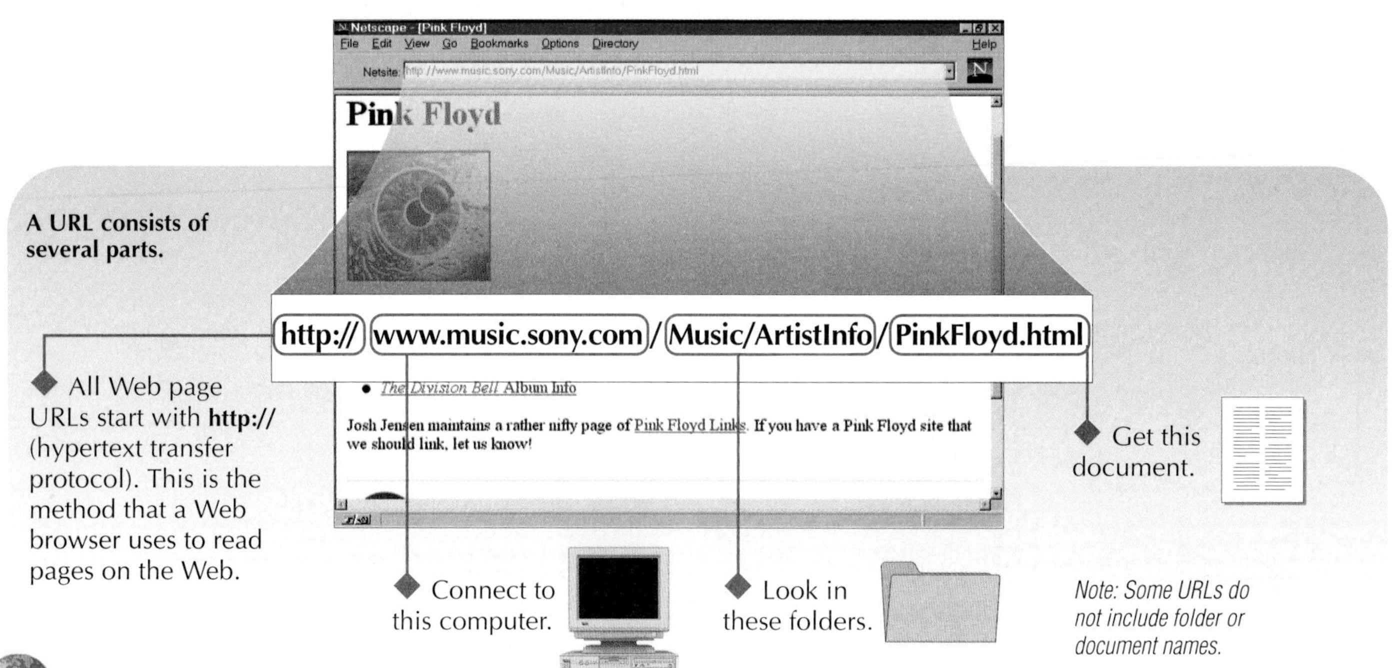

- All Web page URLs start with **http://** (hypertext transfer protocol). This is the method that a Web browser uses to read pages on the Web.
- Connect to this computer.
- Look in these folders.
- Get this document.

Note: Some URLs do not include folder or document names.

GRAPHICS

You can view graphics such as album covers, pictures of celebrities and famous paintings on the Web.

The most common types of graphics files on the Web are:

- Graphics Interchange Format (GIF)
- Joint Photographic Expert Group (JPEG)

10 SECONDS

Text transfers quickly to your computer. This lets you start reading the text on a page right away.

30 SECONDS

Graphics transfer more slowly.

1 MINUTE

You may have to wait a while to clearly view the graphics.

GRAPHICS ON

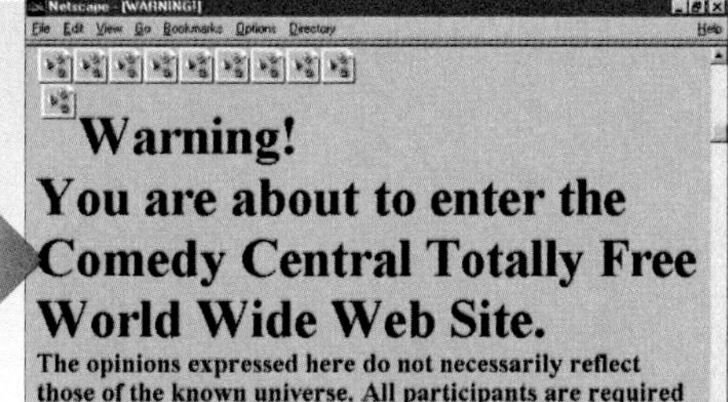

GRAPHICS OFF

TURN OFF GRAPHICS

Graphics on a page are attractive, but transfer slowly to your computer. You can save time by turning off the display of graphics.

SOUND AND VIDEO

SOUND

You can hear sound such as TV theme songs, movie soundtracks, sound effects and historical speeches on the Web.

Sound takes a few minutes to transfer to your computer.

To listen to sound, you need a sound card and speakers. A sound card is a special circuit board that enables a computer to produce high-quality sound.

Note: Most Macintosh computers come with sound cards.

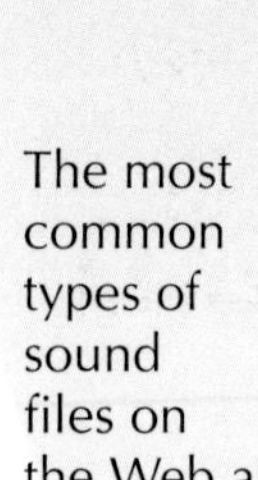

The most common types of sound files on the Web are:

- Audio Player (AU)
- Real Audio (RA) - a new type of sound file that lets you instantly listen to sound without having to wait. The sound quality is similar to AM radio.
- Wave (WAV)

HELPER PROGRAMS

A Web browser needs helper programs to work with certain types of sound, video, animation and graphics that are found on the Web. A helper program (also called a viewer) helps a browser perform tasks it cannot itself perform.

VIDEO AND ANIMATION

You can display video and animation such as movie clips, cartoons and interviews with celebrities on the Web.

Video and animation take a long time to transfer to your computer. For example, a four minute video can take approximately one hour to transfer. Be prepared to wait.

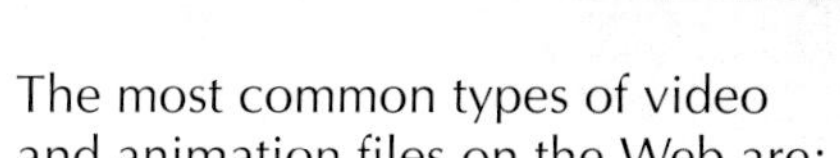

The most common types of video and animation files on the Web are:

- Audio Video Interleaved (AVI)
- Motion Picture Experts Group (MPEG)
- QuickTime (MOV)

INTERESTING WEB SITES YOU CAN VISIT

TV Theme Songs	http://www.tvtrecords.com/tvbytes
Rob's Multimedia Lab	http://www.acm.uiuc.edu/rml
Lights Camera Action! Movie Sounds	http://www.netaxs.com/people/dgresh/snddir.html
Sun-MultiMedia-Site	http://sunsite.unc.edu/pub/multimedia
Internet Underground Music Archive	http://www.iuma.com

VIRTUAL WORLDS

Virtual worlds are the future of the Internet. These three-dimensional worlds provide a more realistic experience than the flat, two-dimensional World Wide Web.

THE WEB

VIRTUAL WORLDS

VRML

Virtual worlds are created using a language called Virtual Reality Modeling Language (VRML).

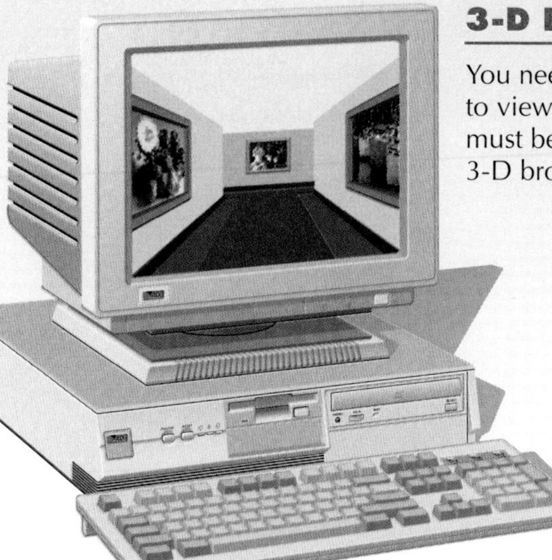

3-D BROWSER

You need a special program, called a 3-D browser, to view and explore virtual worlds. The browser must be able to understand VRML. Two popular 3-D browsers are WebSpace and WebFX.

Tip

Computer programmers hope that one day you will be able to use special goggles and gloves to walk through virtual worlds.

WALK THROUGH VIRTUAL WORLDS

You can use your mouse or keyboard to move through three-dimensional rooms. You can move left and right through hallways and move closer to objects of interest.

When you move closer to an object, the object appears in more detail. Limitations of today's computers prevent virtual worlds from looking totally realistic.

VIRTUAL OBJECTS

You can view a virtual object from any angle. You can walk around a virtual object and move closer or farther away from the object.

A virtual object can be a car, truck, plane, lamp or any other item in the real world.

Virtual objects let you view products produced by various companies without leaving your desk.

YAHOO

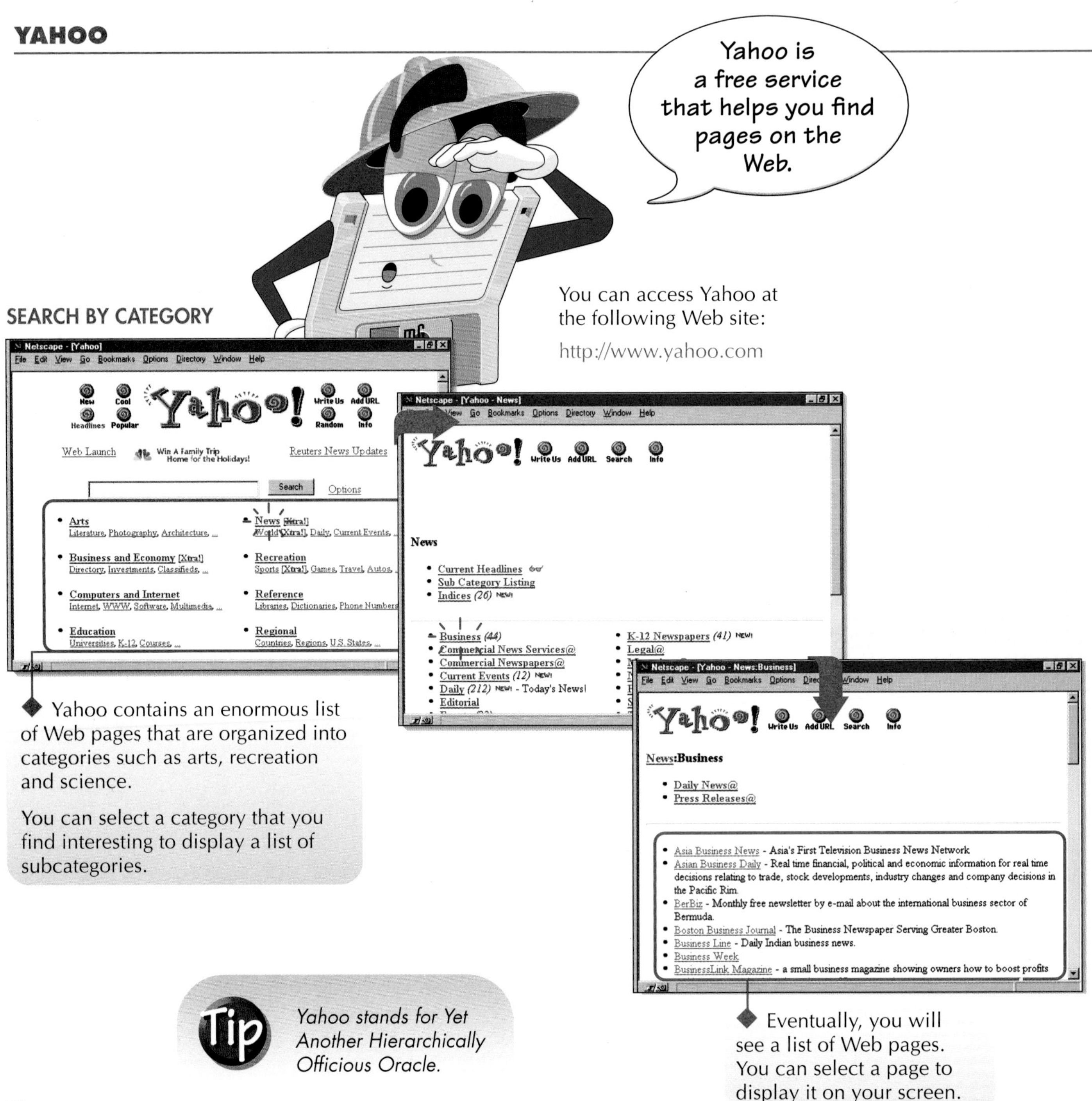

You can access Yahoo at the following Web site:

http://www.yahoo.com

◆ Yahoo contains an enormous list of Web pages that are organized into categories such as arts, recreation and science.

You can select a category that you find interesting to display a list of subcategories.

◆ Eventually, you will see a list of Web pages. You can select a page to display it on your screen.

Tip *Yahoo stands for Yet Another Hierarchically Officious Oracle.*

SEARCH BY NAME

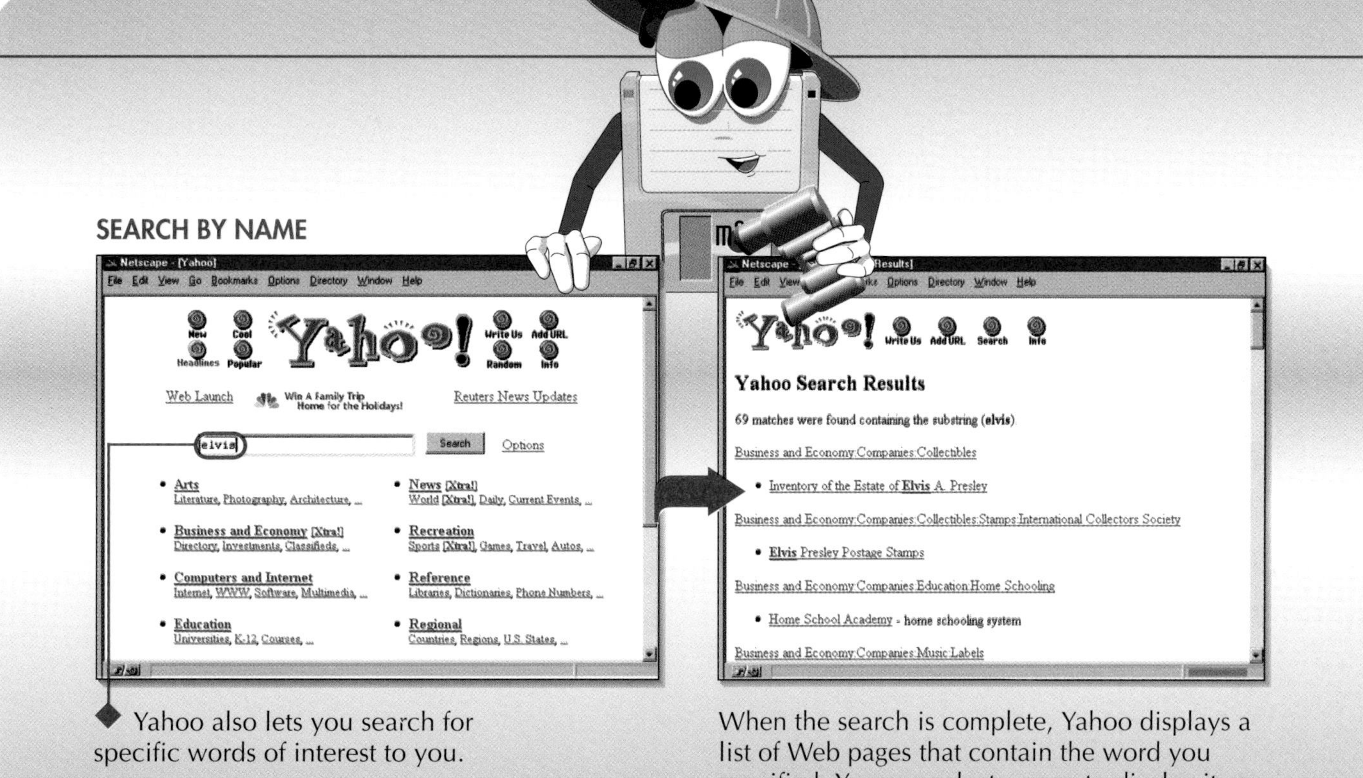

Yahoo also lets you search for specific words of interest to you.

When the search is complete, Yahoo displays a list of Web pages that contain the word you specified. You can select a page to display it on your screen.

ADDITIONAL FEATURES

Yahoo also offers some features that you may find informative and entertaining.

New

Takes you to Web pages recently added to Yahoo.

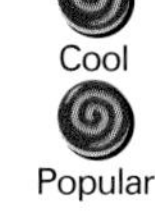

Random

Takes you to randomly selected Web pages listed in Yahoo's enormous database. This is a fun way to view pages on the Web.

Headlines

Gives you news and headlines for various categories, such as politics, entertainment and sports.

Cool

Takes you to Web pages that Yahoo considers innovative and interesting.

Popular

Displays the 50 most popular categories in Yahoo.

LYCOS WEBCRAWLER

LYCOS

Lycos is another free service that helps you find pages on the Web.

Lycos comes from the first five letters of the Latin name for Wolf Spider.

You can access Lycos at the following Web site:

http://www.lycos.com

◆ Lycos lets you search for specific words of interest.

Netscape - [Lycos search: elvis]

2) Elvis Home Page [0.4637]

Outline: The CORRECTION:

Abstract: unofficial **Elvis** Home Page (celebrating over 1 year online!) Point Communications Corp. rated my site in the Top 5% of the Web! Modified September 24, 1995 Contrary to recent reports in various media, there was NO court case between **Elvis** Presley Enterprises and myself. There was NO "settlement" between **Elvis** Presley Enterprises and myself. 8 months ago, I signed the statement they asked me to sign in this letter . This letter was the only commmunication between myself and **Elvis** Presley Enterprises. The **Elvis** Home Page, as it once was, is unavailable due to legal problems. The representatives of **Elvis** Presley Enterprises let it be known that the distribution of
http://calypso.oit.unc.edu/elvis/elvishom.html (6k)

3) Little Known Facts About Elvis Presley [0.3703]

Abstract: Little Known Facts About **Elvis** Presley Little Known Facts... About **Elvis** Presley * **Elvis** Aaron Presley was one of twin boys born to Gladys Smith Presley and Vernon **Elvis** Presley on January 8, 1935. His brother Jesse Garon died, within six hours of birth. *King Creole,

When the search is complete, Lycos displays a list of Web pages that contain the word you specified. You can select a page to display it on your screen.

◆ Lycos ranks the pages with a numerical score. The pages with the best scores are listed first.

There are two ways that a search tool finds pages on the Web.

Some search tools have automated robots that travel around the Web looking for new pages.

People also submit information about pages they have created.

Since hundreds of new pages are created each day, it is impossible for a search tool to find and catalog every new page on the Web.

WEBCRAWLER

WebCrawler was named for its sophisticated way of finding new sites on the Web. You can use WebCrawler to find pages of interest.

You can access WebCrawler at the following Web site:

http://www.webcrawler.com

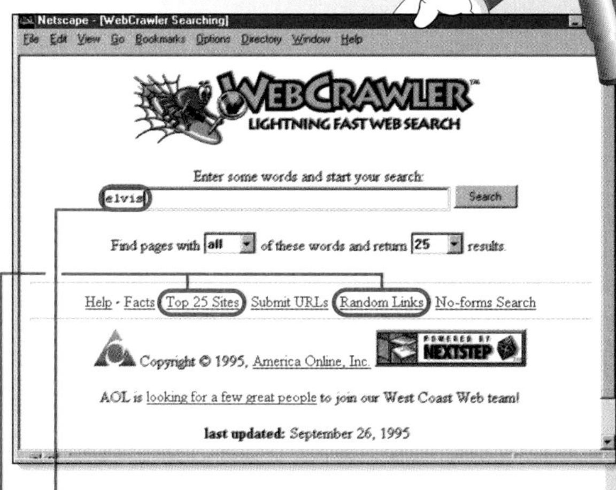

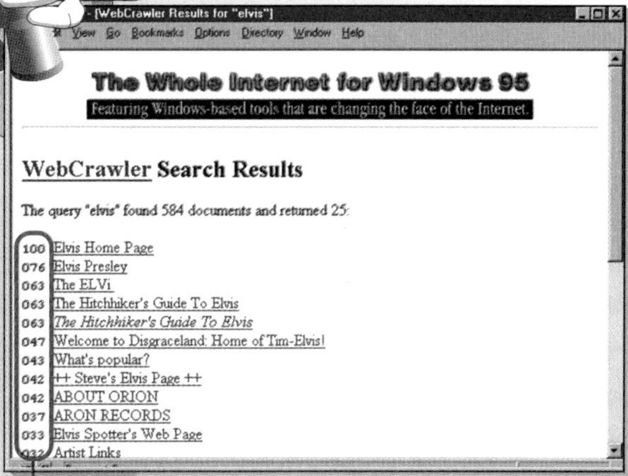

◆ WebCrawler lets you search for specific words of interest.

◆ WebCrawler also offers some features that you may find useful.

Top 25 Sites
Takes you to WebCrawler's 25 most frequently referenced Web pages.

Random Links
Takes you to randomly selected Web pages listed in WebCrawler's enormous database. This is a fun way to view pages on the Web.

When the search is complete, WebCrawler displays a list of Web pages that contain the word you specified. You can select a page to display it on your screen.

◆ WebCrawler gives each page a numerical score out of 100. The pages with the best scores are listed first.

In this chapter you will learn about exchanging electronic mail (e-mail) with people around the world.
judy@sales.maran.com
derek@sales.maran.com

ELECTRONIC MAIL

Introduction to E-mail

E-mail Addresses

E-mail Programs and Features

E-mail Messages

Common E-mail Terms

Mailing Lists

Interesting Mailing Lists

INTRODUCTION TO E-MAIL

You can exchange electronic mail (e-mail) with people around the world. E-mail is the most widely used feature on the Internet.
jmaran@abc.com

SPEED

E-mail is much faster than old-fashioned mail, called "snail mail." A message can travel around the world in seconds.

CONTENT

A message can contain a few lines of text or several hundred. Unlike with the postal service, messages are not charged by weight.

COST

There is usually no charge for sending and receiving electronic mail, even if a message travels around the world. Rather than making long distance calls to colleagues, friends or family, you can save money by using the Internet to exchange messages.

RECEIVING MESSAGES

You do not have to be at your computer to receive a message. Your service provider keeps all your messages until you ask for them. Make sure you regularly check for messages.

When you send a message, do not assume the person receiving the message will read it right away. Some people may not regularly check their messages.

E-MAIL ADDRESSES

You can send a message to anyone around the world if you know their e-mail address.

An address consists of two parts, separated by the @ (at) symbol.

mvickers@sales.abc.com

USER NAME
The name of the person's account. This can be a real name or a nickname.

DOMAIN NAME
The location of the person's account. Periods (.) separate the various parts of the domain name.

Note: An e-mail address cannot contain spaces.

The last few characters in an e-mail address usually indicate the type of organization and/or country the person belongs to. Examples include:

ORGANIZATION

com	commercial	**edu**	education
gov	government	**mil**	military
net	network	**org**	organization (often non-profit)

COUNTRY

au	Australia
ca	Canada
it	Italy
jp	Japan
us	United States

INTERESTING E-MAIL ADDRESSES

Bill Gates – billg@microsoft.com
Fox TV – foxnet@delphi.com
Glamour – glamourmag@aol.com
GQ – gqmag@aol.com
Nightly News – nightly@news.nbc.com
President – president@whitehouse.gov
Rolling Stone, New York – rollingstone@echonyc.com
Time – timeletter@aol.com
USA Today-Letters to the editor – usatoday@clark.net
Wired – editor@wired.com

There is no central listing of e-mail addresses. The best way to find out someone's e-mail address is to phone and ask.

The World Wide Web page located at http://home.netscape.com/home/internet-white-pages.html offers several search tools to help you find e-mail addresses.

E-MAIL PROGRAMS AND FEATURES

E-MAIL PROGRAMS

An e-mail program lets you send, receive and manage your messages.
E-M

Eudora is currently the most popular e-mail program.

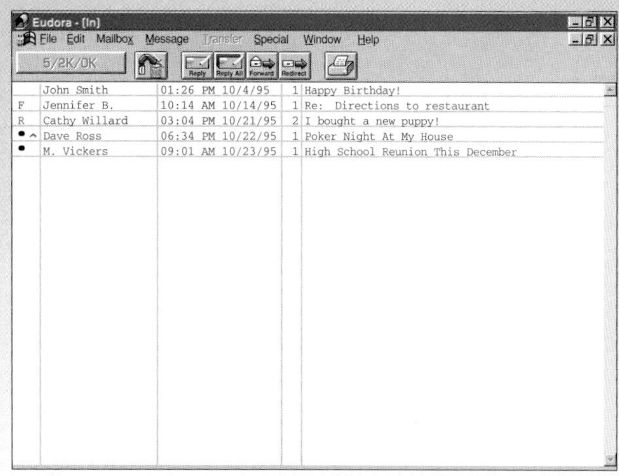

This screen displays a list of all your e-mail messages.

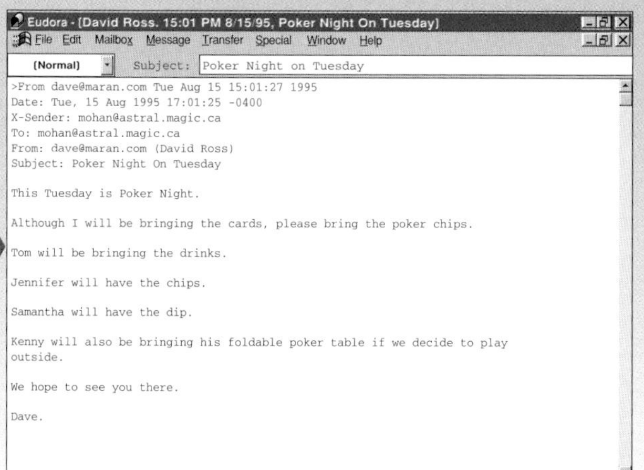

This screen displays a message.

E-MAIL FEATURES

REPLY TO A MESSAGE

You can reply to a message to answer questions or supply additional information. When you send a reply, make sure you include part of the original message. This is called quoting. Quoting helps the reader identify which message you are referring to.

FORWARD A MESSAGE

When you receive a message, you may think of someone else who would be interested in reading the message. E-mail programs let you send a copy of the message, with your comments, to another person.

DELETE A MESSAGE

You can delete messages you no longer need. This prevents mail from accumulating in your mailbox.

STORE MESSAGES

You can store important messages so you can review them again later. E-mail programs let you create folders to organize all your stored messages.

PRINT A MESSAGE

You can print a message to produce a paper copy.

E-MAIL MESSAGES

PARTS OF A MESSAGE

To:
Address of the person who will receive the message.

To: John Smith <jsmith@stay.com>
From: Chris McKenzie <chris@magic.org>
Subject: Our next hockey practice
Cc: David Jones <david@mustang.net>
Bcc: League Commissioner <commish@goal.com>

To John,

The first hockey practice of the season will be held this Saturday at 9 a.m. at Taylorville Arena.

Team goalie Joey Jacobs had his eyes examined during the summer and got contact lenses. He says it is much easier to make saves now that he can see the puck.

Chris McKenzie <chris@magic.org>

Subject:
Identifies the contents of the message. Make sure your subject is informative. Do not use subjects such as "For your information" or "Read this now."

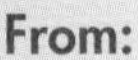

From:
Address of the person sending the message.

Body of the Message
Make sure your message is clear and concise and contains no spelling or grammar errors. Also make sure your message will not be misinterpreted. For example, the reader may not realize a statement is meant to be sarcastic.

Cc:
Stands for carbon copy. This lets you send the same message to several people.

Bcc:
Stands for blind carbon copy. This lets you send the same message to several people without them knowing that others have received the same message. Not all e-mail systems support this feature; therefore it may be unreliable.

Tip

If you want to practice sending a message, send a message to yourself.

SIGNATURE

You can have an e-mail program attach a signature to the end of every message you send. A signature includes information about yourself such as your name, e-mail address, favorite quote or joke. If you use a signature, make sure you limit it to a few lines.

To John,
The first hockey practice of the season will be held this Saturday at 9 a.m. at Taylorville Arena. Hope to see you there!
Chris McKenzie
Assistant Coach

MIME

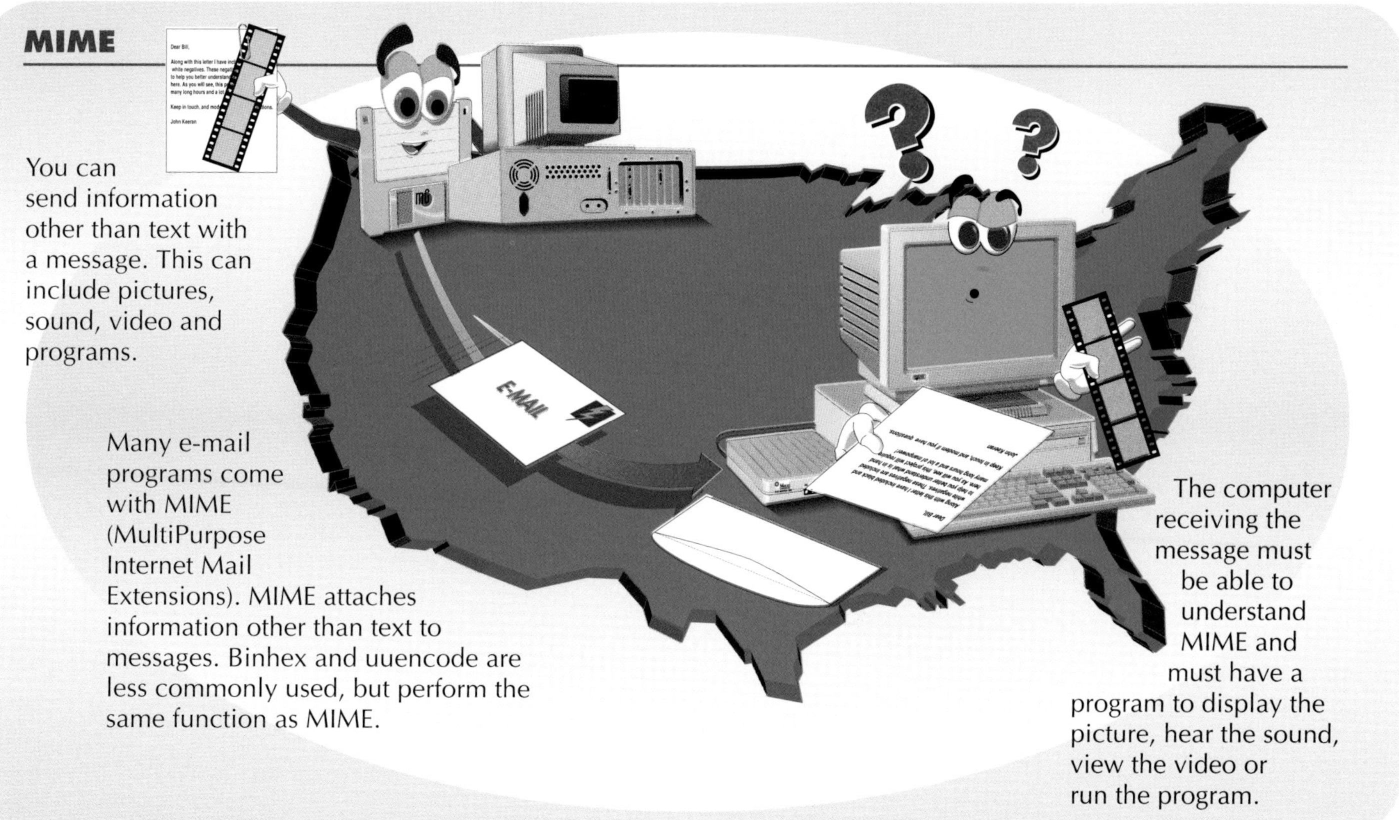

E-MAIL

You can send information other than text with a message. This can include pictures, sound, video and programs.

Many e-mail programs come with MIME (MultiPurpose Internet Mail Extensions). MIME attaches information other than text to messages. Binhex and uuencode are less commonly used, but perform the same function as MIME.

The computer receiving the message must be able to understand MIME and must have a program to display the picture, hear the sound, view the video or run the program.

COMMON E-MAIL TERMS

COMMON E-MAIL TERMS

SMILEYS

Smileys, also called emoticons, are special characters that express emotions and gestures in messages. They represent human faces if you turn them sideways.

<table>
<tr><th>Gesture</th><th>Characters</th></tr>
<tr><td>Cry</td><td>:'-(</td></tr>
<tr><td>Smile</td><td>:-)</td></tr>
<tr><td>Laugh</td><td>:-D</td></tr>
<tr><td>Frown</td><td>:-(</td></tr>
<tr><td>Surprise</td><td>:-0</td></tr>
<tr><td>Wink</td><td>;-)</td></tr>
<tr><td>Santa Claus</td><td>*<|:-)</td></tr>
</table>

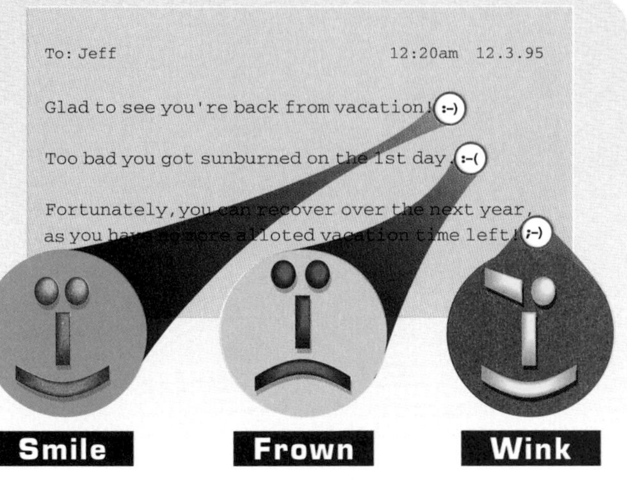

To: Jeff
12:20am 12.3.95
Glad to see you're back from vacation! :-)
Too bad you got sunburned on the 1st day. :-(
Fortunately, you can recover over the next year,
as you have no more alloted vacation time left! ;-)
Smile
Frown
Wink

ABBREVIATIONS

Abbreviations are commonly used in messages to save time typing.

Abbreviation	Meaning
BTW	by the way
FAQ	frequently asked questions
FOAF	friend of a friend
FWIW	for what it's worth
FYI	for your information
IMHO	in my humble opinion
IMO	in my opinion
IOW	in other words

Abbreviation	Meaning
L8R	later
LOL	laughing out loud
MOTAS	member of the appropriate sex
MOTOS	member of the opposite sex
MOTSS	member of the same sex
ROTFL	rolling on the floor laughing
SO	significant other
WRT	with respect to

FLAME

A flame is an angry or insulting message directed at one person.

A flamewar is an argument that continues for a while. Avoid starting or participating in flame wars.

SHOUTING

A MESSAGE WRITTEN IN CAPITAL LETTERS IS ANNOYING AND HARD TO READ. THIS IS CALLED SHOUTING. Always use upper and lower case letters when typing messages.

BOUNCED MESSAGE

A bounced message is a message that returns to you because it cannot reach its destination. A message usually bounces because of typing mistakes in the e-mail address. Before sending a message, check for typing errors.

MAILING LISTS

A mailing list is a discussion group that uses e-mail to communicate.

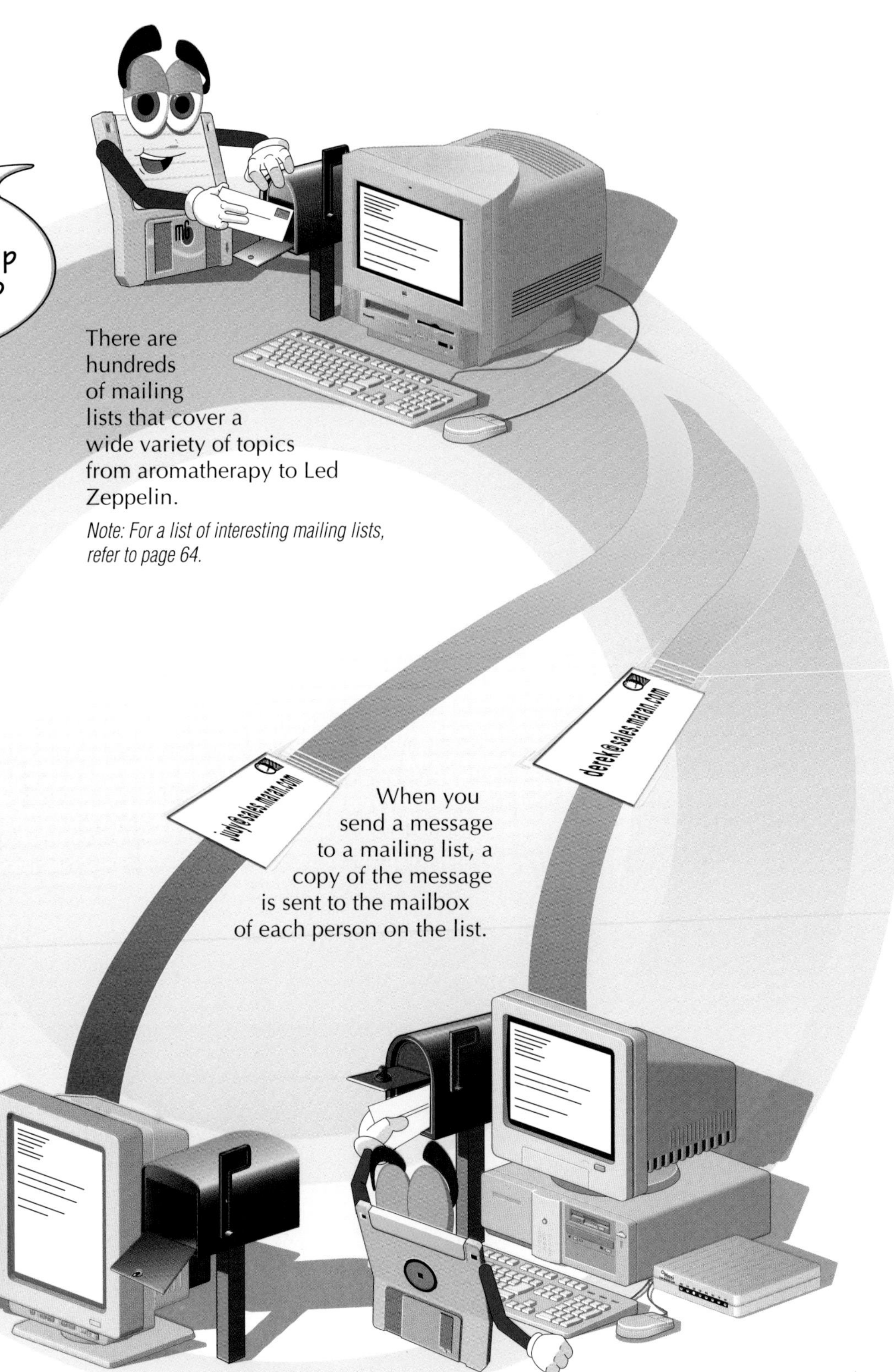

There are hundreds of mailing lists that cover a wide variety of topics from aromatherapy to Led Zeppelin.

Note: For a list of interesting mailing lists, refer to page 64.

When you send a message to a mailing list, a copy of the message is sent to the mailbox of each person on the list.

SUBSCRIBE TO A MAILING LIST

Just as you would subscribe to a magazine, you must subscribe to a mailing list to join the discussion group. You can unsubscribe from a mailing list at any time.

When you subscribe to a mailing list, make sure you frequently check your mailbox. You can receive dozens of messages in a short period of time.

Each mailing list has two addresses. One address receives messages for the entire group and the other address is for administrative purposes. When you subscribe to a mailing list, make sure you send your request to the administrative address.

When you go on vacation, make sure you unsubscribe from all your mailing lists. This will prevent your mailbox from overflowing with messages.

MODERATED MAILING LISTS

Some mailing lists are moderated. In a moderated mailing list, each message is first read by a volunteer who decides if the message is appropriate for the group. If the message meets the guidelines for the group, it is sent to every person on the list.

A moderated mailing list keeps discussions on-topic and removes messages that discuss the same ideas.

In an unmoderated mailing list, all messages are automatically sent to everyone in the group.

DIGESTS

If you receive a lot of messages from a mailing list, check if the list is available as a digest. This groups individual messages together and sends them to you as one message.

For a list of the available mailing lists:

Go to the Web page ***http://www.neosoft.com/internet/paml***

or

Go to the ***news.answers*** *newsgroup and look at the messages with the subject* ***Publicly Accessible Mailing Lists****.*

MAILING LIST ETIQUETTE

Read the messages in a mailing list for a week before submitting a message. This is a good way to learn how people in a mailing list communicate and prevents you from submitting information already read.

You can reply to a message to answer a question or supply additional information.

When you send a reply, make sure you include part of the original message. This is called quoting. Quoting helps readers identify which message you are referring to.

If your reply would not be of interest to others in a mailing list or you want to send a private response, send an e-mail message to the author of the message rather than to the entire list.

Reply to a message only when you have something important to say. Submitting "Me too" or "I agree" is not very informative.

MAILING LISTS

A manually maintained mailing list is managed by an administrator who keeps track of every member.

MANUALLY MAINTAINED LISTS

The e-mail address for a manually maintained list typically contains the word "request" (example: hang-gliding-request@lists.utah.edu).

SUBSCRIBE

To join a manually maintained mailing list, you simply send an e-mail message to the administrative address. Within a few days you will start receiving messages from the mailing list.

To: hang-gliding-request@lists.utah.edu
Subject: subscribe

Please add me to your hang-gliding mailing list. Thank you.

Mary Vickers
mvickers@company.com

UNSUBSCRIBE

To leave a manually maintained mailing list, you simply send an e-mail message to the administrative address.

To: hang-gliding-request@lists.utah.edu
Subject: unsubscribe

Please remove me from your hang-gliding mailing list. Thank you.

James Smith
jsmith@sales.abc.com

AUTOMATED LISTS

An automated mailing list is managed by a program that keeps track of every member.

The e-mail address for an automated list typically starts with the name of the program used to manage the list (example: listproc@chaos.taylored.com). There are three major programs–listproc, listserv and majordomo.

SUBSCRIBE

To join an automated mailing list, you simply send an e-mail message to the administrative address. Within a few days you will start receiving messages from the mailing list.

To: listproc@chaos.taylored.com
SUBSCRIBE X-FILES Bill Norton

UNSUBSCRIBE

To leave an automated mailing list, you simply send an e-mail message to the administrative address.

To: listproc@chaos.taylored.com
SIGNOFF X-FILES

INTERESTING MAILING LISTS

2020 World
Exploration of life in the year 2020.
Contact: majordomo@seatimes.com
Type in message: subscribe 2020world

A Word A Day
Sends you a word and its definition every day.
Contact: wsmith@wordsmith.org
Type in subject line: subscribe Your Name

Andrew Lloyd Webber
For fans of the famous composer/producer.
Contact: majordomo@world.std.com
Type in message: subscribe alw end

Animal Rights Views
Discussion of animal rights.
Contact: ar-views-request@cygnus.com
Type in message: subscribe ar-views

Blister
Lists of people's favorite and least favorite books.
Contact: majordomo@world.std.com
Type in message: subscribe blister

Diabetic
For diabetic patients to exchange ideas and comments.
Contact: listserv@lehigh.edu
Type in message: subscribe diabetic Your Name

Disney Comics
Discussion of Disney comics.
Contact: disney-comics-request@minsk.docs.uu.se

Ghost Stories
Ghost stories and other spooky discussions.
Contact: ghost-stories-request@netcom.com

Homebrewing
Discussion of beer, homebrewing and related issues.
Contact: homebrew-request@hpfcmi.fc.hp.com
Type in message: subscribe

Klingon Language
Discussion of the Klingon language used in Star Trek.
Contact: listserv@kli.org
Type in message: subscribe tlhingan-hol Your Name

Media McLuhan Project
Continuing the exploration of Media Science and Media Ecology.
Contact: mclr@astral.magic.ca
Type in message: subscribe mcluhan-list

Melrose Place
Discussion of the Fox television show Melrose Place.
Contact: melrose-place-request@ferkel.ucsb.edu

Movie Poster
For collectors of movie memorabilia.
Contact: listserv@listserv.american.edu
Type in message: SUBSCRIBE MOPO-L Your Name

New Music
Discussion of new and alternative music.
Contact: majordomo@xmission.com
Type in message: subscribe nm-list

Offroad
Information and discussions about 4x4 and offroad driving.
Contact: offroad-request@ai.gtri.gatech.edu

Pen Pals
Forums for children to correspond electronically with each other.
Contact: pen-pals-request@mainstream.com
Type in message: subscribe pen-pals

Private Eye
For private investigators or people who want to learn how to be an investigator.
Contact: private-eye-request@netcom.com

Rainbow Connection
A support group for people in long distance relationships.
Contact: rainbow-request@rmit.edu.au

Stock Market Secrets
Daily comments on the Stock Market.
Contact: smi-request@world.std.com

Tennis
Tennis news, surveys and notices.
Contact: racquet-notices-request@tenagra.com

Trepan-L
Publication of weird news items.
Contact: listserv@brownvm.brown.edu
Type in message: SUB TREPAN-L Your Name

Veggie
Discussion of issues relevant to vegetarians.
Contact: veggie-request@maths.bath.ac.uk

Weights
Discussion of all aspects of weights and exercise.
Contact: weights-request@fa.disney.com

Wine
For people interested in fine wines, making wine and tasting wine.
Contact: majordomo@niagara.com
Type in message: subscribe wine

In this chapter you will learn about newsgroups and chat groups. These groups let you discuss various topics with people around the world.
soc. women
talk. rumors
talk. origins
alt. drugs. culture
alt. horror
alt. books. reviews
rec. food. cooking

CHAPTER 4

NEWSGROUPS AND CHAT

Introduction to Newsgroups

Netiquette

Newsreader

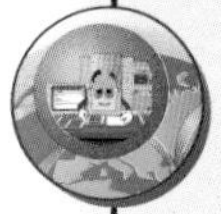

News Server

Internet Relay Chat

3-D Chat

Voice Chat

INTRODUCTION TO NEWSGROUPS

Usenet, short for Users Network, is the largest discussion forum in the world. Usenet allows people with common interests to communicate with one another.

NEWSGROUPS

Usenet consists of thousands of discussion groups, called newsgroups, on every subject imaginable. Each newsgroup discusses a particular topic such as chemistry, UFOs or basketball.

sci.chem

alt.ufo.reports

ARTICLE

An article is a message that an individual sends to a newsgroup. An article can be just a few lines of text or the length of a small book.

I just bought a new dog & can't decide what to name him. Any suggestions?

What about "Muffin"?

I think "Fluffy" is a great name for a dog.

I like the name "Bunny".

THREAD

A thread is the original article and all replies to the article. It can include an initial question and the answers from other readers.

rec.sport.basketball.pro

NEWSGROUP NAME

The name of a newsgroup describes the type of information it discusses. A name consists of two or more words, separated by periods.

rec.sport.basketball.pro

- The first word describes the main topic area (example: **rec** for recreation).
- Each of the following words narrows the topic area.

INTRODUCTION TO NEWSGROUPS

SUBSCRIBE

Similar to subscribing to a magazine, you subscribe to newsgroups that you want to read on a regular basis. When you subscribe to a newsgroup, a program (called a newsreader) keeps track of which articles you have and have not read.

READ AN ARTICLE

New articles are sent to newsgroups every day. Just as you would read the morning paper, you can select which articles you want to read.

Original Article
I am a vampire and I want to meet others like me. Call me at (555) 321-2632. But don't call after 10 because it will wake up my parents.
Reply Article
I am a vampire and I want to meet others like me. Call me at (555) 321-2632. But don't call after 10 because it will wake up my parents.
I am a vampire too. Let's meet for a bite and a drink. Call (555) 323-7575
GLUE

REPLY TO AN ARTICLE

You can reply to an article to answer a question or supply additional information.

Reply to an article only when you have something important to say. Replying "Me too" or "I agree" is not very informative.

◆ When you send a reply, make sure you include part of the original article. This is called quoting. Quoting helps readers identify which article you are referring to.

MODERATED NEWSGROUPS

Some newsgroups are moderated. In a moderated newsgroup, each message is first read by a volunteer who decides if the message is appropriate for the group. If the message meets the guidelines for the group, it is posted for all to read. Moderated newsgroups may have the word "moderated" at the end of the newsgroup name (example: sci.military.moderated).

In an unmoderated newsgroup, all messages are automatically posted for everyone to read.

POST AN ARTICLE

When you send an article to a newsgroup, you are "posting" the article.

If you want to practice posting an article to a newsgroup, send the article to the **alt.test** newsgroup. You will receive automated replies to let you know you posted correctly.

If your reply would not be of interest to others in a newsgroup or you want to send a private response, send an e-mail message to the author of the article rather than sending it to the entire newsgroup.

Similar to newsgroups, there are hundreds of mailing lists that let you discuss topics of interest with people around the world. Mailing lists are usually more specific than newsgroups and the messages are delivered directly to your mailbox.

Note: For more information, refer to page 58.

Netiquette refers to the proper way to behave on the Internet.

NETIQUETTE

READ ARTICLES

Read the articles in a newsgroup for a week before posting an article. This is called lurking. Lurking is a good way to learn how people in a newsgroup communicate and prevents you from posting information already read.

READ THE FAQ

The FAQ (Frequently Asked Questions) is a document that contains a list of questions and answers that regularly appear in a newsgroup.

The FAQ prevents new readers from asking the same questions over and over again. Make sure you read the FAQ before posting any articles to a newsgroup.

The **news.answers** newsgroup provides frequently updated FAQs for a wide variety of newsgroups. This lets you learn about many different topics in a short period of time.

CAREFULLY CHOOSE YOUR WORDS

An article that you post to a newsgroup can be read by tens of thousands of people around the world. Make sure you carefully re-read an article before posting.

- Make sure your article will not be misinterpreted. For example, not all readers will realize a statement is meant to be sarcastic.
- Make sure your article is clear and concise and contains no spelling or grammar errors.

CHOOSE AN INFORMATIVE SUBJECT HEADING

The subject of an article is the first item people read. Make sure your subject heading clearly identifies the contents of your article. For example, the subject heading "Read this now" or "For your information" is not very informative.

POST TO THE APPROPRIATE NEWSGROUP

Make sure you post an article to the appropriate newsgroup. Posting to several inappropriate newsgroups is called "spamming." Spamming is particularly annoying when the article serves a commercial purpose such as selling a product or service.

A newsreader is a program that lets you read and send articles to newsgroups.

NEWSREADER

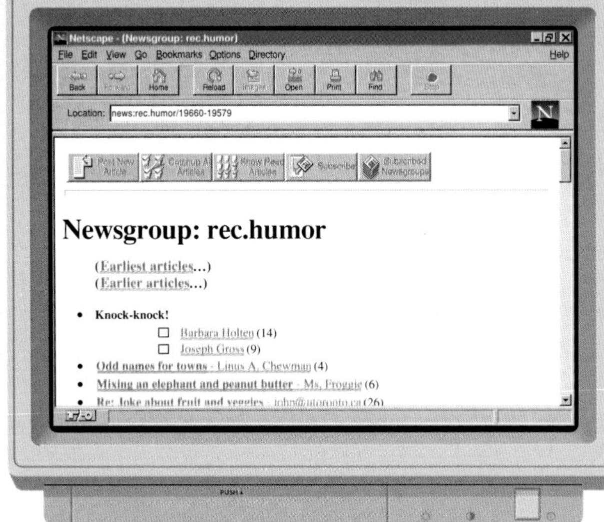

This screen lists the articles in the **rec.humor** newsgroup.

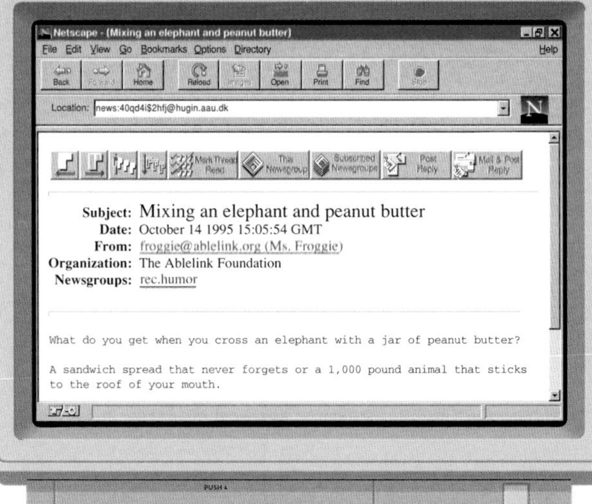

This screen displays an article.

ENCODED ARTICLES

An article can contain information other than text, such as a graphic or a sound recording. To send this type of information to a newsgroup, you must use a special program such as uuencode to change the information to a text format.

◆ An encoded article looks like a series of meaningless characters.

◆ To return an article to its original format, you must use a special program such as uudecode.

NEWS SERVER

Newsgroup articles are stored on thousands of news servers around the world.

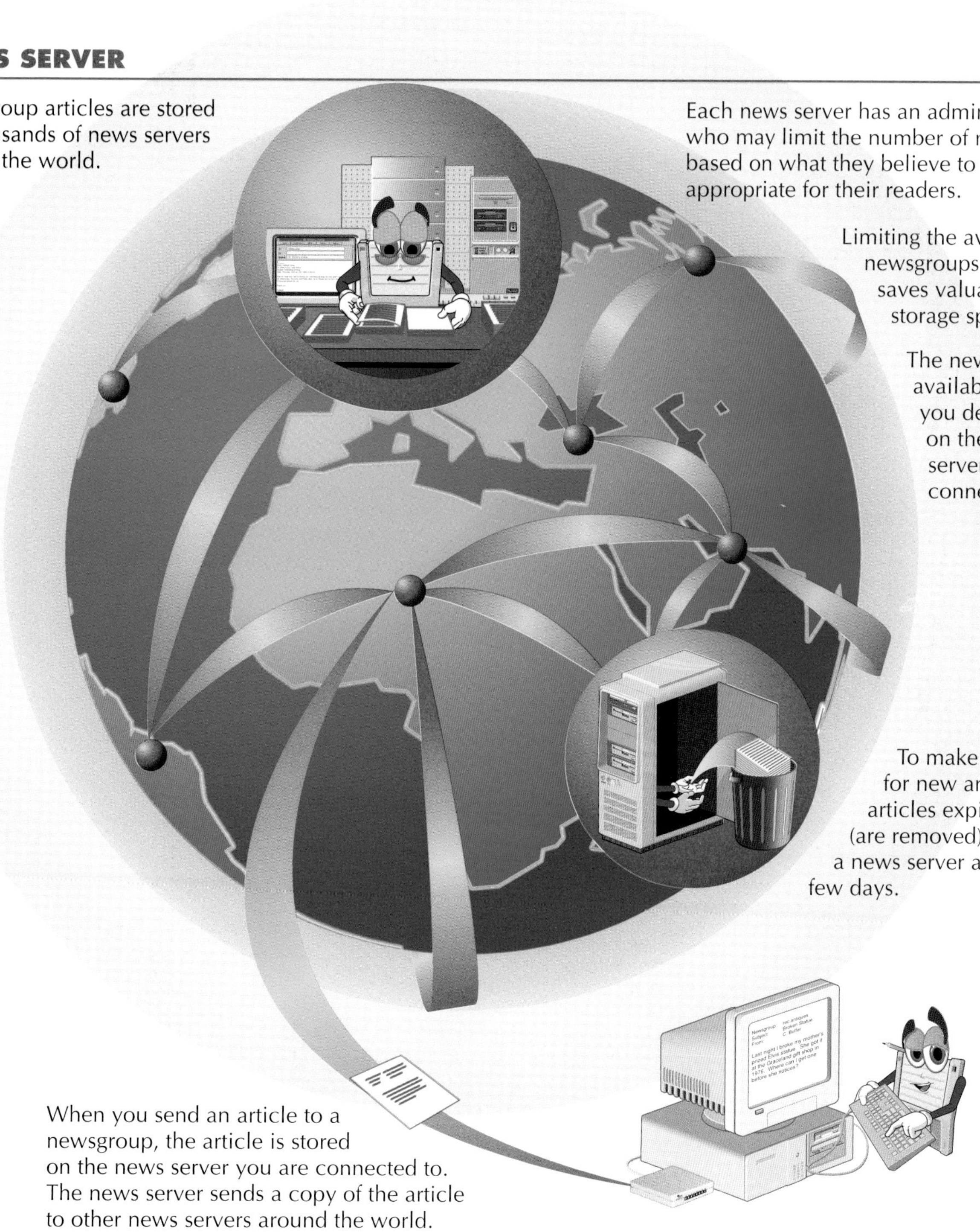

Each news server has an administrator who may limit the number of newsgroups based on what they believe to be appropriate for their readers.

Limiting the available newsgroups also saves valuable storage space.

The newsgroups available to you depend on the news server you are connected to.

To make room for new articles, articles expire (are removed) from a news server after a few days.

When you send an article to a newsgroup, the article is stored on the news server you are connected to. The news server sends a copy of the article to other news servers around the world.

INTERNET RELAY CHAT

Internet Relay Chat is a feature on the Internet that lets you instantly communicate with people around the world.

INTERNET RELAY CHAT (IRC)

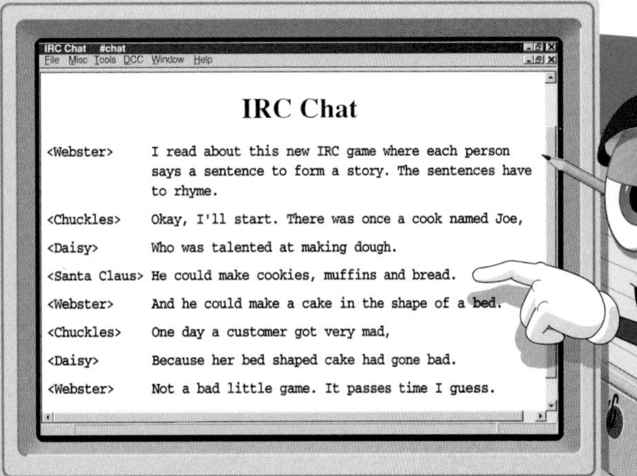

Similar to talking on the telephone, IRC lets you have conversations with one or more individuals on the Internet by simply typing back and forth. This is a great way to meet people and exchange ideas.

When you type text, it immediately appears on the screen of every person involved in the conversation.

Unlike talking on the telephone, IRC lets you chat with friends and colleagues in other cities, states or countries without paying long distance charges.

NICKNAMES

Every person on a channel gives themselves a nickname. This lets people know who is talking and lets people chat anonymously. If you see a nickname starting with @, such as @robotman, this is a program that manages the group.

When participating on a channel, do not assume that people are really who they say they are.

CHANNELS

Chat groups, called channels, usually focus on specific topics. The name of each channel begins with the # symbol and often tells you the theme of the discussion, such as #cars, #disney, #football or #poker. Look for channels that interest you.

Celebrities sometimes make publicized appearances in chat groups.

You need a special program to chat on the Internet. The following sites offer a chat program free of charge.

mIRC program
http://huizen.dds.nl/~mirc/index.htm

Global Chat
http://www.prospero.com/globalchat

3-D CHAT

Just like at a cocktail party, you can meet people on the Internet by walking through three-dimensional rooms and chatting with people you encounter.

WORLDS CHAT

Worlds Chat is the leading 3-D chat program. You can get this program for free at the **http://www.worlds.net** Web site.

An object represents each person. An object is called an Avatar and can be a man, fish, penguin or any other object.

To listen to music and sound effects while walking through three-dimensional rooms, you need a 16-bit sound card and speakers.

You can use your mouse or arrow keys to walk through rooms. You can move left and right through hallways and move closer to people who interest you.

You can use the Internet to talk to people in other cities, states and countries without paying long distance charges.

VOICE CHAT

With voice chat, usually only one person can talk at a time. If you have a full duplex sound card, two people can talk at a time. The sound may seem fuzzy, but advances in technology will soon make the sound as clear as conversations over the telephone.

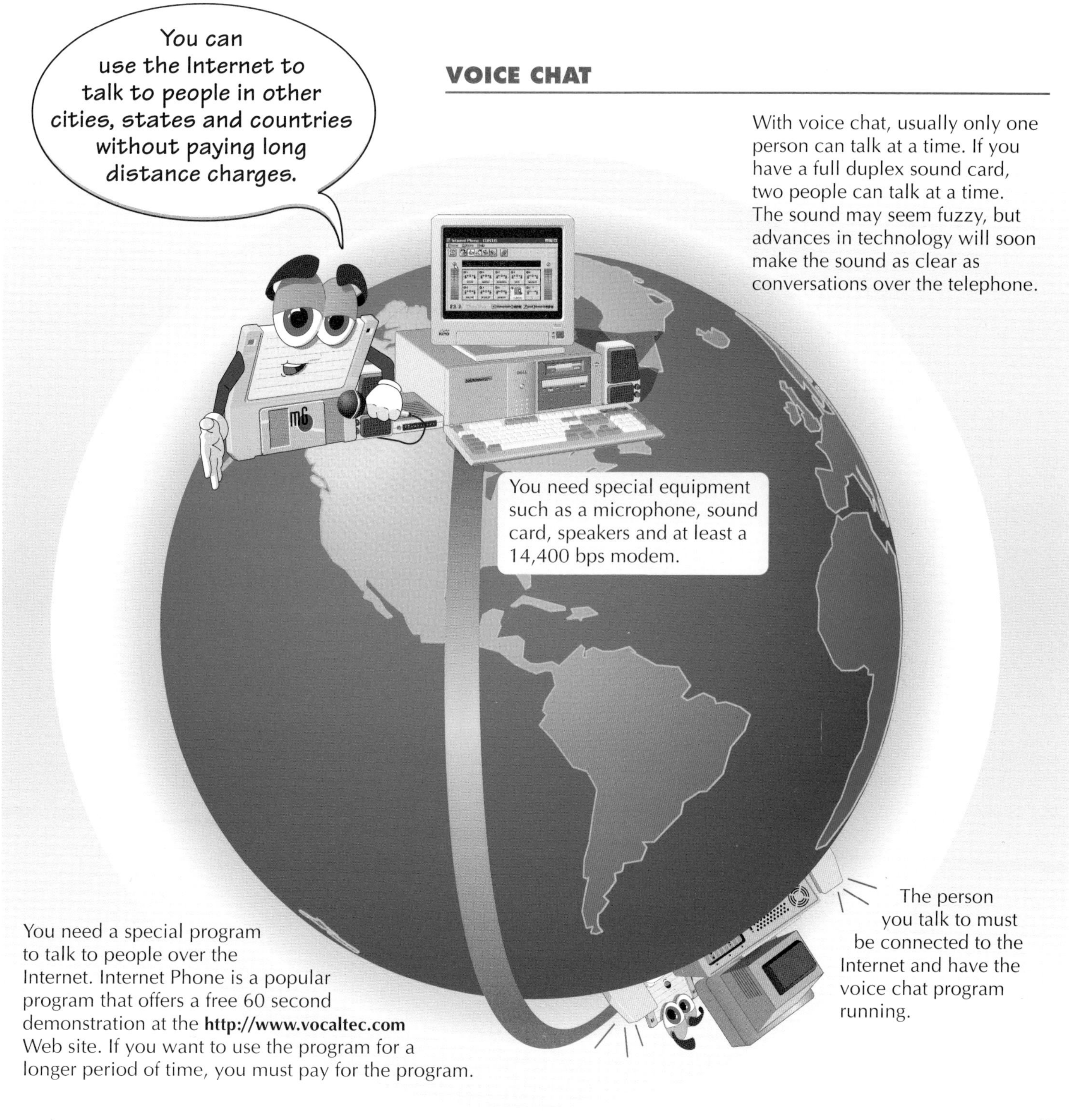

You need special equipment such as a microphone, sound card, speakers and at least a 14,400 bps modem.

You need a special program to talk to people over the Internet. Internet Phone is a popular program that offers a free 60 second demonstration at the **http://www.vocaltec.com** Web site. If you want to use the program for a longer period of time, you must pay for the program.

The person you talk to must be connected to the Internet and have the voice chat program running.

In this chapter you will learn about using FTP and Gopher to access information stored around the world.
FTP SITE

CHAPTER 5

FTP AND GOPHER

Introduction to FTP

Files at FTP Sites

Archie

Gopher

Veronica and Jughead

INTRODUCTION TO FTP

File Transfer Protocol (FTP) lets you look through files stored on computers around the world. You can copy files that interest you.

DOWNLOAD

When you receive information from another computer, you are downloading information.

Note: When you send information to another computer, you are uploading information.

FTP SITE

An FTP site is a university, government agency, company or individual that stores files you can copy to your computer.

FILES AVAILABLE

Each FTP site can only let a certain number of people use the site at once. If you get an error message when you try to connect, the site may already have as many people connected as it can handle. Try accessing FTP sites during off-peak hours, such as nights and weekends.

Popular FTP Sites

Library of Congress	ftp.loc.gov
Microsoft Corporation	ftp.microsoft.com
SunSite Site	sunsite.unc.edu/pub
Washington University	wuarchive.wustl.edu
Wiretap Library	wiretap.spies.com

ANONYMOUS FTP

Universities, government agencies and companies around the world have made files available to the public at no charge. You can access and copy files of interest without needing a password. This way of accessing and transferring files is called "anonymous" FTP.

You can view a list of most FTP sites at the following Web site:
http://hoohoo.ncsa.uiuc.edu/ftp-interface.html

You can also find FTP site listings in the ***comp.answers*** *and* ***news.newusers.questions*** *newsgroups.*

MIRROR SITE

Many popular FTP sites have other sites that provide the same information. These sites are called mirror sites. Mirror sites help reduce the traffic on popular sites by giving people alternative locations they can use. This ensures a faster and more reliable connection and lets people obtain information from computers that are physically closer. Mirror sites are updated on a regular basis.

FILES AT FTP SITES

Browsing through the contents of an FTP site is similar to flipping through files in a filing cabinet.
FTP SITE
Directory

Every FTP site stores files in different directories. Like the folders in a filing cabinet, a directory helps organize information. A directory can contain other directories and files.

FILENAMES

Every file has a name.

NAME

A name describes the contents of a file.

Note: A period (.) separates the name and the extension.

EXTENSION

An extension usually identifies the program used to create the file.

Note: For common file extensions, *refer to page 86.*

This is an example of what you would see on the screen when you access an FTP site.

```
Netscape - [Directory of /]
File  Edit  View  Go  Bookmarks  Options  Directory                Help

VocalTec FTP Site.

The latest version of the Internet Phone is located in the directory
/pub
        iphone13.exe - self extracting image of the Internet Phone
        ircsrvrs.ini - the latest Internet-Phone servers list.

If you have problem accessing the software you can download it
from one of our mirror sites:

Host: ubique.com        file: /pub/outgoing/vocaltec/iphone13.exe
Host: ftp.fast.net      file: /vocaltec/iphone13.exe

incoming/                    Tue Jul 25 05:51:00 1995 Directory
lib/                         Wed May 03 16:02:00 1995 Directory
outgoing/                    Mon Jul 17 17:47:00 1995 Directory
pub/                         Sat Jul 22 16:52:00 1995 Directory
usr/                         Mon Feb 27 20:31:00 1995 Directory
welcome.msg     408 bytes Tue Jun 06 16:18:00 1995

ftp://ftp.vocaltec.com/pub/
```

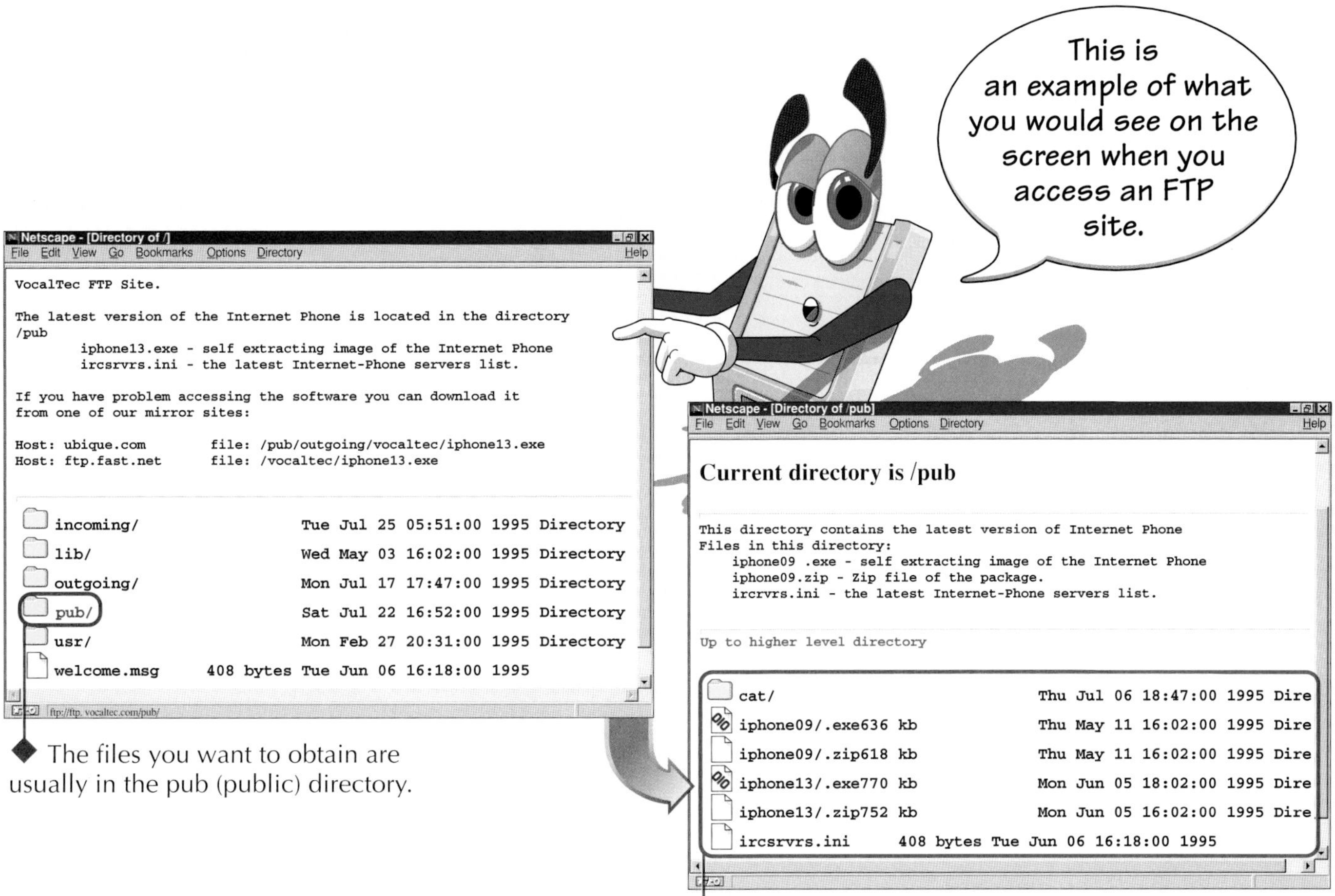

The files you want to obtain are usually in the pub (public) directory.

```
Netscape - [Directory of /pub]
File  Edit  View  Go  Bookmarks  Options  Directory                Help

Current directory is /pub

This directory contains the latest version of Internet Phone
Files in this directory:
    iphone09 .exe - self extracting image of the Internet Phone
    iphone09.zip - Zip file of the package.
    ircrvrs.ini - the latest Internet-Phone servers list.

Up to higher level directory

cat/                             Thu Jul 06 18:47:00 1995 Dire
iphone09/.exe636 kb              Thu May 11 16:02:00 1995 Dire
iphone09/.zip618 kb              Thu May 11 16:02:00 1995 Dire
iphone13/.exe770 kb              Mon Jun 05 18:02:00 1995 Dire
iphone13/.zip752 kb              Mon Jun 05 16:02:00 1995 Dire
ircsrvrs.ini     408 bytes Tue Jun 06 16:18:00 1995
```

When you select a directory, a list of files you can copy to your computer appears.

Make sure you only get files for your type of computer. Many FTP sites have separate directories for Macintosh and IBM-compatible computers. Just because you can transfer a file to your computer does not mean that you can use the file.

TYPES OF FILES AVAILABLE AT FTP SITES

TEXT

You can obtain interesting documents for research projects or for enjoyment. You can get books, computer manuals, government documents and academic papers.

Look for these extensions:
.doc .htm .html .txt

GRAPHICS

You can obtain computer-generated art, museum paintings and pictures of famous people. To view most graphics, you need special software.

Look for these extensions:
.bmp .eps .gif
.jpg .pict .png

SOUND

You can obtain theme songs, sound effects, clips of famous speeches and lines from television shows and movies. To hear sound, you need special hardware and software.

Look for these extensions:
.au .wav

VIDEO

You can obtain movie clips, cartoons, educational videos and computer-generated animation. To view video, you need special hardware and software.

Look for these extensions:
.avi .mov .mpg

PROGRAMS

You can obtain thousands of useful programs such as word processors, spreadsheets, and numerous games.

Look for these extensions:
.bat .com .exe .zip

Types of Programs

Freeware is any program available on the Internet that you can use and copy for free. You cannot sell freeware programs, but you can give copies away to friends and colleagues.

Shareware is any program available on the Internet that you can try for free. If you like the program and want to continue using it, you must pay the creator of the program.

FILES AT FTP SITES

TEXT AND BINARY FILES

Every file stored at an FTP site is either a text file or a binary file.

TEXT FILES

A text file contains just text and usually gives basic information, such as a list of frequently asked questions. The names of text files often end with .txt (example: manual.txt). Any type of computer can use a text file. Documents created in word processors are not text files because they include formatting. Text files are also called ASCII files.

BINARY FILES

A binary file contains more than just text. A binary file can be a program, picture, sound or video.

COMPRESSED FILES

Many large files stored at FTP sites are compressed or squeezed to reduce their size. This is commonly done for programs and sound. Compressed files save storage space and transfer more quickly to your computer.

Popular compression programs include PKZip for the IBM and Stuffit for the Macintosh.

When you receive a compressed file, you must use a decompression program to expand the file to its original form. You can usually get the decompression program for free at the site where you got the file.

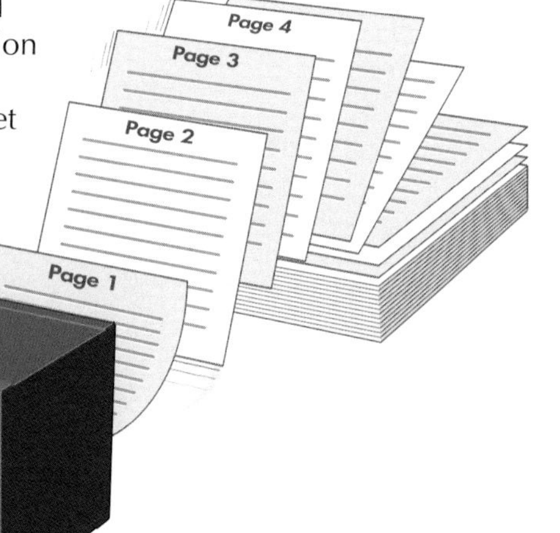

For IBM-compatible compressed files, look for these extensions:
.arc .arj .lhz .pak .zip

For Macintosh compressed files, look for these extensions:
.bin .seq .sit

ARCHIVED FILES

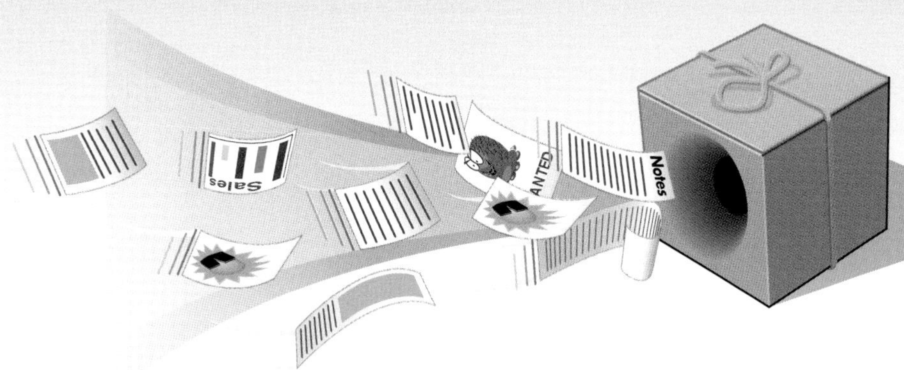

Programs stored at FTP sites usually require a large group of files to operate. These files are usually packaged, or archived, into a single file so you do not have to transfer each file individually to your computer.

ARCHIE

Archie helps you find publicly available files stored on FTP sites around the world.
AVAILABLE FILES

Archie was named after the *Archie* comic book character.

ARCHIE SITE

An Archie site is a computer on the Internet that contains a huge listing of publicly available files. You can search the listing for files that interest you. Archie sites periodically update their file listings by searching FTP sites locally or around the world.

This is an example of what you would see on the screen when you access an Archie site.

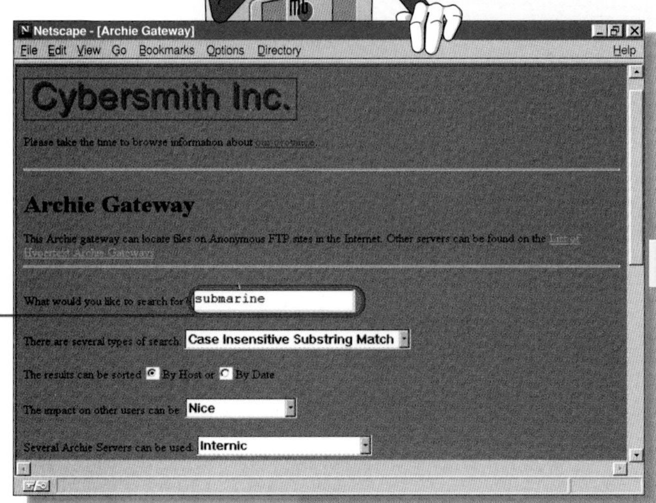

To find a file, you type part or all of the file name.

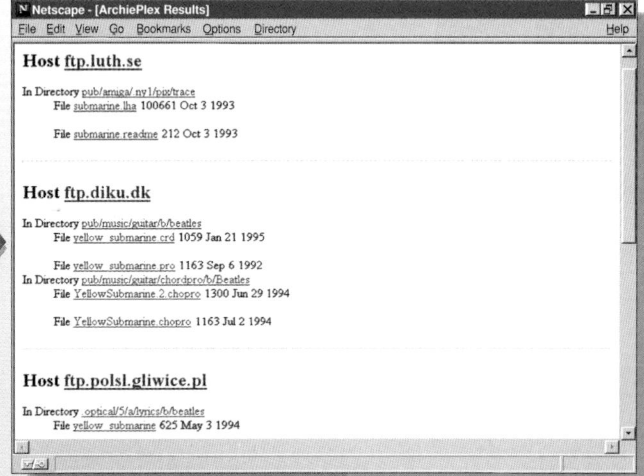

When the search is complete, Archie gives you a list of matching files and the FTP sites that store the files. The search can take about 5 minutes, so be prepared to wait. To save time, try using Archie during off-peak hours, such as nights and weekends.

Tip

Archie is useful when you have heard or read about a file and want to know where you can find the file.

POPULAR ARCHIE SITES ON THE WEB

Cybersmith
http://lydian.csi.nb.ca/archie

NASA
http://www.lerc.nasa.gov/archieplex

NCSA
http://hoohoo.ncsa.uiuc.edu/archie.html

Rutgers University
http://www-ns.rutgers.edu/htbin/archie

GOPHER

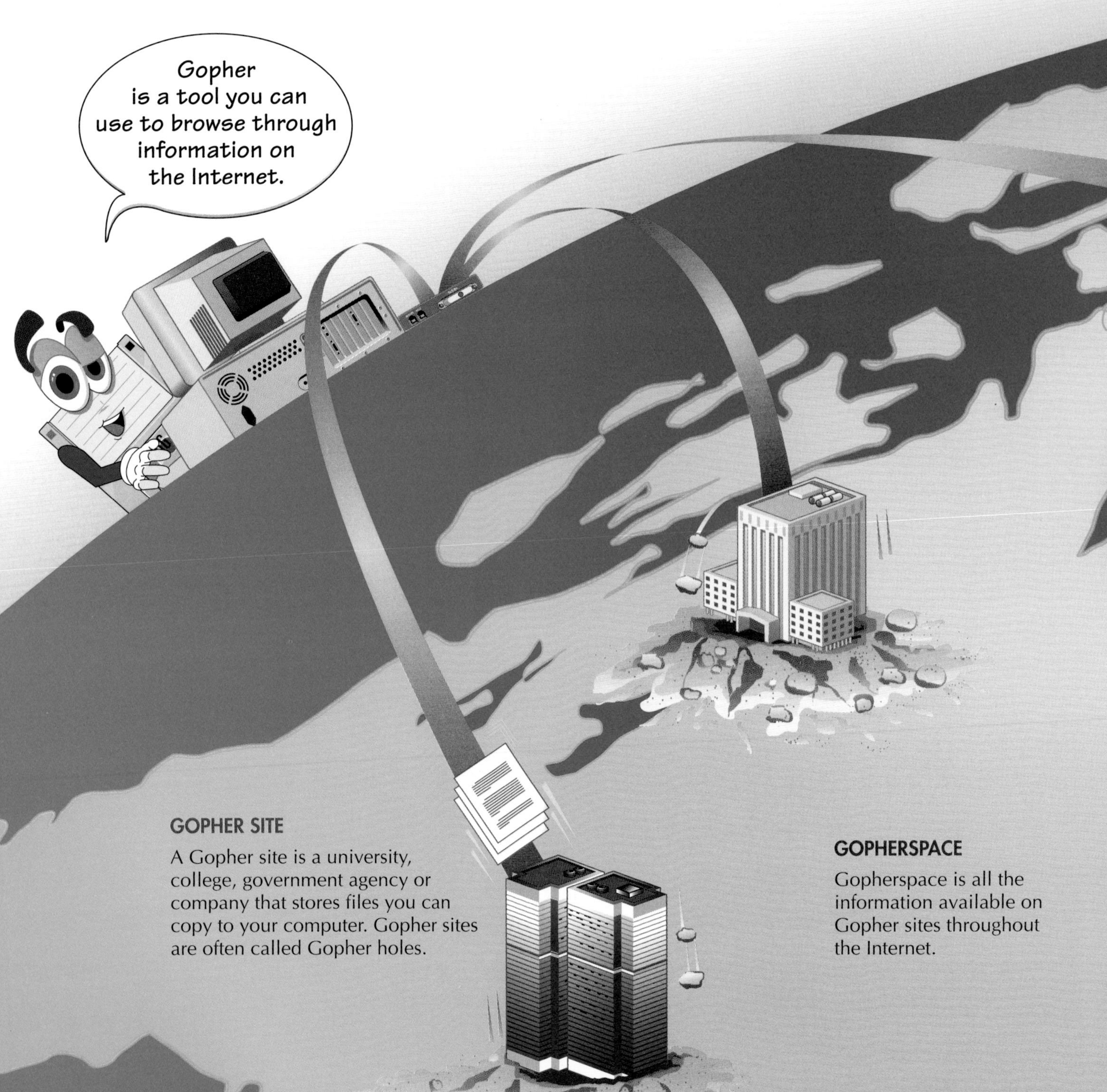

Gopher is a tool you can use to browse through information on the Internet.

GOPHER SITE

A Gopher site is a university, college, government agency or company that stores files you can copy to your computer. Gopher sites are often called Gopher holes.

GOPHERSPACE

Gopherspace is all the information available on Gopher sites throughout the Internet.

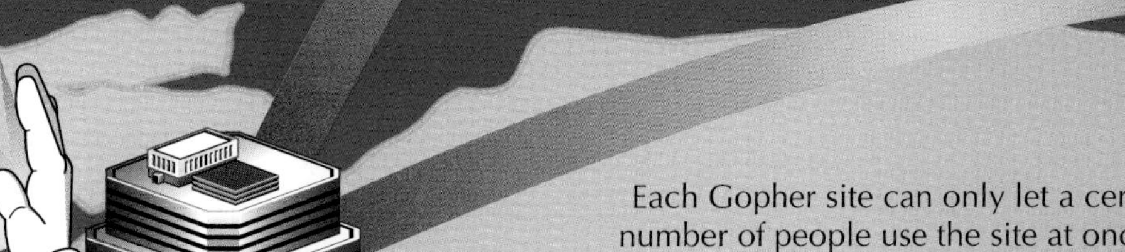

Each Gopher site can only let a certain number of people use the site at once. If you get an error message when you try to connect, the site may already have as many people connected as it can handle. Try accessing Gopher sites during off-peak hours, such as nights and weekends.

Popular Gopher Sites

Electronic Text Archives	gopher.etext.org
House of Representatives	gopher.house.gov
Library of Congress	gopher.loc.gov
Peabody Museum of History	gopher.peabody.yale.edu
United Nations	gopher.undp.org
University of Minnesota	gopher.tc.umn.edu
World Health Organization	gopher.who.ch

The first Gopher site appeared at the University of Minnesota where Gopher was developed. The Golden Gopher is the mascot of the university. This site gives you the locations of most Gopher sites on the Internet.

VERONICA AND JUGHEAD

GOPHER MENUS

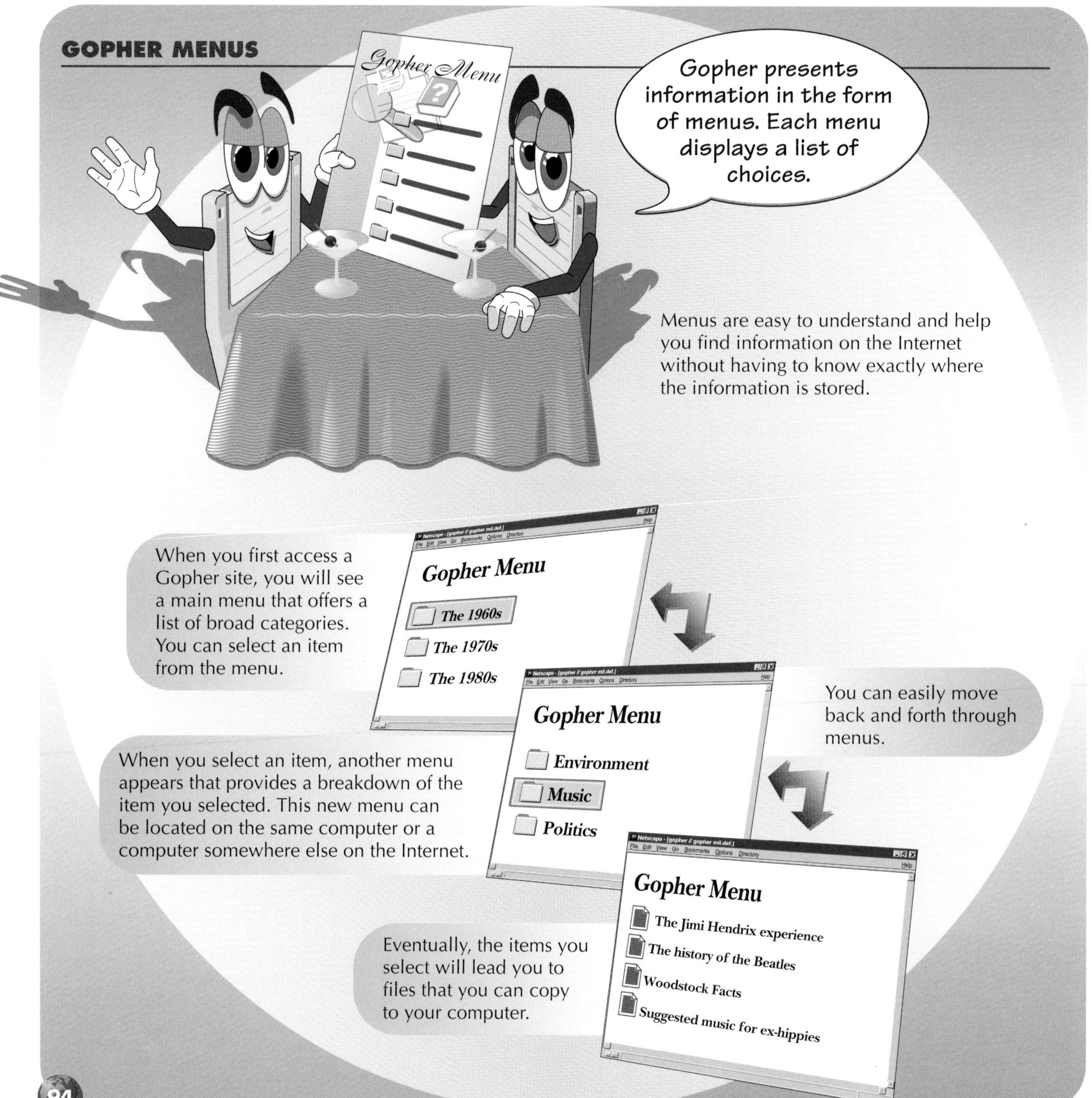

Menus are easy to understand and help you find information on the Internet without having to know exactly where the information is stored.

When you first access a Gopher site, you will see a main menu that offers a list of broad categories. You can select an item from the menu.

You can easily move back and forth through menus.

When you select an item, another menu appears that provides a breakdown of the item you selected. This new menu can be located on the same computer or a computer somewhere else on the Internet.

Eventually, the items you select will lead you to files that you can copy to your computer.

VERONICA AND JUGHEAD

Veronica and Jughead both help you find information stored on Gopher sites around the world.

Most Gopher sites offer either Veronica or Jughead to help you search for information.

VERONICA

Veronica contains a catalog of all directory and document names on Gopher menus around the world.

JUGHEAD

Jughead is a faster version of Veronica that contains a catalog of all directory and some document names on Gopher menus around the world.

To find a word of interest, you simply type the word.

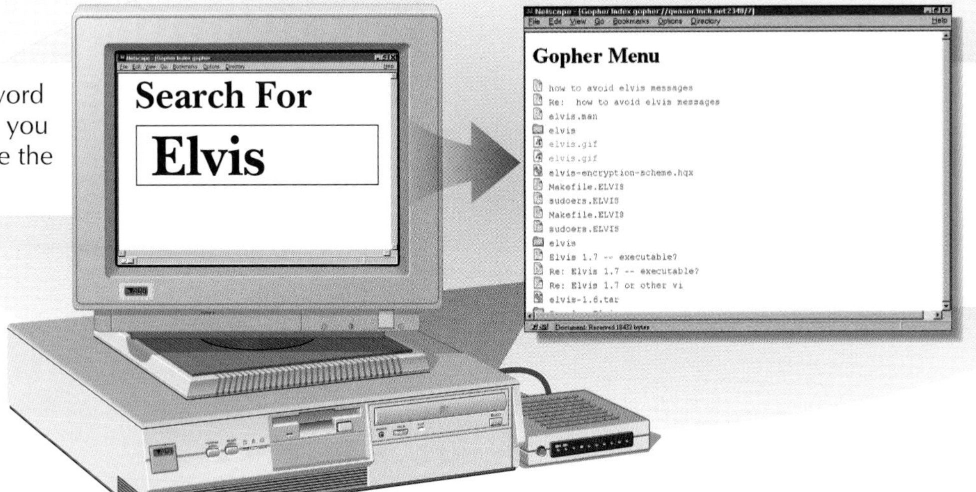

When the search is complete, the results appear in a Gopher menu. The menu lists the items that match the word you specified.

Like the Archie FTP search tool, Veronica and Jughead were also named after Archie comic book characters.

In this chapter you will learn about security issues and shopping on the Internet.

ONLINE SECURITY AND SHOPPING

Internet Security

Shopping on the Internet

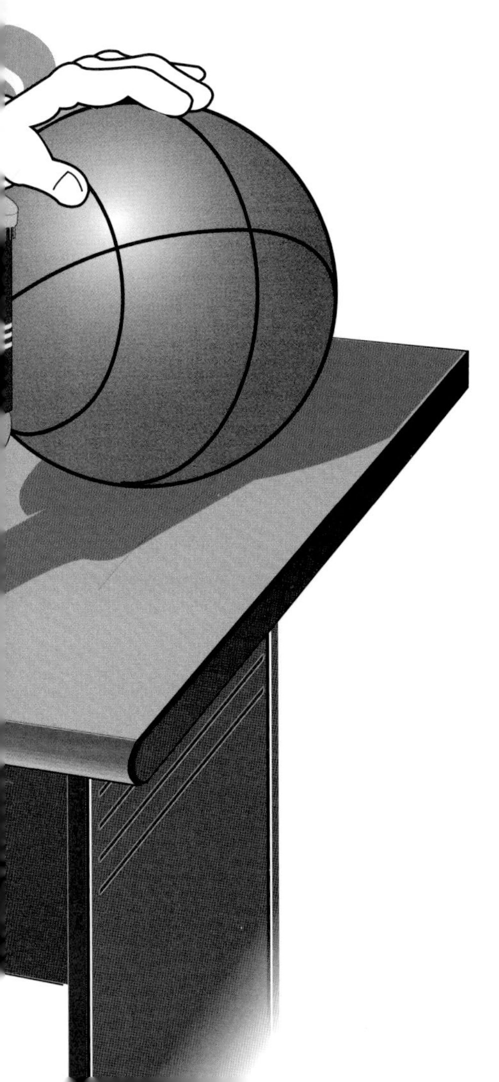

COMMON SECURITY TERMS

HACKER

A hacker is a person who enjoys working with computers and spends numerous hours writing programs. Some hackers, called crackers, test their skills by breaking into computer systems for fun or to steal information.

FIREWALL

A firewall is a program that restricts information passing between two networks. Many organizations use firewalls to prevent unauthorized individuals on the Internet from accessing a private network.

PHREAKER

A phreaker is a person who breaks into phone systems to make free long distance calls, obtain calling card numbers and much more. Phreakers often exchange tips and techniques with other phreakers on the Internet.

PASSWORD

You must enter a password each time you connect to the Internet. A password is a secret code that restricts unauthorized access to your account.

When creating a password, make sure it is at least 8 characters long and contains both letters and numbers (example: easy@123). Do not use obvious passwords, such as your name or birth date, and never give your password to anyone.

VIRUS

A virus is a computer program that can replicate itself and disrupt the normal operation of a computer. Viruses cause a variety of problems, from the appearance of annoying messages to the destruction of information.

Most viruses attach themselves to programs. If you get a program from the Internet, make sure you use virus detection software to check the program. Virus detection software is freely available on the Internet. You can also buy the software at most computer stores.

ENCRYPTION

Encryption scrambles information so it can transfer privately over the Internet.

ENCRYPTION

The sending computer converts the original text into coded information. The coded information appears as a series of meaningless characters.

There are several encryption methods used today.

PGP

Pretty Good Privacy (PGP) is commonly used to make e-mail messages private. PGP is very controversial since no one, not even the government, can crack the code.

ROT13

Rotate 13 (rot13) is used to make newsgroup messages private.

Only individuals who have a special code can read the information.

DECRYPTION

The receiving computer uses a special code to convert the information back to regular text.

SHTTP

Secure HyperText Transfer Protocol (SHTTP) is commonly used for security on the World Wide Web.

SSL

Secure Sockets Layer (SSL) is used for security on the Internet and the World Wide Web.

CLIPPER CHIP

The clipper chip is an encryption method proposed by the United States government. This chip has caused controversy because only the government knows the key to decode information. This will allow law enforcement agencies, with a court order, to monitor all electronic communications.

SHOPPING ON THE INTERNET

SHOPPING ON THE INTERNET

There are several shopping malls on the Internet. These shopping malls let you browse through products offered by many companies and let you buy products online.

Note: For popular shopping sites on the World Wide Web, refer to page 142.

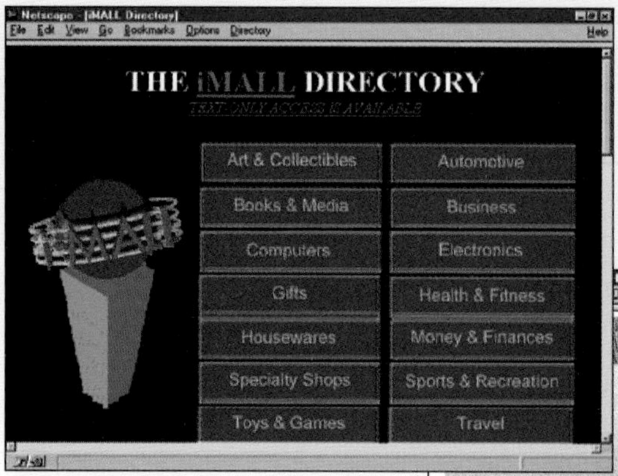

Many companies, such as American Airlines, have their own sites on the Web. You can get product information and often buy products online.

There are a variety of products you can buy on the Internet, such as antiques, books, cars, clothing, computers, flowers, food, games, office supplies, paintings, programs, music and much more.

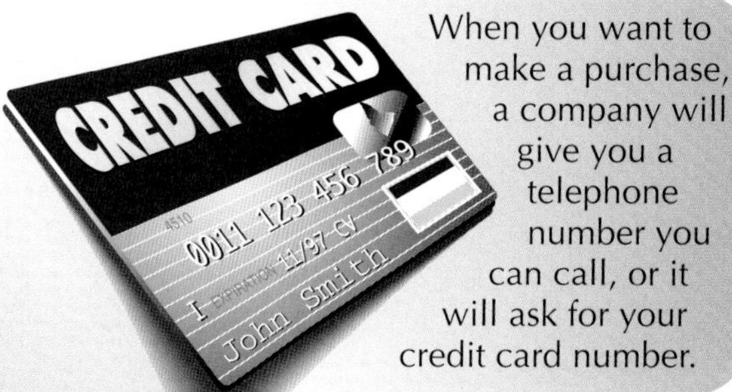

When you want to make a purchase, a company will give you a telephone number you can call, or it will ask for your credit card number.

You can easily and effortlessly view information about thousands of products sold around the world. Products available on the Internet are delivered to your door and are usually less expensive because of the lower overhead.

Although shopping on the Internet has many advantages, you may like to touch or try products before using them. You also have to wait for products to be delivered, which may take a few weeks.

GAMBLING

Gambling is becoming more popular on the Internet. You can play card games for free or try to win money. Other forms of gambling, such as betting on sports, will soon appear on the Internet.

Here are some popular gambling sites on the World Wide Web:

Internet Casino
http://www.casino.org/places.html

Virtual Vegas
http://www.virtualvegas.com

This chapter includes a list of the newsgroups that you can join.

CHAPTER 7

INTERESTING NEWSGROUPS

alt. (alternative)

biz. (business)

comp. (computers)

misc. (miscellaneous)

news.

rec. (recreation)

sci. (science)

soc. (social)

talk.

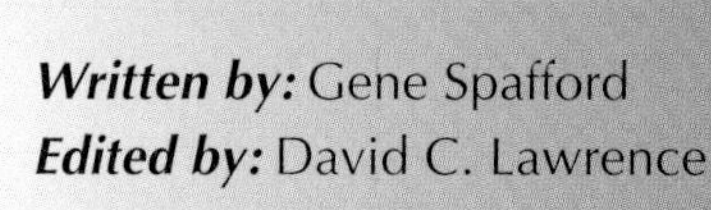
Written by: Gene Spafford
Edited by: David C. Lawrence

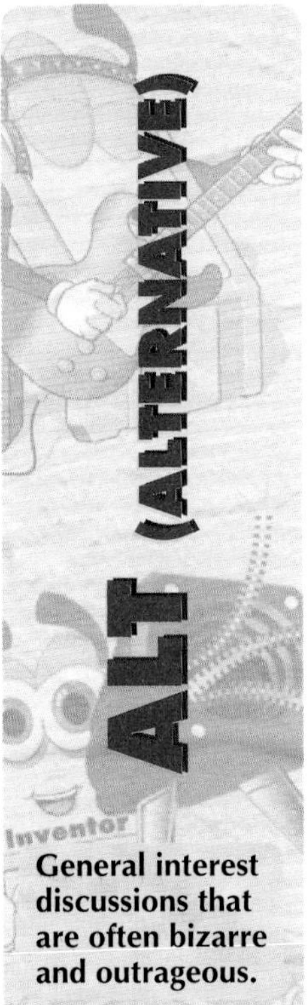

ALT (ALTERNATIVE)

General interest discussions that are often bizarre and outrageous.

alt.2600
The magazine or the game system. You decide.

alt.3d.misc
Three-dimensional imaging.

alt.activism
Activities for activists.

alt.adoption
For those involved with or contemplating adoption.

alt.anarchism
Anarchists of the world, unite.

alt.animals.bears
Who's gonna win the Super Bowl? Da Bears.

alt.animals.dolphins
Flipper, Darwin, and all their friends.

alt.animals.felines
Cats of all types.

alt.animals.foxes
For those wild and crazy guys.

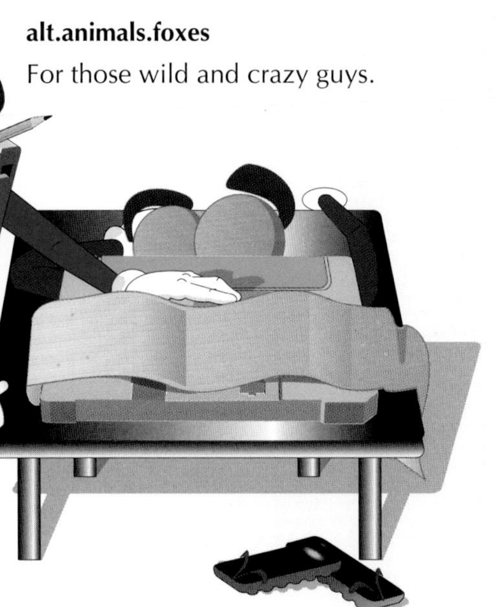

Newsgroup: alt.animals.felines
Subject: Urgent cat problem
From: Pete Lilly

Please help me! The kitten I adopted turned out to be a lion cub–and it's now full grown. I'm trapped in my bedroom, and I hear hungry growls outside the door. I need an experienced lion tamer to call me at (555) 845-2309.

alt.answers
As if anyone on alt has the answers. (Moderated)

alt.archery
Robin Hood had the right idea.

alt.architecture
Building design/construction and related topics.

alt.astrology
Twinkle, twinkle, little planet.

alt.atheism
Godless heathens.

alt.athiesm
Illiterate Godless heathens.

alt.backrubs
Lower...to the right...aaaah.

alt.best.of.internet
It was a time of sorrow, it was a time of joy.

alt.bigfoot
Dr. Scholl's gone native.

alt.binaries.sounds.movies
Sounds from copyrighted movies.

alt.binaries.sounds.tv
Sounds from copyrighted television shows.

alt.books.reviews
If you want to know how it turns out, read it.

alt.books.stephen-king
The works of horror writer Stephen King.

alt.censorship
Discussion about restricting speech/press.

alt.child-support
Raising children in a split family.

alt.christnet
Gathering place for Christian ministers and users.

alt.coffee
Another group worshipping caffeine.

alt.conspiracy
Be paranoid—they're out to get you.

alt.consumers.free-stuff
Free offers and how to take advantage of them.

alt.cows.moo.moo.moo
Like cows would cluck or something.

alt.crime
Crime in general, not just the crimes in alt.

alt.cult-movies
Movies with a cult following.

alt.current-events.usa
What's new in the United States.

alt.cyberpunk
High-tech low-life.

alt.disasters.misc
General discussion of disaster issues.

alt.dreams
What do they mean?

alt.education.alternative
School doesn't have to suck.

alt.evil
Tales from the dark side.

alt.fan.actors
Discussion of actors, male and female.

Newsgroup: alt.evil
Subject: Update on evil force
From: Shirley Nelson

Thanks to everyone who sent me advice on how to deal with the evil force in my basement. It turns out, however, there is no evil force. Several stray cats had snuck through a basement window. Does anyone want a cat?

ALT (CONTINUED)

alt.fan.bill-gates
Fans of the original micro-softie.

alt.fan.elvis-presley
The late, great Elvis the Pelvis.

alt.fan.jay-leno
Fans of The Tonight Show with Jay Leno.

alt.fan.letterman
One of the top 10 reasons to get the alt groups.

alt.fan.letterman.top-ten
Top Ten lists from the Letterman show. (Moderated)

alt.fan.newt-gingrich
Conservatives return with a vengeance.

alt.fan.noam-chomsky
Noam Chomsky's writings and opinions.

alt.fan.tlc
Discussion of TLC rap/hip-hop group.

alt.fan.u2
The Irish rock band U2.

alt.flame
Alternative, literate, pithy, succinct screaming.

alt.guitar
You axed for it, you got it.

alt.horror
The horror genre.

alt.humor.best-of-usenet
What readers think is funniest in netnews. (Moderated)

alt.hypnosis
When you awaken, you will forget about this newsgroup.

alt.individualism
Philosophies where individual rights are paramount.

alt.internet.media-coverage
The coverage of the Internet by the media.

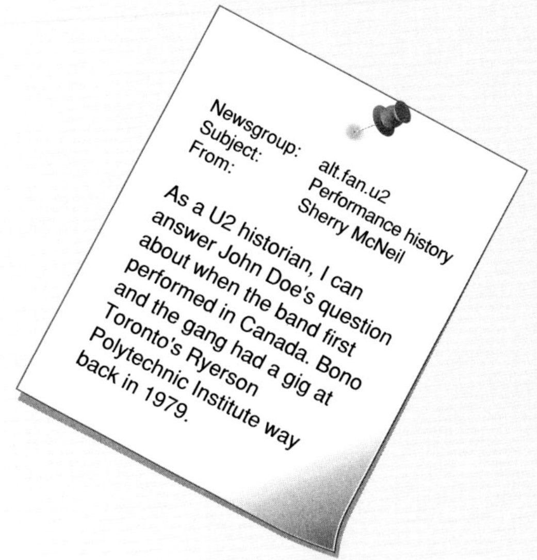

Newsgroup: alt.fan.u2
Subject: Performance history
From: Sherry McNeil
As a U2 historian, I can answer John Doe's question about when the band first performed in Canada. Bono and the gang had a gig at Toronto's Ryerson Polytechnic Institute way back in 1979.

Newsgroup: alt.inventors
Subject: Marketing advice
From: Andrea Bartell

I have invented a device that I figure will sell millions, especially to the kindhearted. It is a rat trap that simply yells, "Get outa my house, rodent!" without actually harming the little animal.

How can I market my invention and retire early?

alt.internet.services
The different features of the Internet.

alt.inventors
People with new ideas.

alt.irc
Internet Relay Chat material.

alt.jokes.limericks
There once was a group in alt.

alt.journalism
Shop talk by journalists and journalism students.

alt.journalism.criticism
I write, therefore, I'm biased.

alt.kids-talk
A place for the pre-college set on the Net.

alt.life.sucks
Another upbeat newsgroup.

alt.magic
For discussion about stage magic.

alt.magick
For discussion about supernatural arts.

alt.meditation
General discussion of meditation.

alt.movies.independent
Films put out by independent producers.

alt.movies.monster
Godzilla, The Wolfman, The Thing and so on.

alt.movies.visual-effects
Discussion of visual f/x for movies and TV.

alt.music.abba
Swedish pop.

alt.music.african
African music.

alt.music.alternative
For groups having 2 or fewer platinum-selling albums.

alt.music.beastie-boys
The Beastie Boys.

ALT (CONTINUED)

alt.music.billy-joel
Discussion of Billy Joel.

alt.music.bjork
For fans of Bjork and the late Sugarcubes.

alt.music.blues-traveler
For "All fellow travelers."

alt.music.blur
Fandom of the uniquely British group Blur.

alt.music.bon-jovi
For fans of Jon and the gang.

alt.music.boyz-2-men
The harmonizing tunes of Boyz II Men.

alt.music.brian-eno
Apparently too popular to warrant further description.

alt.music.bruce-springsteen
New Jersey's finest.

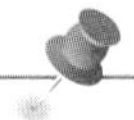

Newsgroup: alt.music.bruce-springsteen
Subject: Secret backwards messages
From: Danyael Halprin

It's true, it's true! Play "Streets of Philadelphia" backwards and you hear The Boss speaking eloquently on rocket science, brain surgery and the ancient Greek philosophers. Wild stuff!

alt.music.celine-dion
The music and art of the international star Celine Dion.

alt.music.chicago
Discussion of the band Chicago.

alt.music.ct-dummies
Discussion of the musical group Crash Test Dummies.

alt.music.dance
Music to dance to.

alt.music.dave-matthews
The Dave Matthews Band.

alt.music.elo
The Electric Light Orchestra.

alt.music.enya
Gaelic set to spacey music.

alt.music.genesis
Genesis, in all their incarnations.

alt.music.green-day
The band Green Day.

alt.music.hawaiian
The music of the Hawaiian islands.

alt.music.karaoke
Givin' it from the (usually drunken) heart.

Newsgroup: alt.music.ramones
Subject: Farewell tour
From: Adam Bain

I can't believe that *Adios Amigos* is really the final album. It's so hard to imagine the alternative rock scene without the immortal Ramones. How can a longtime fan club member secure tickets and maybe even backstage passes for the upcoming farewell tour?

alt.music.lyrics
Discussion of song lyrics.

alt.music.michael-jackson
The enigmatic Michael Jackson.

alt.music.midi
Music from MIDI devices.

alt.music.monkees
Hey, hey, they were the Monkees.

alt.music.nin
Nine Inch Nails.

alt.music.paul-simon
Discussion of Paul Simon's music.

alt.music.pearl-jam
The music of the alternative rock band Pearl Jam.

alt.music.pet-shop-boys
The music of the Pet Shop Boys.

alt.music.peter-gabriel
So, it's the music of Peter Gabriel, sans frontier.

alt.music.pink-floyd
Sold-out shows everywhere.

alt.music.primus
Discussions related to the music group Primus.

alt.music.queen
The band Queen and related solo acts.

alt.music.ramones
For discussion of the kings of punk rock.

alt.music.smash-pumpkins
The Smashing Pumpkins.

alt.music.sondheim
The life and music of Stephen Sondheim.

alt.music.soundgarden
The band Soundgarden.

alt.music.techno
Bring on the bass.

alt.music.tom-waits
Discussion of works of artist Tom Waits.

alt.music.tragically-hip
The rock band The Tragically Hip.

ALT (CONTINUED)

alt.music.u2
Another group for the band U2. See also alt.fan.u2.

alt.music.van-halen
For discussion of topics related to Van Halen.

alt.music.weird-al
Parodies-R-Us.

alt.music.world
Discussion of music from around the world.

alt.mythology
Zeus rules.

alt.newbie
The altnet housewarming committee.

alt.news-media
Don't believe the hype.

alt.obituaries
Notices of dead folks.

alt.online-service
Large commercial online services, and the Internet.

Newsgroup: alt.personals
Subject: Mate wanted
From: John Doe

Foul-mouthed person with two ferocious dogs and a large, poisonous snake seeks same. Must enjoy trailer park culture and daytime TV.

alt.paranormal
Phenomena which are not scientifically explicable.

alt.pave.the.earth
Damn the environmentalists, full speed ahead.

alt.personals
Do you really want to meet someone this way?

alt.philosophy.debate
Back to basics.

alt.politics.media
How the mass media is involved in shaping politics.

alt.politics.org.cia
The United States Central Intelligence Agency.

alt.politics.org.fbi
The United States Federal Bureau of Investigation.

alt.politics.org.nsa
The ultrasecret security arm of the U.S. government.

alt.politics.usa.congress
Discussions relating to U.S. House and Senate.

alt.privacy
Privacy issues in cyberspace.

alt.prose
Postings of original writings, fictional and otherwise.

alt.rave
Techno-culture: music, dancing, drugs, dancing, etc.

alt.revenge
Two wrongs trying to make a right.

alt.rock-n-roll
Counterpart to alt.sex and alt.drugs.

alt.romance
Discussion about the romantic side of love.

alt.rush-limbaugh
Fans of the conservative activist radio announcer.

alt.save.the.earth
Environmentalist causes.

alt.security
Security issues on computer systems.

alt.sex
Postings of a prurient nature.

alt.sport.bowling
In the gutter again.

alt.sport.falconry
Hunting with birds of prey.

alt.sport.lacrosse
The game of lacrosse.

Newsgroup: alt.sports.badminton
Subject: Footwear
From: Steve Scott
I am thinking about joining a badminton club at the local gym. Is there special footwear I should buy before I get started? I'm concerned that my old jogging shoes won't quite cut it.

alt.sport.officiating
Being a referee.

alt.sport.racquetball
All aspects of indoor racquetball and related sports.

alt.sport.squash
With the proper technique, vegetables can go very fast.

alt.sports.badminton
Discussion about badminton.

alt.stagecraft
Technical theatre issues.

alt.startrek.creative
Stories and parodies related to Star Trek.

alt.support
Dealing with emotional situations and experiences.

ALT (CONTINUED)

alt.surrealism
Surrealist ideologies and their influences.

alt.test
Alternative subnetwork testing.

alt.true-crime
Criminal acts around the world.

alt.tv.x-files
Extraterrestrial coverup conspiracies.

alt.usenet.kooks
I have a theory about why we have such crazy theories.

alt.vampyres
Discussion of vampires and related writings, films, etc.

Newsgroup: alt.vampyres
Subject: I am a vampire.
From: Dr. Death

I am a vampire, and I want to meet others like me. Call me at (321) 555-2632. But don't call after 10 because it will wake up my parents.

alt.video.games.reviews
Reviews of video games.

alt.war
Discussion of war and related topics.

alt.women.attitudes
The different attitudes that women have.

alt.www.hotjava
Discussions of Sun Microsystems' Java language.

alt.yoga
All forms and aspects of yoga.

alt.zines
Small magazines, mostly noncommercial.

BIZ (BUSINESS)

Business discussions that are usually more commercial in nature than those of other groups. Advertising is allowed and lists of job openings are available.

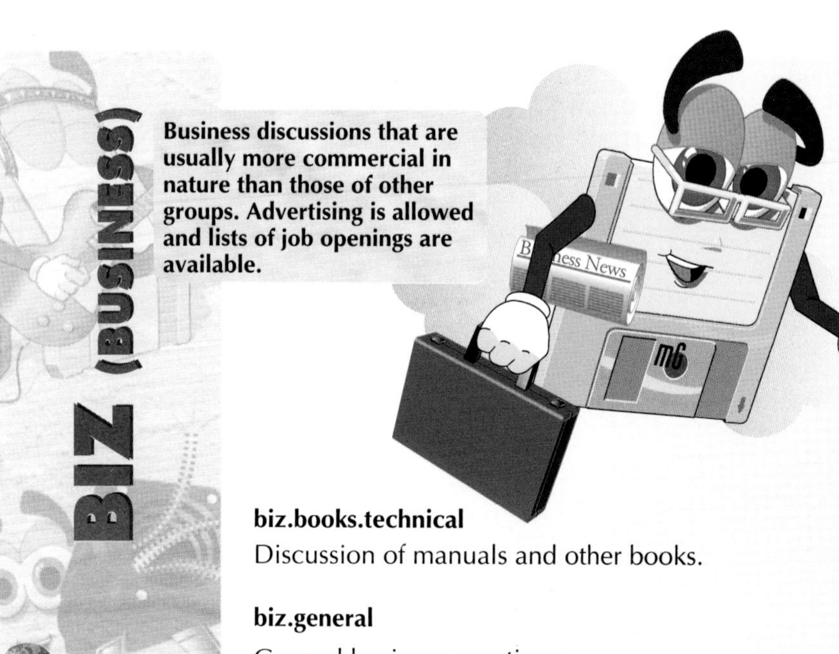

biz.books.technical
Discussion of manuals and other books.

biz.general
General business questions.

biz.jobs.offered
Find a job on the Internet.

biz.marketplace.computers.discussion
How much is your computer worth?

biz.marketplace.international
Discussing international business.

biz.misc
Various business issues.

biz.newgroup
New business newsgroups.

biz.test
For test messages.

COMP (COMPUTERS)

Discussions of computer hardware, software and computer science.

comp.admin.policy
Discussions of site administration policies.

comp.ai
Artificial intelligence discussions.

comp.answers
Repository for periodic Usenet articles. (Moderated)

comp.fonts
Typefonts—design, conversion, use, etc.

comp.graphics.apps.photoshop
Adobe Photoshop techniques and help.

comp.graphics.misc
Computer graphics miscellany.

comp.human-factors
Issues related to human-computer interaction (HCI).

comp.infosystems
Any discussion about information systems.

comp.infosystems.www.announce
World Wide Web announcements. (Moderated)

TAC
TAC
TAC
TAC

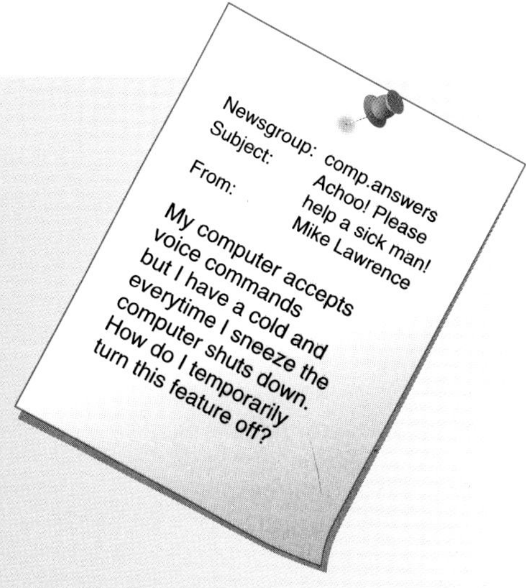
Newsgroup: comp.answers
Subject: Achoo! Please help a sick man!
From: Mike Lawrence
My computer accepts voice commands but I have a cold and everytime I sneeze the computer shuts down. How do I temporarily turn this feature off?

comp.infosystems.www.authoring.html
Writing HTML for the Web.

comp.infosystems.www.browsers.mac
Web browsers for the Macintosh platform.

comp.infosystems.www.browsers.ms-windows
Web browsers for MS Windows.

comp.internet.library
Discussing electronic libraries. (Moderated)

comp.lang.c++
The object-oriented C++ language.

comp.lang.misc
Different computer languages not specifically listed.

comp.lang.pascal.borland
Borland's Pascal.

comp.lang.perl.misc
The Perl language in general.

comp.os.ms-windows.advocacy
Speculation and debate about Microsoft Windows.

comp.os.ms-windows.win95.misc
Miscellaneous topics about Windows 95.

COMP (CONTINUED)

comp.os.os2.advocacy
Supporting and flaming OS/2.

comp.patents
Discussing patents of computer technology. (Moderated)

comp.protocols.tcp-ip
TCP and IP network protocols.

comp.robotics.misc
All aspects of robots and their applications.

comp.security.misc
Security issues of computers and networks.

comp.society
The impact of technology on society. (Moderated)

comp.society.folklore
Computer folklore and culture, past and present. (Moderated)

comp.sys.intel
Discussions about Intel systems and parts.

comp.sys.laptops
Laptop (portable) computers.

comp.sys.mac.advocacy
The Macintosh computer family compared to others.

comp.sys.powerpc
General PowerPC discussion.

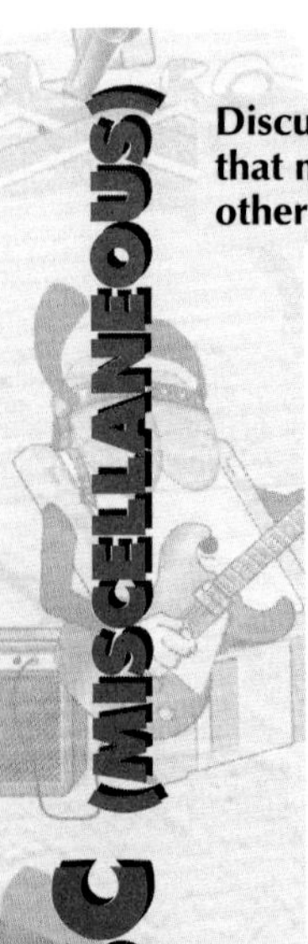

MISC (MISCELLANEOUS)

Discussions of miscellaneous topics that may overlap topics discussed in other categories.

misc.activism.militia
Citizens bearing arms for the common defense. (Moderated)

misc.answers
Repository for periodic Usenet articles. (Moderated)

misc.books.technical
Discussion of books about technical topics.

misc.consumers
Consumer interests, product reviews, etc.

misc.consumers.house
Discussion about owning and maintaining a house.

misc.creativity
Promoting the use of creativity in all human endeavors.

misc.education
Discussion of the educational system.

misc.emerg-services
Forum for paramedics and other first responders.

misc.entrepreneurs
Discussion on operating a business.

misc.fitness.misc
General fitness topics.

misc.handicap
Items of interest for/about the handicapped. (Moderated)

misc.health.aids
AIDS issues and support.

misc.health.alternative
Alternative, complementary and holistic health care.

misc.health.diabetes
Discussion of diabetes management in day-to-day life.

Newsgroup: misc.fitness.misc
Subject: Wimpy Feet!
From: R. Tuff

I'm a pretty athletic guy and I pump iron every day. But I find that my feet are still tiny and weak. What can I do to give myself rough and tough feet?

PUFF! PUFF!

misc.jobs.offered
Announcements of positions available.

misc.jobs.offered.entry
Job listings only for entry-level positions.

misc.legal
Legalities and the ethics of law.

misc.legal.computing
Discussing the legal climate of the computing world.

misc.taxes
Tax laws and advice.

misc.writing
Discussion of writing in all of its forms.

Discussions about the Usenet. Topics range from news and information about the network to advice on how to use it.

news.admin.misc
General topics of network news administration.

news.announce.newsgroups
Calls for newsgroups and announcements of same. (Moderated)

news.announce.newusers
Explanatory postings for new users. (Moderated)

news.answers
Repository for periodic Usenet articles. (Moderated)

news.groups
Discussions and lists of newsgroups.

news.lists
News-related statistics and lists. (Moderated)

news.misc
Discussions of Usenet itself.

news.newusers.questions
Q and A for users new to the Usenet.

INTERESTING NEWSGROUPS

REC (RECREATION)

Discussions of recreational activities and hobbies.

rec.antiques
Discussing antiques and vintage items.

rec.arts.animation
Discussion of various kinds of animation.

rec.arts.books
Books of all genres, and the publishing industry.

rec.arts.books.childrens
All aspects of children's literature.

rec.arts.books.reviews
Book reviews. (Moderated)

rec.arts.comics.alternative
Alternative (non-mainstream) comic books.

rec.arts.comics.dc.universe
DC Comics' shared universe and characters.

rec.arts.comics.marvel.universe
Marvel Comics' shared universe and characters.

Newsgroup: rec.antiques
Subject: Broken Statue
From: C. Buffer

Last night I broke my mother's prized Elvis statue. She got it at the Graceland gift shop in 1976. Where can I get one before she notices?

rec.arts.comics.misc
Comic books, graphic novels, sequential art.

rec.arts.dance
Any aspects of dance not covered in another newsgroup.

rec.arts.disney.announce
FAQs, lists, info, announcements. (Moderated)

rec.arts.disney.misc
General topics pertinent to the Disney Company.

rec.arts.drwho
Discussion about Dr. Who.

rec.arts.misc
Discussions about the arts not in other groups.

rec.arts.movies.production
Filmmaking, amateur and professional.

rec.arts.movies.reviews
Reviews of movies. (Moderated)

rec.arts.puppetry
For discussion of puppets in any form or venue.

rec.arts.sf.misc
Science fiction lovers' newsgroup.

rec.arts.sf.movies
Discussing SF motion pictures.

rec.arts.startrek.current
New Star Trek shows, movies and books.

rec.arts.startrek.fandom
Star Trek conventions and memorabilia.

rec.arts.startrek.info
Information about the universe of Star Trek. (Moderated)

rec.arts.startrek.misc
General discussions of Star Trek.

rec.arts.theatre.misc
Miscellaneous topics and issues in theatre.

rec.arts.theatre.musicals
Musical theatre around the world.

rec.arts.theatre.plays
Dramaturgy and discussion of plays.

Newsgroup: rec.arts.tv.soaps.abc
Subject: General Asylum
From: June Burke

I missed yesterday's episode of General Asylum and I need an update. Did Rachel's evil twin sister marry her ex-husband's gardener? Did Samantha's long-lost brother come out of his coma and reveal that Tiffany's fourth husband is the murderer? I can't wait to find out!

rec.arts.tv
The boob tube, its history, and past and current shows.

rec.arts.tv.soaps.abc
Soap operas produced by or for the ABC network.

rec.arts.tv.soaps.cbs
Soap operas produced by or for the CBS network.

rec.arts.tv.soaps.misc
Postings of interest to all soap opera viewers.

rec.autos.antique
Discussing all aspects of automobiles over 25 years old.

rec.autos.driving
Driving automobiles.

rec.autos.tech
Technical aspects of automobiles, et. al.

rec.aviation.answers
Frequently asked questions about aviation. (Moderated)

rec.aviation.student
Learning to fly.

rec.bicycles.misc
General discussion of bicycling.

rec.birds
Hobbyists interested in bird watching.

rec.boats
Hobbyists interested in boating.

REC (CONTINUED)

rec.climbing
Climbing techniques, competition announcements, etc.

rec.collecting
Discussion among collectors of many things.

rec.equestrian
Discussion of things equestrian.

rec.folk-dancing
Folk dances, dancers, and dancing.

rec.food.cooking
Food, cooking, cookbooks, and recipes.

rec.food.recipes
Recipes for interesting food and drink. (Moderated)

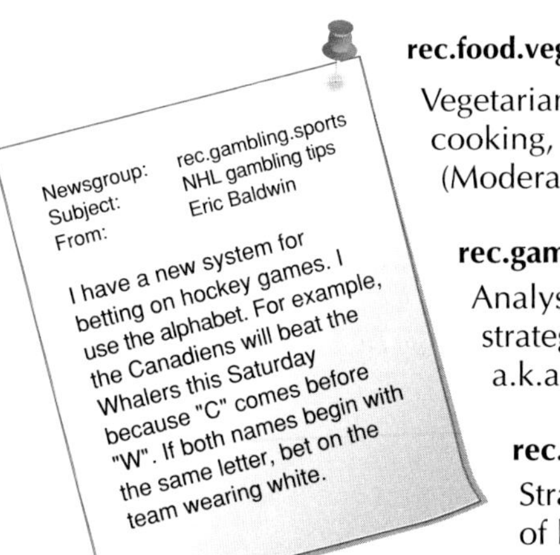

Newsgroup: rec.gambling.sports
Subject: NHL gambling tips
From: Eric Baldwin
I have a new system for betting on hockey games. I use the alphabet. For example, the Canadiens will beat the Whalers this Saturday because "C" comes before "W". If both names begin with the same letter, bet on the team wearing white.

rec.food.veg.cooking
Vegetarian recipes, cooking, nutrition. (Moderated)

rec.gambling.blackjack
Analysis of and strategy for blackjack, a.k.a. 21.

rec.gambling.lottery
Strategy and news of lotteries and sweepstakes.

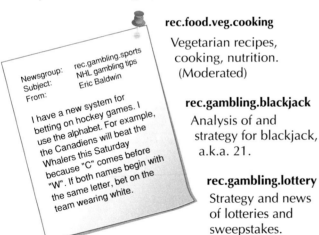

rec.gambling.poker
Analysis and strategy of live poker games.

rec.gambling.sports
Wagering on human sporting events.

rec.games.frp.cyber
Discussions of cyberpunk-related roleplaying games.

rec.games.frp.dnd
Fantasy roleplaying with TSR's Dungeons and Dragons.

rec.games.miniatures.misc
Miniatures and various tabletop wargames.

rec.games.video.nintendo
All Nintendo video game systems and software.

rec.games.video.sega
All Sega video game systems and software.

rec.gardens
Gardening methods and results.

rec.humor
Jokes and the like. May be somewhat offensive.

rec.humor.funny
Jokes that are funny, in the moderator's opinion. (Moderated)

rec.hunting
Discussions about hunting. (Moderated)

rec.org.mensa
Talking with members of the high–IQ society Mensa.

rec.pets
Pets, pet care, and household animals in general.

rec.pets.cats
Discussion about domestic cats.

rec.pets.dogs.misc
All other topics, chat, humor, etc.

rec.photo.misc
General issues related to photography.

rec.photo.moderated
The art and science of photography. (Moderated)

rec.puzzles
Puzzles, problems, and quizzes.

rec.running
Running for enjoyment, sport, exercise, etc.

rec.scuba
Hobbyists interested in SCUBA diving.

rec.skydiving
Hobbyists interested in skydiving.

rec.sport.archery
All aspects of archery for archers of any skill level.

rec.sport.baseball
Discussion about baseball.

rec.sport.basketball.college
Hoops on the collegiate level.

rec.sport.basketball.pro
Talk of professional basketball.

rec.sport.boxing
Boxing in all its pugilistic facets and forms.

rec.sport.fencing
All aspects of swordplay.

rec.sport.football.college
U.S.-style college football.

rec.sport.football.pro
U.S.-style professional football.

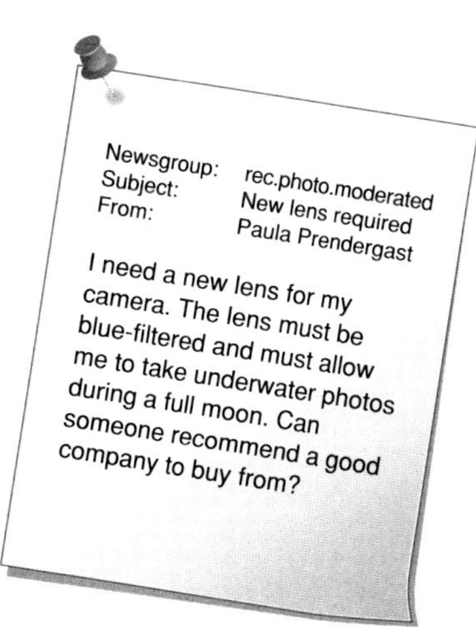

Newsgroup: rec.photo.moderated
Subject: New lens required
From: Paula Prendergast
I need a new lens for my camera. The lens must be blue-filtered and must allow me to take underwater photos during a full moon. Can someone recommend a good company to buy from?

REC (CONTINUED)

rec.sport.golf
Discussion about all aspects of golfing.

rec.sport.hockey
Discussion about ice hockey.

rec.sport.rowing
Crew for competition or fitness.

rec.sport.rugby
Discussion about the game of rugby.

rec.sport.soccer
Discussion about soccer (Association Football).

rec.sport.squash
Forum for all aspects of squash.

rec.sport.swimming
Training for and competing in swimming events.

Newsgroup: rec.sport.golf
Subject: Help needed on golf swing
From: Joey Marlin

Could someone please recommend an instructional book on how to improve the accuracy of my golf swing? So far, I have broken the windows in three houses, two cars and a restaurant. I may have to get a second job to pay these bills!

rec.sport.tennis
Things related to the sport of tennis.

rec.sport.unicycling
All sorts of fun on one wheel.

rec.sport.volleyball
Discussion about volleyball.

rec.video
Video and video components.

rec.windsurfing
Riding the waves as a hobby.

rec.woodworking
Hobbyists interested in woodworking.

SCI (SCIENCE)

Discussions about science, including research, applied science and the social sciences.

sci.agriculture
Farming, agriculture and related topics.

sci.answers
Repository for periodic Usenet articles. (Moderated)

sci.anthropology
All aspects of studying humankind.

sci.archaeology
Studying antiquities of the world.

sci.astro
Astronomy discussions and information.

sci.chem
Chemistry and related sciences.

sci.cognitive
Perception, memory, judgment and reasoning.

sci.cryonics
Theory and practice of biostasis, suspended animation.

sci.electronics
Circuits, theory, electrons and discussions.

sci.energy
Discussions about energy, science and technology.

sci.engr
Technical discussions about engineering tasks.

sci.environment
Discussions about the environment and ecology.

sci.math
Mathematical discussions and pursuits.

sci.med
Medicine and its related products and regulations.

sci.med.pharmacy
The teaching and practice of pharmacy.

sci.military.moderated
Military technology. (Moderated)

sci.physics
Physical laws, properties, etc.

sci.psychology.misc
General discussion of psychology.

sci.space.news
Announcements of space-related news items. (Moderated)

sci.virtual-worlds
Virtual Reality technology and culture. (Moderated)

SOC (SOCIAL)

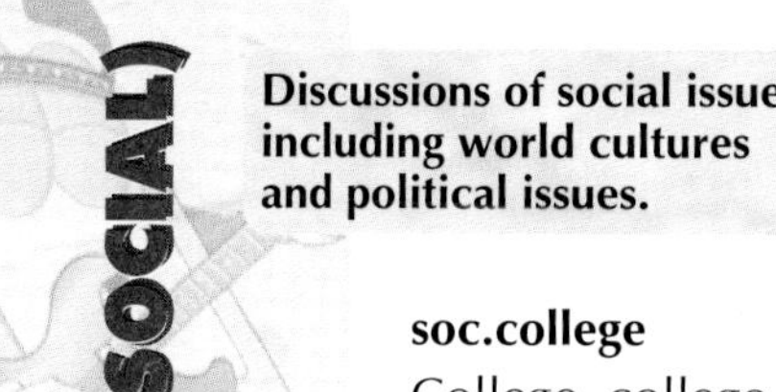

Discussions of social issues, including world cultures and political issues.

soc.college
College, college activities, campus life, etc.

soc.college.grad
General issues related to graduate schools.

soc.culture.afghanistan
Discussion of Afghan society.

soc.culture.african.american
Discussions about Afro-American issues.

soc.culture.australian
Australian culture and society.

soc.culture.british
Issues about Britain and those of British descent.

SOC (CONTINUED)

soc.culture.canada
Discussions of Canada and its people.

soc.culture.caribbean
Life in the Caribbean.

soc.culture.celtic
Irish, Scottish, Breton, Cornish, Manx and Welsh.

soc.culture.china
About China and Chinese culture.

soc.culture.europe
Discussing all aspects of all-European society.

soc.culture.greek
Group about Greeks.

soc.culture.italian
The Italian people and their culture.

soc.culture.japan
Everything Japanese, except the Japanese language.

soc.culture.mexican
Discussion of Mexico's society.

soc.culture.russian
All things Russian, in the broadest sense.

soc.culture.south-africa
South African society, culture, and politics.

soc.culture.spain
Spain and the Spanish.

soc.culture.taiwan
Discussion about things Taiwanese.

soc.culture.ukrainian
The lives and times of the Ukrainian people.

Newsgroup: soc.history.living
Subject: Civil War re-enactment errors
From: Steve Wilson

I wish all participants in U.S. Civil War re-enactments would review history books about the time period in question. At an event last weekend, several soldiers were disappointed when told they couldn't use cellular phones, Army Jeeps and portable computers. Please study!

soc.feminism
Discussion of feminism and feminist issues. (Moderated)

soc.history
Discussions of things historical.

soc.history.living
Living history and reenactment, issues and info.

soc.penpals
In search of net.friendships.

soc.politics
Political problems, systems, solutions. (Moderated)

soc.rights.human
Human rights and activism (e.g., Amnesty International).

soc.veterans
Social issues relating to military veterans.

soc.women
Issues related to women, their problems and relationships.

Debates and long discussions, often about controversial subjects.

talk.abortion
All sorts of discussions and arguments on abortion.

talk.answers
Repository for periodic Usenet articles. (Moderated)

talk.environment
Discussion on the state of the environment and what to do.

talk.origins
Evolution versus creationism (sometimes hot!).

Newsgroup: talk.rumors
Subject: Ghost of Elvis
Name: Jen White

Sightings of the ghost of Elvis have increased dramatically. The King's spirit has been spotted in Chicago, Los Angeles, Denver and New York in the last month. Be on the lookout– Elvis may be coming to your neighborhood soon!

talk.philosophy.misc
Philosophical musings on all topics.

talk.politics.animals
The use and/or abuse of animals.

talk.politics.guns
The politics of firearm ownership and (mis)use.

talk.rumors
For the posting of rumors.

REGIONAL

There are newsgroups available that focus on topics of interest to people living in specific geographical regions. For example, aus for Australia, bc for British Columbia and ca for California.

In this chapter you will find interesting Web sites that you can visit.
http://www.maran.co
Netscape - [maranGraphics]
File Edit View Go Bookmarks Options Directory
Windows '95
All Other Titles Ordering Info.

CHAPTER 8

INTERESTING WEB SITES

WEB SITE RATINGS

★	*Good*
★★	*Very Good*
★★★	*Excellent*
★★★★	*Superb*
★★★★★	*A Masterpiece*

ANIMALS

Animal Game ★★

This Web site asks you a series of questions to determine what animal you are thinking of.

 http://www.cs.wustl.edu/~brian/Animals

Animal Science ★★★

Information on all your favorite barnyard animals.

 http://www.okstate.edu/OSU_Ag/ansci.html

AquaLink ★★★

All the fish information your heart desires.

 http://weber.u.washington.edu/~aqualink

Cats on the Internet ★

This site provides links to cat home pages around the world.

 http://http2.sils.umich.edu/~dtorres/cats/cats.html

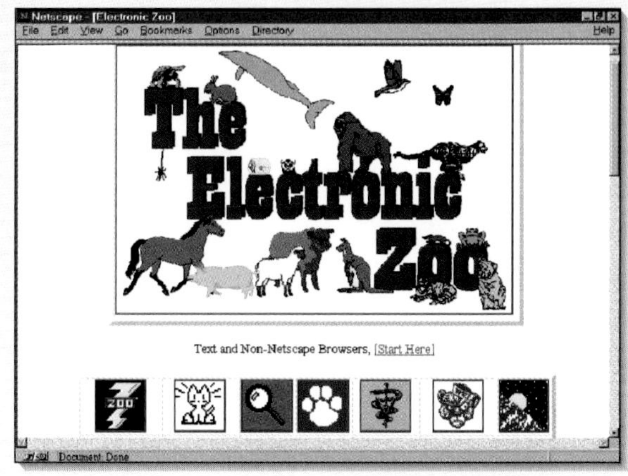

Electronic Zoo ★★★★★

All of the fun without the hair and that peculiar smell.

 http://netvet.wustl.edu/e-zoo.htm

FINS ★★★★

The Fish Information Service provides information about aquariums.

http://www.actwin.com/fish

Fish Cam ★

Netscape displays a constantly updating picture of their office fish tank.

http://home.netscape.com/fishcam

NetVet Resources ★★★

A great place to find veterinary and animal resources.

 http://netvet.wustl.edu

Petscape ★★

A pet-oriented version of the Netscape home page.

 http://hisurf.aloha.com/petscape

Socks The Cat ★★

See Socks Clinton, the First Cat of the United States of America.

 http://www.whitehouse.gov/White_House/Family/html/Life.html

Useless Pet Pages ★

An Internet user has compiled a list of the most useless pet home pages on the Internet.

 http://www.primus.com/staff/paulp/useless/pets.html

Virtual Pet Cemetery ★★

As morbid and depressing as it is, this site allows people to post small obituaries of their lost pets.

 http://www.lavamind.com/pet.html

ART

African Art Exhibit ★

This site exhibits African art and describes African culture.

 http://www.lib.virginia.edu/dic/exhib/93.ray.aa/African.html

Andy Warhol ★★

This site offers information on The Andy Warhol Museum in Pittsburgh, PA.

 http://www.warhol.org/warhol

Art on the Net ★★★

Artists, writers and musicians from around the world use this site to share their work.

 http://www.art.net

Body Modification Ezine ★★★★

That's right—body piercing and tattooing are now known as Body Art.

 http://www.io.org/~bme

ART (CONTINUED)

DaliWeb ★★★★★

An online gallery dedicated to Salvador Dali, the man famous for his melting clocks.

 http://www.highwayone.com/dali/daliweb.html

Dan's Gallery of the Grotesque ★

This gallery of disturbing images is not for the faint of heart.

 http://zynet.com/~grotesk

Electronic Gallery ★★★

This site offers many paintings that you can view and even buy if you like.

 http://www.egallery.com/egallery

Kaleidospace ★★★★

This site offers a wide variety of work from independent artists.

 http://kspace.com

Leonardo da Vinci ★★★

You can view many works by the famous artist and engineer.

 http://www.leonardo.net/main.html

Museum of Bad Art ★★★★

The place for art too bad to be ignored.

 http://glyphs.com/moba

Photo Perspectives ★★

A photographic museum of society and culture.

 http://www.i3tele.com/photo_perspectives_museum/faces/perspectives.home.html

Studio M ★

An artist has put a few of his paintings online in a virtual studio.

 http://astral.magic.ca/~bfp/studiom.html

Time Life Photo Sight ★★

A collection of photographs from Time's archives.

http://www.pathfinder.com/pathfinder/photo/sighthome.html

WebMuseum ★★★★★

You can view works of art by some of the most famous painters in the world, including Michelangelo, Renoir, Monet and Picasso.

http://www.emf.net/louvre

ASTRONOMY

Internet UFO Group ★★

This site lets you read articles and catch up on the latest UFO sightings.

http://users.aol.com/iufog

NASA ★★★

NASA presents pictures, information and links to all major NASA research locations in the U.S.

http://www.nasa.gov

National Space Science Data Center ★★★★★

This site contains a photo gallery and various space-related information.

http://nssdc.gsfc.nasa.gov

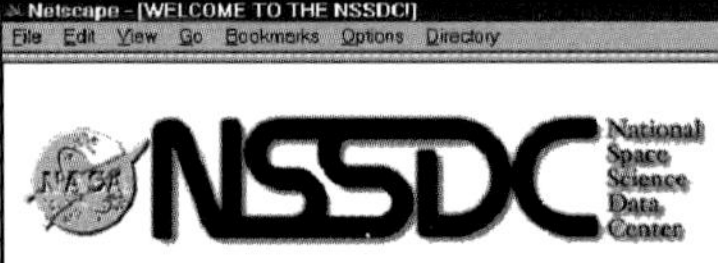

WELCOME TO THE NSSDC!

National Space Science Data Center, NASA Goddard Space Flight Center, Greenbelt, MD 20771, USA

The National Space Science Data Center (NSSDC) provides access to a wide variety of astrophysics, space physics, solar physics, lunar and planetary data from NASA space flight missions, in addition to selected other data and some models and software. NSSDC provides access to online information bases about NASA and non-NASA data at the NSSDC and elsewhere as well as the spacecraft and experiments that have or will provide public access data. NSSDC also provides information and support relative to data management standards and technologies.

Shuttle Web ★★

NASA's status report keeps you up-to-date on the space shuttle.

http://shuttle.nasa.gov

Stars and Galaxies ★★★

This great guide to the universe is taken from a multimedia CD-ROM.

http://www.eia.brad.ac.uk/btl

Views Of The Solar System ★★★

Travel light years away with the click of your mouse.

http://www.c3.lanl.gov/~cjhamil/SolarSystem/homepage.html

INTERESTING WEB SITES

BIOLOGY

BIO Online ★★

One of the top sites for information on biotechnology.

URL http://www.bio.com

Biosciences ★★★★

A guide to biology on the Internet.

URL http://golgi.harvard.edu/biopages/all.html

Cell Online ★

A collection of biology journals.

URL http://www.cell.com

Dictionary Of Cell Biology ★★★★

You can find those important definitions for your next biology essay.

URL http://www.mblab.gla.ac.uk/~julian/Dict.html

Entomology ★★

Colorado State's collection of bug information.

URL http://www.colostate.edu/Depts/Entomology/ent.html

Interactive Frog Dissection ★

Learn about frog anatomy without the mess.

URL http://curry.edschool.virginia.edu/~insttech/frog

USGS Biology ★★★

A directory of biological science sites on the Web.

URL http://info.er.usgs.gov/network/science/biology/index.html

Virology Server ★★★★★

Articles, pictures and information concerning various viruses.

URL http://www.bocklabs.wisc.edu/Welcome.html

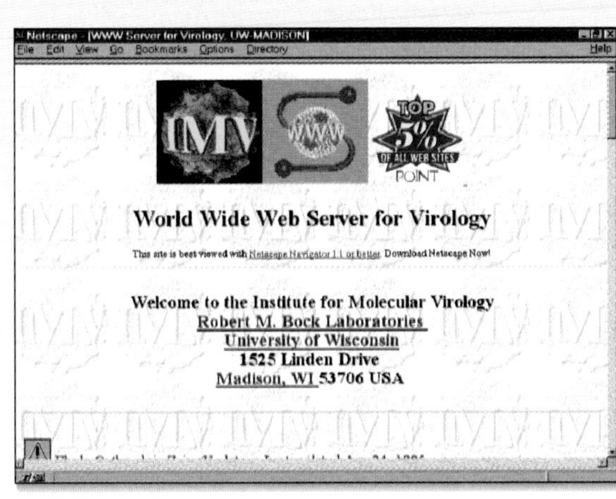

BIZARRE

50 Greatest Conspiracies ★★★★
Read excerpts from a book about the 50 greatest lies of all time.

 http://www.webcom.com:80/~conspire

Anagram Maker ★★★
Give this Web page a phrase and it will use the letters to make another sentence.

 http://Infobahn.COM:80/pages/anagram.html

Blue Dog ★★
A dog will bark the answer to the math question you ask.

 http://hp8.ini.cmu.edu:5550/bdf.html

Britannica's Lives ★★★★
Find out what famous people were born today.

 http://www.eb.com/cgi-bin/bio.pl

Captain Kirk Sing-A-Long Page ★
William Shatner croons his heart out on this quirky page.

 http://www.ama.caltech.edu/users/mrm/kirk.html

Carlos' Coloring Book ★★
Color a picture of anything from a house to a snowman at this site.

 http://robot0.ge.uiuc.edu/~carlosp/color

Crash Site ★★
This Cool Site of the Year nominee has a bit of everything.

 http://www.crashsite.com/Crash

Cyrano Server ★★★★
This site will write a love letter based on the personal information you provide.

 http://www.nando.net/toys/cyrano.html

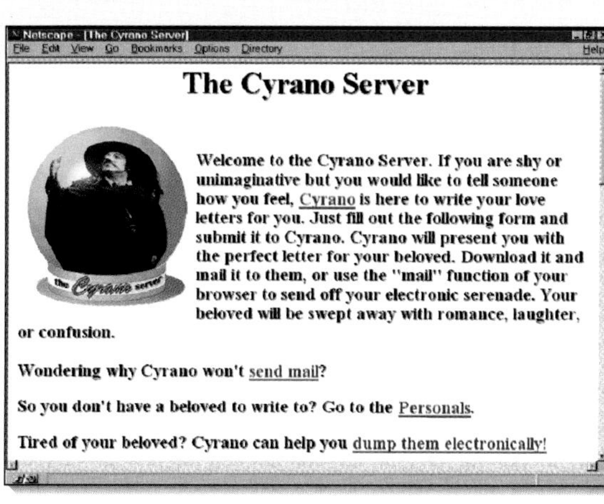

BIZARRE (CONTINUED)

Mr. Edible Starchy Tuber Head ★★

An online toy that just happens to look like the Mr. Potatohead doll.

URL http://winnie.acsu.buffalo.edu/potatoe

Paranoia Home Page ★★★★

This site promotes freedom of thought and eclectic interests on the Internet.

URL http://www.paranoia.com

Plastic Princess Collector's Page ★★★★

A great place for barbie doll collectors. This site includes information on doll shows, price guides and links to other Web sites.

URL http://d.armory.com/~zenugirl/barbie.html

Send A Virtual Postcard ★★★

Send a postcard to someone else on the Internet via this site at MIT.

URL http://postcards.www.media.mit.edu/Postcards

The Spot ★★★★

Live vicariously through nine online teenagers. This site was voted Cool Site of the Year.

 http://www.thespot.com

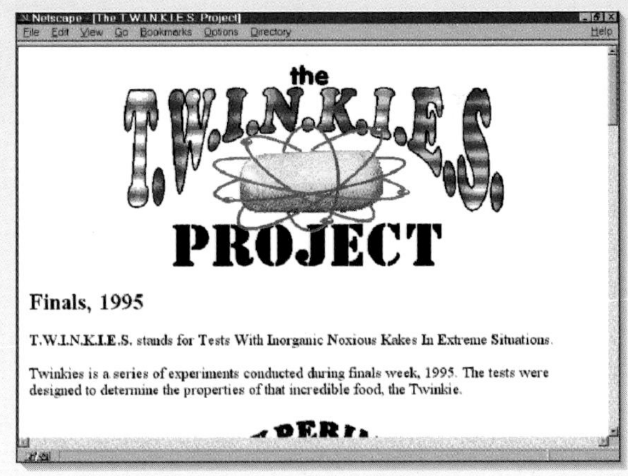

T.W.I.N.K.I.E.S ★

Tests With Inorganic Noxious Kakes In Extreme Situations. That's right, you can watch Twinkies blow up into a million pieces.

URL http://www.rice.edu/~gouge/twinkies.html

Underground Net ★★★★★

Truly bizarre, it's never the same site twice.

URL http://bazaar.com

Virtual Confession Booth ★★

Your chance to confess your sins from the comfort of your home.

URL http://anther.learning.cs.cmu.edu/priest.html

Who's Cool In America Project ★★★

The battle to control the use of the word "cool" on the Internet.

URL http://www.getcool.com/~getcool

BOOKS AND LANGUAGE

Amazon.com ★★★★

The Internet's largest bookstore, with over 1 million books for sale.

URL http://www.amazon.com

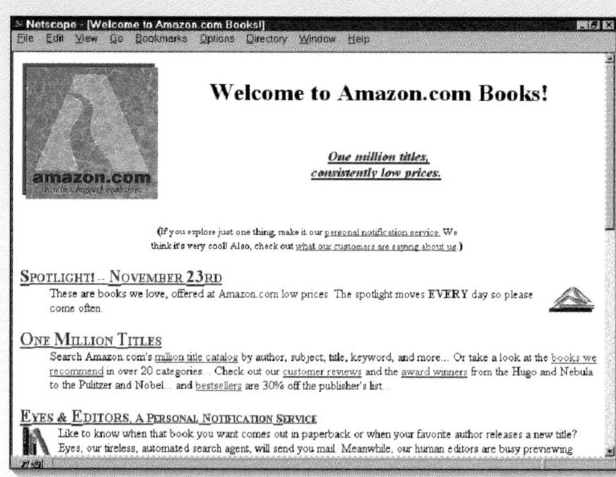

AudioBooks ★★

A catalog of books on tape.

 http://www.audiobooks.com

Bantam Doubleday Dell ★★

One of North America's largest publishers has information on their books and a daily puzzle.

 http://www.bdd.com

Book Stacks ★★★

Another of the Internet's major online book stores.

 http://www.books.com

BookWire ★★

A good place to start if you're looking for book information.

URL http://www.bookwire.com

Children's Literature ★★★

A guide to books for the little ones.

URL http://www.ucalgary.ca/~dkbrown/index.html

BOOKS AND LANGUAGE (CONTINUED)

Elementary Grammar ★

Remember—I before E, except after C. This site offers grammar lessons.

 http://www.hiway.co.uk/~ei/intro.html

English Server ★★★★

Carnegie Mellon University uses this site to distribute research, novels, criticism and much more.

 http://english-www.hss.cmu.edu

IDG Books ★★★★

IDG publishes the Dummies series, the 3-D Visual series and many others.

 http://www.idgbooks.com

Internet Public Library ★★★★★

Many reference books are available here, including a thesaurus and dictionary.

 http://ipl.sils.umich.edu

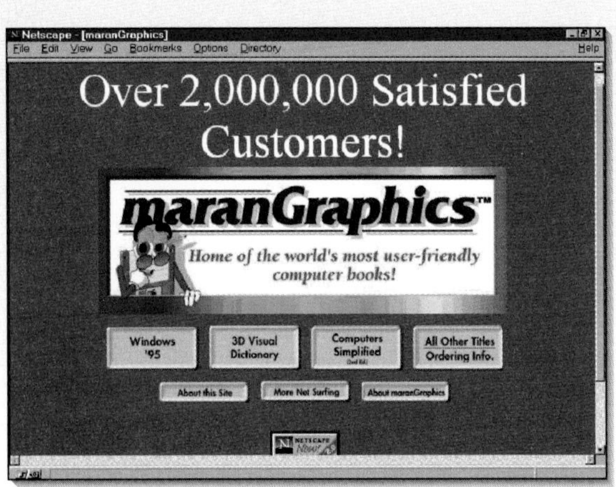

Library of Congress ★★★

You can't read the books online, but you can search for one of interest.

 http://lcweb.loc.gov/homepage/lchp.html

maranGraphics ★★★★★

Find out more about the world's most user-friendly computer books.

 http://www.maran.com

On-line Books ★★★

A collection of books at Carnegie Mellon University.

 http://www.cs.cmu.edu/Web/books.html

Project Gutenberg ★★★

You can find entire books here, such as Moby Dick and Anne of Green Gables.

 http://jg.cso.uiuc.edu/PG/welcome.html

Shakespeare Web ★★

A good place to start if you want to learn more about Shakespeare.

 http://www.shakespeare.com

Virtual Reference Desk ★★★★

Use a thesaurus, dictionary or phone book here.

 http://thorplus.lib.purdue.edu/reference/index.html

BUSINESS: COMPANIES

American Airlines ★★★

Browse through airline schedules, fares and much more.

 http://www.amrcorp.com/aa_home/aa_home.htm

AT&T ★★

AT&T offers a wide variety of telecommunications services.

 http://www.att.com

Canadian Airlines ★★★

Browse through airline schedules, inflight movies, special meals and much more.

 http://www.CdnAir.ca

Crayola ★★

This site tells you how crayons are made and the colors the company produces.

 http://www.crayola.com/crayola

FAO Schwarz ★★

More toys than you can imagine.

 http://faoschwarz.com

FedEX ★

Track your package online and make sure it arrives safely.

 http://www.fedex.com

BUSINESS: COMPANIES (CONTINUED)

Guinness ★

The beer, not the Book of World Records.

 http://www.itl.net/guinness

JCPenney ★★★

This chain of department stores lets you browse through their products from the comfort of your own home.

 http://www.jcpenney.com

Joe Boxer ★★★★

This site is less about underwear and more about having fun.

 http://www.joeboxer.com

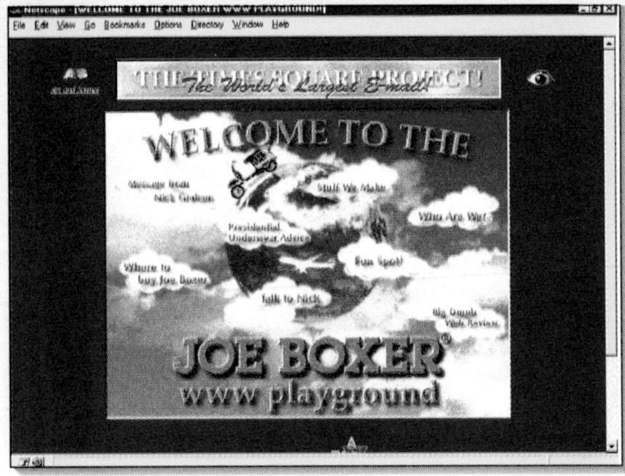

Kodak ★★★

This site offers a great collection of digital images.

 http://www.kodak.com

Leggs Pantyhose ★

You can buy pantyhose online at this site.

 http://www.pantyhose.com

Lego ★★

That's right, the multi-colored children's blocks.

http://legowww.homepages.com

Magnavox ★★★

You can find information on the company, its products and electronics in general.

http://www.magnavox.com

Molson ★★

Information on Molson and its products.

 http://www.molson.com

Ragu ★★★★★

This is a top-notch site with recipes, contests and guides to speaking Italian.

URL http://www.eat.com

Sharper Image ★★★

Neat gizmos you never thought existed can always be found at this site.

URL http://www.sharperimage.com/tsi

Sprint ★★

Find out all about the long distance company at this site.

URL http://www.sprint.com

TicketMaster ★★★

Look up events, read interviews and win free concert tickets!

URL U.S. http://www.ticketmaster.com

URL Canada http://www.ticketmaster.ca

Time Warner Inc. ★★★★

All the news, sports and entertainment information you could ask for.

URL http://www.pathfinder.com

UPS ★

Use the United Parcel Service site to track your package across the country.

URL http://www.ups.com

Virtual Vineyards ★★

Read about wine at this site or buy your favorite bottle.

URL http://www.virtualvin.com

Wal-Mart ★

The management team's quote of the day and much more.

URL http://www.wal-mart.com

BUSINESS: FINANCE

BarterWire ★★

Don't pay cash—barter for it!

 http://www.itex.net

Citibank ★

One of the largest banks in the U.S.

 http://www.citicorp.com

Coin Universe ★★★

Resources for collectors, dealers and anyone else interested in coins from around the world.

 http://www.coin-universe.com/index.html

Finance On The WWW ★★

This site in Denmark is filled with links to business and finance.

 http://www.wiso.gwdg.de/ifbg/finance.html

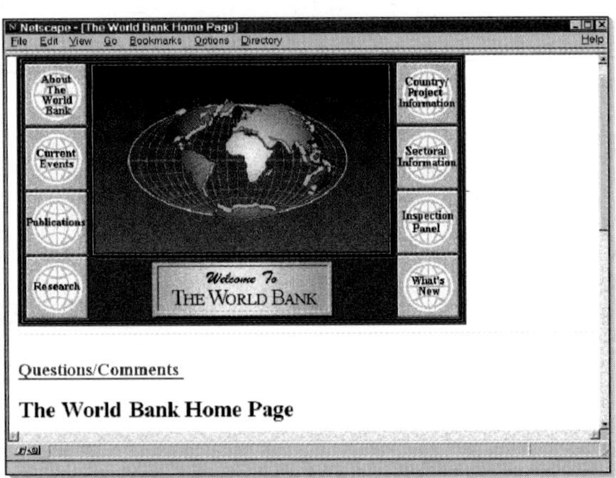

Internal Revenue Service ★

This site gives you access to IRS tax information and services.

 http://www.ustreas.gov/treasury/bureaus/irs/New_irs.html

Money and Investing Update ★★★★

The Wall Street Journal's financial news page.

 http://update.wsj.com

Money Magazine ★★★

A great source of financial information, from loan rates to investment ideas.

 http://www.pathfinder.com/money

Mutual Fund Charts ★★

Check out what mutual funds are hot and what funds are not.

 http://www.ai.mit.edu/stocks/mf.html

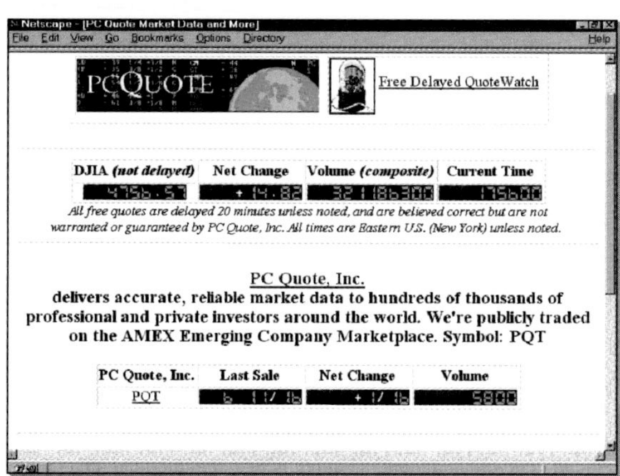

Ohio State University Financial Data Finder ★★

This site has a list of financial and economic data available on the Web.

URL http://www.cob.ohio-state.edu:80/dept/fin/osudata.htm

Online Banking and Financial Service Home Page ★★★

Yet another list of money-related sites on the Web.

URL http://www.orcc.com/orcc/banking.htm

PCQuote ★★★★★

A great place to get delayed stock quotes free of charge.

URL http://www.pcquote.com

Security APL ★★★★

Security APL provides stock quotes to the public.

URL http://www.secapl.com

Stock Market Charts ★

Find out what stocks are hot and what stocks are not.

URL http://www.ai.mit.edu/stocks/graphs.html

USA Today - Money ★★★

Read about what's new in the financial world.

URL http://www.usatoday.com/money/mfront.htm

Wells Fargo ★★

The oldest bank in the West has a wide variety of services on the Internet.

URL http://www.wellsfargo.com

World Bank ★★★

Find out all about the World Bank at this site.

URL http://www.worldbank.org

BUSINESS: SHOPPING

Access Market Square ★

You can find many unique products and gifts at this site.

 http://www.icw.com/ams.html

CommerceNet ★★★★

This site provides an index of commercial products and services available on the Internet.

 http://www.commerce.net

eMall ★★★

Products, services and information—this site has something for everyone.

 http://eMall.com

Global Shopping Network ★★

You can purchase all of your fishing and boating needs at this site.

URL http://www.gsn.com

imall ★★★

This site offers links to other products and services on the Internet.

 http://www.imall.com

Internet Mall ★★★

Find out where you can purchase food, clothing, furniture, gifts and much more.

URL http://www.internet-mall.com

Internet Shopping Network ★★★★★

A site with hot deals and Internet specials.

 http://www.internet.net

Malls Of Canada ★★★

Canada's largest Internet shopping mall offers goods and services from across Canada.

 http://www.canadamalls.com/provider

NECX Direct ★★★

Over 20,000 computer products are available here.

 http://www.necx.com

ParentsPlace ★★

Everything for parents and children—books, diapers, toys and more.

 http://www.parentsplace.com/shopping/index.html

Shopping2000 ★★★★

Find products and services from the world's leading merchants at Shopping2000.

 http://www.shopping2000.com

The Shopper ★

A directory of many large shopping malls on the Internet.

 http://www.hummsoft.com/hummsoft/shopper.html

CARS

Alamo Rent A Car ★★

Reserve a car online and check out the weather for where you are headed.

 http://www.freeways.com

AutoBANK ★

Find a vehicle that matches your criteria.

 http://www.spyder.org/autobank

Autoscape ★★★

Advertised as "The Internet's Premier Auto Mall."

 http://www.autoscape.com

Cadillac ★

You can find information on the new Cadillacs or check out upcoming Cadillac-sponsored events.

 http://www.cadillac.com

CARS (CONTINUED)

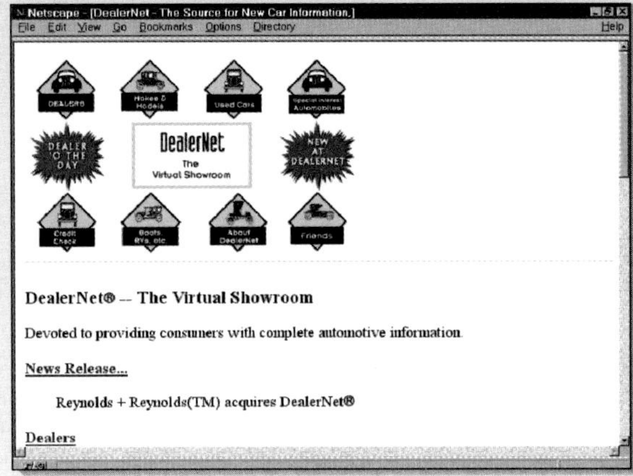

DealerNet ★★★★★

A great place to look for information on a variety of vehicles.

 http://www.dealernet.com

Ford ★★★

All the Ford information your heart desires.

 http://www.ford.com

Goodyear ★★★

They've got lots of tires and a very big blimp.

 http://www.goodyear.com

Harley Davidson Motorcycles of Stamford ★★★★

Okay, so it's not a car—it still has wheels.

 http://www.hd-stamford.com

International Auto Mall ★

Find out what cars your local dealers have in stock.

 http://www.mindspring.com/~mikea/dealer.html

Jeep ★★★

For those who crave the rugged outdoors.

 http://www.jeepunpaved.com

Saturn ★★

This site is geared towards Saturn owners, but prospective buyers should also check it out.

 http://www.saturncars.com

Toyota ★★★★

You can find information on Toyota's vehicles, dealers and much more.

 http://www.toyota.com

Virtual Vehicle Showroom ★★★
A guide to automotive resources on the Internet.

URL http://ism.idirect.com:80/canautonet

Volvo ★★
Check out the new line of Volvos or locate the dealer nearest you.

URL http://www.volvocars.com

CHEMISTRY

Chemistry Hypermedia Project ★★★
Provides resources and educational material for chemistry students.

URL http://www.chem.vt.edu/chem-ed/vt-chem-ed.html

Chemistry Virtual Library ★★★★
This site provides links to chemistry sites around the world.

URL http://www.chem.ucla.edu/chempointers.html

Chemist's Art Gallery ★★★
Pictures and animations of molecules and other aspects of chemistry.

URL http://www.csc.fi/lul/chem/graphics.html

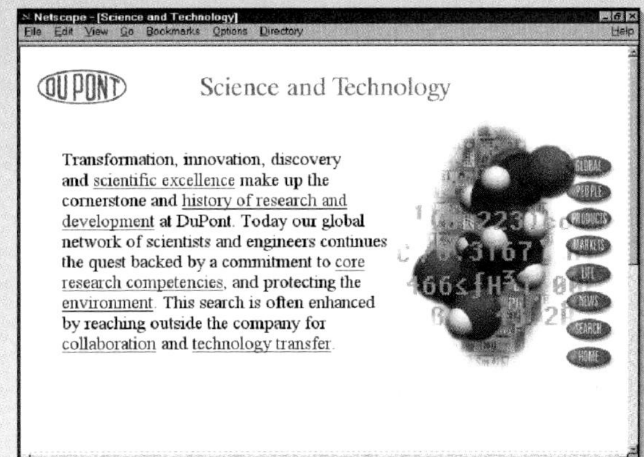

DuPont ★★
Find information on the chemical company and its products.

URL http://www.dupont.com

Ethics in Science ★★★
Find information on the ethics of chemistry and science in general.

URL http://www.chem.vt.edu/ethics/ethics.html

CHEMISTRY (CONTINUED)

Hazardous Chemical Database ★★★★
Look up information on over 1,300 dangerous chemicals.

 http://odin.chemistry.uakron.edu/erd

Internet Chemistry Index ★★★★★
A list of chemistry FTP, Gopher and WWW sites on the Internet.

 http://www.chemie.fu-berlin.de/chemistry/index

Internet Chemistry Resources ★★★
This site provides links to other chemistry sites and gives you access to databases, catalogs and much more.

 http://www.rpi.edu/dept/chem/cheminfo/chemres.html

Journal of Biological Chemistry ★★★
This site offers extensive articles on biological chemistry.

 http://www-jbc.stanford.edu/jbc

National Academy of Sciences ★
A list of scientific committees and resources across the U.S.

 http://www.nas.edu

Royal Society of Chemistry ★★
This site is for students, teachers or anyone interested in chemistry.

 http://chemistry.rsc.org/rsc

COMPUTERS: PICTURES

Dan's Gallery of the Grotesque ★
Not for the faint of heart.

 http://zynet.com/~grotesk

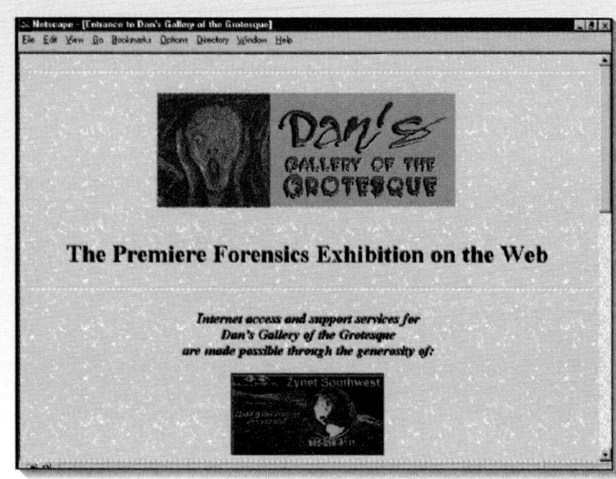

Kite Site ★★
Pictures of all sorts of kites.

 http://www.latrobe.edu.au/Glenn/KiteSite/Kites.html

Lighthouses ★★

Pictures of lighthouses from around the world.

URL http://http2.sils.umich.edu/~superman/LIGHTHOUSE/LightHome.html

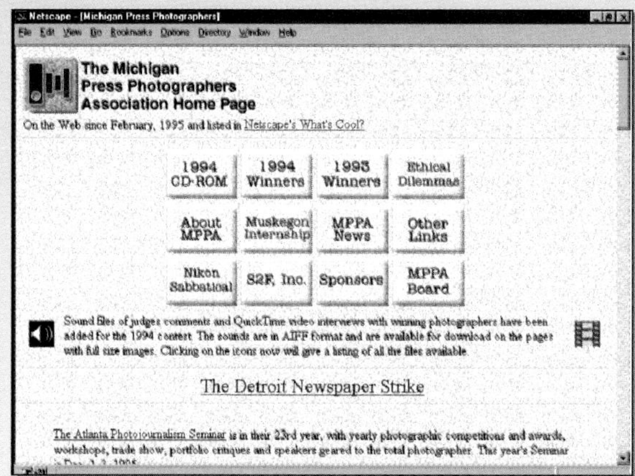

Michigan Press Photographers Association ★★★

Browse through the winning photos in the Pictures of the Year contest.

URL http://www.cris.com/~mppa

National Park Photos ★★★

Excellent photos of America's best national parks.

URL http://anansi.panix.com:80/~wizjd/cgi-bin/getphoto.cgi

NSSDC Photo Gallery ★★★★★

The National Space Science Data Center has pictures of planets, asteroids and more.

URL http://nssdc.gsfc.nasa.gov/photo_gallery

Photo Exhibits ★★

A list of photo exhibits on the Web.

URL http://math.liu.se/~behal/photo/exhibits.html

Stamps ★

Pictures of U.S. Government stamps from the past two years.

URL http://www.usps.gov/images/stamps/stamps.html

SunSite Archive ★★★★

A huge list of pictures sorted into categories.

URL http://sunsite.unc.edu/pub/multimedia/pictures

Swedish FTP Archive ★★★★

Pictures of almost anything you can imagine.

URL http://ftp.sunet.se/pub/pictures

COMPUTERS: PICTURES (CONTINUED)

Time Life Photo Sight ★★★

The best of Time Life's large collection of photos.

 http://www.pathfinder.com/pathfinder/photo/sighthome.html

ZooNet Archive ★★★

Pictures of animals you would find in a zoo.

 http://www.mindspring.com/~zoonet/gallery.html

COMPUTERS: RESOURCES

Adobe ★★★

The creators of Photoshop, Illustrator and other graphics programs.

 http://www.adobe.com

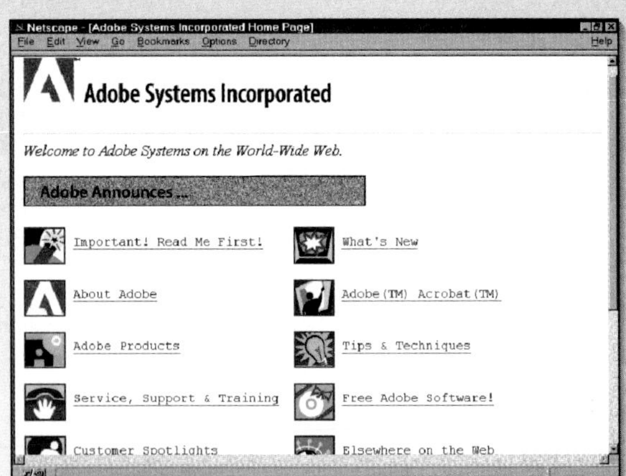

Borland ★

Borland creates database and programming software.

 http://www.borland.com

Compaq ★★

One of North America's largest manufacturers of personal computers.

 http://www.compaq.com

Computer Museum ★★★★

Find interactive exhibits, the history of computing and more at this site.

 http://www.net.org

Dell ★★

One of Compaq's biggest competitors.

 http://www.dell.com

Hewlett-Packard ★★★

One of the top manufacturers of printers, computers and scanners.

 http://www.hp.com

IBM ★★

The giant computer conglomerate known as "Big Blue."

URL http://www.ibm.com

Intel ★

Intel creates the main processor used in most personal computers.

URL http://www.intel.com

Intro to C ★★★

Learn the basics of C, a programming language.

URL http://www.iftech.com/classes/c/c0.htm

Java ★★★★

A guide to Java, the new programming language used on the Internet.

URL http://java.sun.com/progGuide/index.html

McAfee ★★★

One of the leading manufacturers of virus-protection software.

URL http://www.mcafee.com

Microsoft ★★★★

This computer software giant has landed on the Web.

URL http://www.microsoft.com

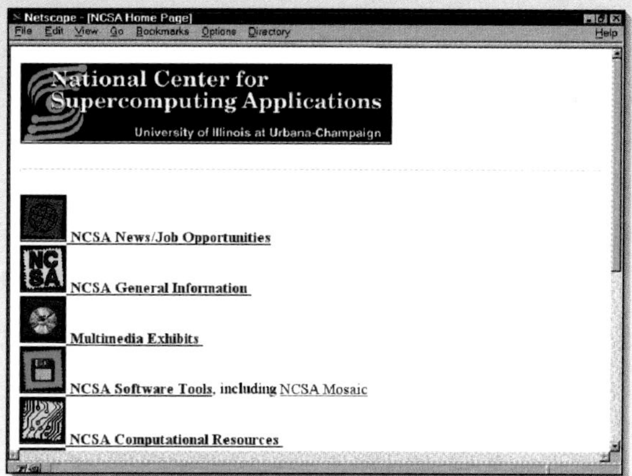

NCSA at UIUC ★★★

The National Center for Supercomputing Applications created NCSA Mosaic, the first graphical Web browser.

URL http://www.ncsa.uiuc.edu

Novell ★★★

Novell software runs many networks around the world.

URL http://www.novell.com

COMPUTERS: RESOURCES (CONTINUED)

Silicon Graphics ★★★★
Known for their high-end computers and for WebSpace, their VRML browser.

 http://www.sgi.com

Team OS/2 Online ★
All you need to know about IBM's OS/2 operating system.

 http://www.teamos2.org/os2web

COMPUTERS: SOUNDS

Blue Dog ★★
A dog will bark the correct answer to a math question you ask.

 http://kao.ini.cmu.edu:5550/bdf.html

Bong ★★
This page features different and unusual forms of instrumental music.

 http://www.apple.is/Bong/Sounds/Sounds.html

Creative Labs ★★
Creators of the ever-popular Sound Blaster sound card.

 http://www.creaf.com

Historical Speeches ★★★
Listen to speeches by Richard Nixon, JFK and many others.

http://www.webcorp.com/sounds/index.htm

Internet Underground Music Archive ★★★★
A cool place to hear independent artists and bands.

http://www.iuma.com

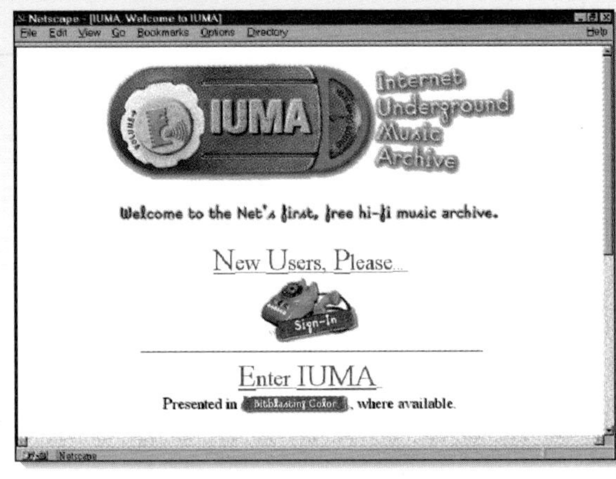

Japanese Sound Archive ★★
The sounds have nothing to do with Japan, but sound travels quickly from this site to your computer.

 http://sunsite.sut.ac.jp/multimed/sounds

John Lennon Sound Files ★
This site is very popular because you can copy previously unreleased songs to your computer.

 http://www.missouri.edu/~c588349/sounds.html

Movie Sounds ★★
Sounds from all your favorite movies.

 http://www.netaxs.com/people/dgresh/snddir.html

RealAudio ★★★★★
Hear sound instantly, without a wait!

 http://www.realaudio.com

SunSite Sounds ★★★
You can find songs, quotes and more at this large sound collection.

URL http://sunsite.unc.edu/pub/multimedia/pc-sounds

Text to Speech ★
Type something and this Web site will actually say it back.

URL http://wwwtios.cs.utwente.nl/say

TV Themes ★★★
This site offers a huge collection of TV theme songs you can listen to.

URL http://www.parkhere.com/tvbytes

Vincent Voice Library ★★★★
A selection of historical speeches and lectures.

URL http://web.msu.edu/vincent/index.html

Warsaw University ★★
Warsaw is one of many universities around the world that have collections of sound.

URL http://info.fuw.edu.pl/multimedia/sounds

DANCE AND DANCE MUSIC

Belly Dance Home Page ★
An entire Web site dedicated to the art of belly dancing.

 http://cie-2.uoregon.edu/bdance

Breaks ★★★
A site dedicated to breakbeat music.

 http://www.breaks.com

Dancescape ★★★★
Your guide to the world of ballroom dancing.

 http://wchat.on.ca/dance/pages/dscape1.htm

Dancing On a Line ★★
You will find information on performances, reviews and links to other Web sites.

 http://www.cipsinc.com/dance/doal.html

Danclink International ★★★★
At this site, you can learn new dance steps in the virtual studio or even find a dance partner.

URL http://www.cts.com/~danclink

Henry's Dance Hotlist ★
An Internet user named Henry has a list of sites about different types of dancing.

URL http://zeus.ncsa.uiuc.edu:8080/~hneeman/dance_hotlist.html

Hyperreal ★★★
A collection of rave culture and music resources.

URL http://www.hyperreal.com

Let's Dance ★★
You can flip through an online catalog for all your dancewear needs.

URL http://letsdance.com

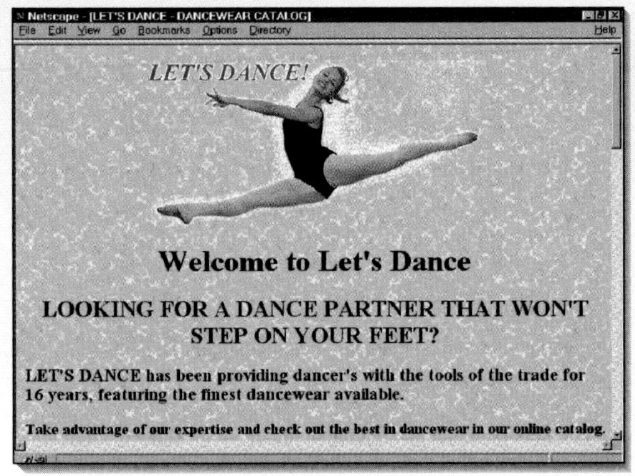

National Ballet of Canada ★★★

News and information about the company's upcoming shows and ticket prices.

URL http://www.ffa.ucalgary.ca/nbc/nbc_main.html

Rare Groove ★★

Bits of information about dance music.

URL http://rg.media.mit.edu/RG/RG.html

Streetsound ★★★★★

A site designed for dance music DJs and fans.

URL http://www.streetsound.com/zone

Tango ★★★

Includes the history and culture surrounding the tango.

URL http://litwww.epfl.ch/tango

VIBE Magazine Online ★★

The online version of VIBE, the dance music magazine.

URL http://www.pathfinder.com/vibe

EDUCATION

AskERIC ★★★★★

This service is well-known for its resources for teachers.

URL http://ericir.syr.edu

CollegeNeT ★★

A searchable database of over 2,000 universities and colleges.

 http://www.collegenet.com

EDUCATION (CONTINUED)

EdLinks ★
Links to educational sites of every size and shape.

 http://www.marshall.edu/~jmullens/edlinks.html

EdWeb ★★★
Find out about technology and school reform at this site.

 http://k12.cnidr.org:90

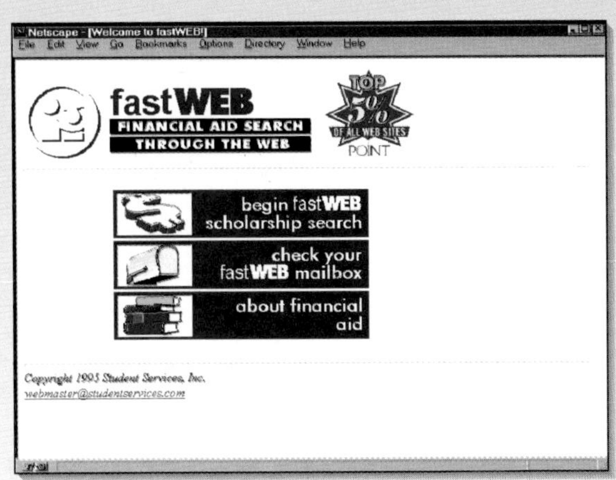

FastWeb ★★★
A guide to finding university and college scholarships.

 http://www.studentservices.com/fastweb

Global SchoolNet Foundation ★★★★
This site is dedicated to linking kids around the world and offers projects, contests and much more.

 http://gsn.org

Global Show-n-Tell ★
Kids can show their stuff to other kids around the world.

 http://www.manymedia.com/show-n-tell

K-16 Science Education ★★★
A collection of science and mathematics resources available on the Web.

 http://www-sci.lib.uci.edu/SEP/SEP.html

Kidlink ★★
This site offers several different forums that allow 10- to 15-year-old students around the world to communicate.

 http://www.kidlink.org

KidPub ★★★
Where kids and classes can post their stories and poems.

 http://escrime.en-garde.com/kidpub

Kids' Space ★★★★

A fantastic place for kids to share their imaginations with other kids.

URL http://plaza.interport.net/kids_space

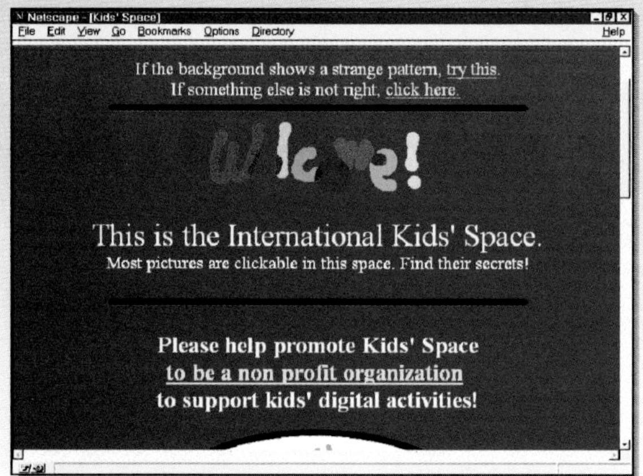

Media Literacy On-Line Project ★★★

A collection of information about the influence of the media in our lives.

 http://interact.uoregon.edu/MediaLit/HomePage

Online Educational Resources ★★

A collection of educational resources for students and teachers.

URL http://quest.arc.nasa.gov/OER

Teaching and Learning on the Web ★★★★

This site is for more than just net surfing—you can search for sites of interest here.

URL http://www.mcli.dist.maricopa.edu/cgi-bin/index_tl

You Too Can Learn Spanish! ★★

Que pasa? Learn the basics of the Spanish language here.

URL http://www.willamette.edu/~tjones/Spanish/lesson1.html

ENVIRONMENT AND WEATHER

Daily Planet ★

This site has links to several weather resources on the World Wide Web.

 http://www.atmos.uiuc.edu

EcoNet ★★

EcoNet works with many environmental organizations to put information on the WWW.

 http://www.igc.apc.org/econet

EnviroLink Network ★★★★

The largest online source of environmental information.

 http://envirolink.org

ENVIRONMENT AND WEATHER (CONTINUED)

Environmental News Network ★★★

Stay on top of environmental issues at this up-to-date site.

 http://www.enn.com

Environmental Protection Agency ★

Learn how the government is making a difference.

 http://www.epa.gov

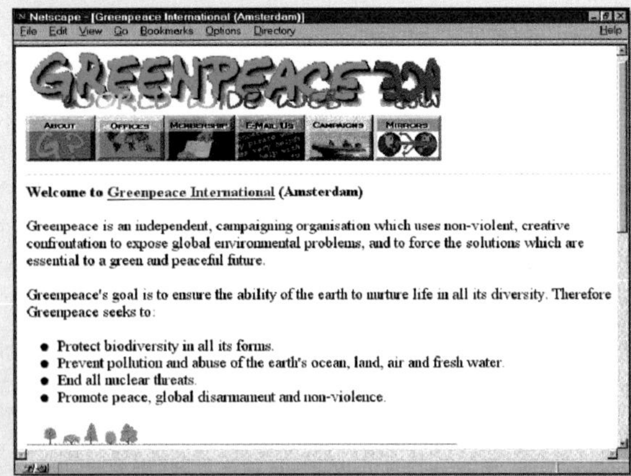

Netscape - [Greenpeace International (Amsterdam)]

File Edit View Go Bookmarks Options Directory Help

About | Offices | Membership | E-Mail Us | Campaigns | Mirrors

Welcome to Greenpeace International (Amsterdam)

Greenpeace is an independent, campaigning organisation which uses non-violent, creative confrontation to expose global environmental problems, and to force the solutions which are essential to a green and peaceful future.

Greenpeace's goal is to ensure the ability of the earth to nurture life in all its diversity. Therefore Greenpeace seeks to:

- Protect biodiversity in all its forms.
- Prevent pollution and abuse of the earth's ocean, land, air and fresh water.
- End all nuclear threats.
- Promote peace, global disarmament and non-violence.

Greenpeace ★★★★★

While you can't race alongside an oil tanker online, this WWW site gives you a taste of Greenpeace.

 http://www.greenpeace.org

Human Wildlife Project ★

As crazy as it sounds, a group of individuals want to live in the middle of the woods for a year and see what happens.

 http://www.fys.uio.no/~kjetikj/HumanWild

INTELLiCast ★★★★

Check out the weather around the world.

 http://www.intellicast.com

Internet Disaster Information Network ★★★

Information on the latest disasters around the world.

 http://www.disaster.net/index.html

National Oceanic and Atmospheric Administration ★★

Find out what the U.S. government is doing about the ozone layer, endangered species and more.

 http://www.noaa.gov

Rainforest Workshop ★

This site helps students and teachers learn more about the rainforest.

 http://mh.osd.wednet.edu

Recycler's World ★★

A site dedicated to recycling.

 http://www.sentex.net/recycle

USA Today Weather ★★★

Weather information from one of the largest newspapers in the U.S.

 http://www.usatoday.com/weather/wfront.htm

Weather Information Superhighway ★★

This site offers links to many weather-related Web pages.

 http://thunder.met.fsu.edu:80/nws/public_html/wxhwy.html

FOOD AND DRINK

Beer Page ★

This site provides information and recipes for homebrewers.

 http://www-personal.umich.edu/~spencer/beer

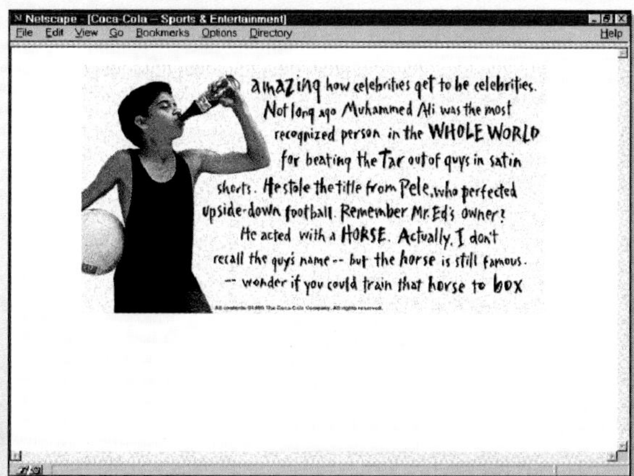

Coca-Cola ★★

This site has information on the company and its products, as well as little things to amuse you.

 http://www.cocacola.com

Godiva Chocolates ★★★

This site includes recipes and a Godiva catalog you can look through.

 http://www.godiva.com

Gumbo Pages ★★★

You can find information on the food, music and culture of New Orleans.

 http://www.webcom.com/~gumbo

Hershey Foods Corporation ★★

The company known for its chocolate kisses.

http://www.microserve.net/~hershey/welcome.html

FOOD AND DRINK (CONTINUED)

Ketchum Kitchen ★★★
Recipes, discussions and much more.
URL http://www.recipe.com

Perrier ★★★
This site has contests, a gallery of art bottles and much more.
URL http://www.perrier.com

Recipe Archive ★★★★
Learn to make everything from lasagna to cheesecake at this site.
URL http://www.vuw.ac.nz/~amyl/recipes

Rubbermaid ★★
Find information on the products that keep your food fresh!
URL http://home.rubbermaid.com

Star Chefs ★★★
Get recipes and tips from great chefs and cookbook authors.
URL http://starchefs.com

Vegetarian Pages ★★★
News, recipes, a list of famous vegetarians and much more.
URL http://www.veg.org/veg

Veggies Unite! ★★★★
At this site, you can pick a recipe and then quickly create a grocery list of ingredients.
URL http://www.honors.indiana.edu/~veggie/recipes.cgi

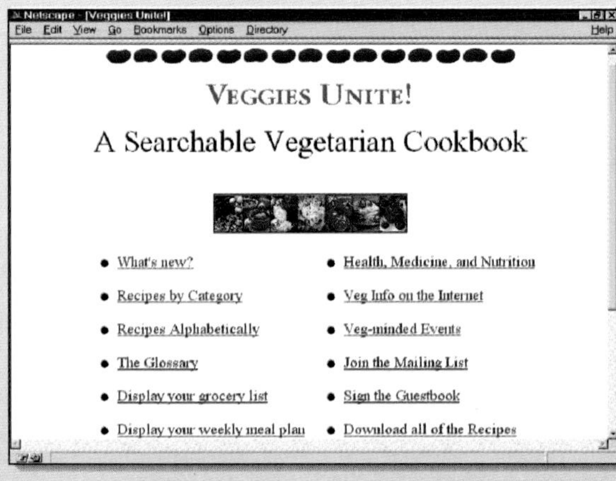

GAMES

Duck Hunt ★★★

Find the ducks hidden at this site.

 http://aurora.york.ac.uk/ducks.html

Electronic Arts ★★

One of the top game-makers in North America.

 http://www.ea.com

Games Domain ★★★★

This popular site offers free games and tips on some of the most popular computer games on the market.

 http://wcl-rs.bham.ac.uk/GamesDomain

Hyper-Jeopardy! ★★★

An online interactive game inspired by the TV game show.

 http://www.hype.com/game_show

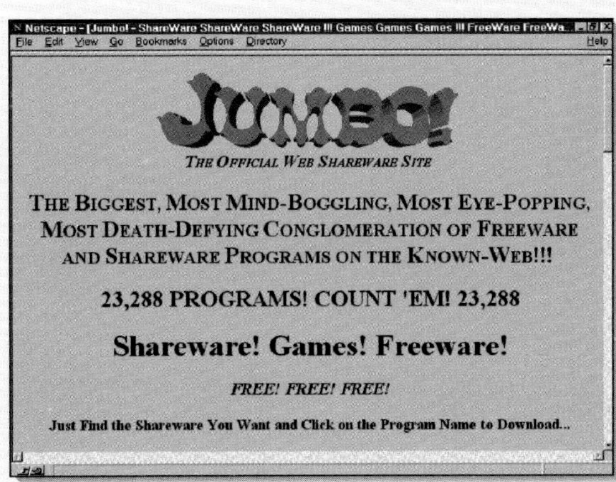

Jumbo ★★★★★

A collection of free programs for DOS, Windows and Macintosh computers.

 http://www.jumbo.com

Letter R.I.P. ★

The 90's version of the classic Hangman game.

 http://www.dtd.com/rip

LucasArts ★

Creators of many top-rated computer games like Full Throttle and Dark Forces.

 http://www.lucasarts.com/menu.html

Madlib ★★

This site creates a wacky story based on a few words you enter.

 http://www.ii.uib.no/~tor/cgi/madlib.html

GAMES (CONTINUED)

Magic: The Gathering ★★★

This card game is popular with Internet users and offers hints for players.

 http://www.itis.com:80/deckmaster/magic

Nintendo Power ★★

Nintendo offers information on its products and links to other cool sites you can visit.

 http://www.nintendo.com

Riddler ★★★★

Solve puzzles and riddles for cash and prizes.

 http://www.riddler.com

Sega Online ★★★

Find out more about Genesis, Game Gear and Saturn from this video game giant.

 http://www.segaoa.com

Virtual Software Library ★★★

This powerful tool helps you find programs that you can copy to your computer.

 http://vsl.cnet.com

Virtual Vegas ★★

Virtual Vegas has blackjack, poker, roulette and more for the gambler in you.

 http://www.virtualvegas.com

GEOGRAPHY

CityNet ★★★★★

One of the most popular sites on the Internet, CityNet provides information on most major cities worldwide.

URL http://www.city.net

GPS World ★★

An online magazine for people interested in the Global Positioning System.

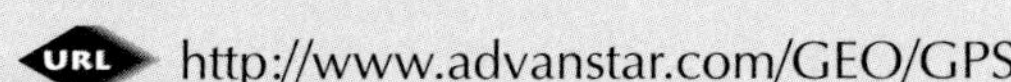
URL http://www.advanstar.com/GEO/GPS

Grand Canyon ★★

View pictures and learn the history of this Arizona landmark.

URL http://www.kbt.com/gc/gc_home.html

How far is it? ★★★

Enter two places and this Web site will tell you the distance between them.

URL http://gs213.sp.cs.cmu.edu/prog/dist

Map Viewer ★★

This site offers maps of the world and plans to add more features in the future.

URL http://pubweb.parc.xerox.com/map

Mt. Rushmore Home Page ★★★

Don't you just wish your face was up there too?

URL http://www.state.sd.us./state/executive/tourism/rushmore/rushmore.html

National Climatic Data Center ★★

Find out where it's hot and where it's not.

URL http://www.ncdc.noaa.gov

GEOGRAPHY (CONTINUED)

National Earthquake Information Center ★★★
Find out what's shakin'.

URL http://gldfs.cr.usgs.gov

NCGIA ★★★★
Find out about the National Center for Geographic Information and Analysis.

URL http://www.ncgia.ucsb.edu

PCL Map Collection ★★★★
The mother of all map collections.

URL http://www.lib.utexas.edu/Libs/PCL/Map_collection/Map_collection.html

U.S. Geological Survey ★★
This site provides information to help you better understand earth sciences.

URL http://www.usgs.gov

GOVERNMENT AND INFORMATION ON CANADA

Canada Net Pages ★★★
A great place to find Canadian business and finance information on the Web.

 http://www.visions.com/netpages

CanadaInfo ★★
A list of Canadian Web sites.

 http://www.clo.com/~canadainfo

Canada's SchoolNet ★★★
One of the most ambitious education and technology projects in North America.

 http://schoolnet2.carleton.ca

Canadiana ★★★★★
A huge list of Canadian Web sites.

 http://www.cs.cmu.edu/Web/Unofficial/Canadiana/README.html

CBC ★★★

Information on the national TV and radio broadcasting service.

URL http://www.cbc.ca

Champlain: Canadian Information Explorer ★★★★

Explore information on the Canadian government.

URL http://info.ic.gc.ca/champlain/champlain.html

Department of Justice of Canada ★

Keep up-to-date on the latest news, laws and government initiatives of the Great White North.

URL http://canada.justice.gc.ca/index_en.html

Environment Canada ★★

They keep Canada clean and green.

URL http://www.doe.ca

GIFT ★★★

You can search the Government of Canada's document collections at this site.

URL http://www.gc.ca/search.html

National Atlas Information Service ★★

Your guide to Canadian geography.

URL http://www-nais.ccm.emr.ca

Parliamentary Internet ★★★★

A guide to Canadian Parliament.

URL http://www.parl.gc.ca/english

Statistics Canada ★★★★

Find out the population of Canada, flip through the consumer price index and much more at this site.

URL http://WWW.StatCan.CA

GOVERNMENT AND INFORMATION ON THE U.S.

Air Force ★★

This site lets you access most U.S. Air Force bases nationwide.

URL http://w3.af.mil

Army ★★★

You can flip through Soldiers, an online magazine, visit other army-related sites and much more.

URL http://www.army.mil

Census Bureau ★

Find out how many people are currently living in the U.S.

URL http://www.census.gov

CIA ★

This is a public site, so you won't find the government's deepest, darkest secrets here.

URL http://www.odci.gov/cia

Coast Guard ★★

This isn't Baywatch.

URL http://www.webcom.com/~d13www/welcome.html

DefenseLINK ★★

The U.S. Defense Department's online handbook.

URL http://www.dtic.dla.mil/defenselink

Department of Education ★

This site provides information for both students and teachers.

URL http://www.ed.gov

Department of Justice ★★★

They fight to protect your rights. This site has links to many agencies, including the FBI.

URL http://www.usdoj.gov

Department of the Treasury ★★★

The people who make all our coins. This site provides information on the programs and activities of the Department of the Treasury.

 http://www.ustreas.gov

FBI ★★★

Find out about the FBI and keep up-to-date on the latest investigations.

 http://www.fbi.gov

FBI's Most Wanted ★★

Find information on America's most wanted fugitives from the privacy of your own computer.

 http://www.fbi.gov/toplist.htm

Federal Budget ★★★

Find out where all your money is going.

 http://ibert.org

Netscape - [B/CS Presidential Campaign Tour & Opinion Page]
File Edit View Go Bookmarks Options Directory Help
IPT Selected as One of the Top 5% Web Sites by PointCom
On The Road to the White House
In preparation for the 1996 Presidential Voting Season Internet Publishing Technologies is providing a collection of Candidate information and links to various goverment and party related sites throughout the Web. We have also included a Virtual Voting Booth where our Web Visitors can cast their votes on who they think will win the election. You may also feel free to add your own "candidate" to the list. If you have any additional sites or ideas for

TOP
5%
OF ALL WEB SITES
POINT

FedWorld ★

A one-stop site for government information.

http://www.fedworld.gov

House of Representatives ★★

This site provides information on legislation, committees and organizations of the house.

http://www.house.gov

Library of Congress ★★★

While you can't read many of the books, you can search for details on almost any publication in North America.

 http://lcweb.loc.gov

NavyOnLine ★★

The complete guide to the U.S. Navy.

http://www.navy.mil

GOVERNMENT AND INFORMATION ON THE U.S. (CONTINUED)

NSA ★
Find information on the National Security Agency.

 http://www.nsa.gov:8080

On The Road to the White House ★★★★
At this site you will find information on the candidates and a virtual voting booth where you can cast your vote.

 http://www.ipt.com/vote

PoliticsUSA ★★★
Check out the movers and shakers in American politics.

 http://PoliticsUSA.com

Postal Service ★
Look up a zip code, find a postage rate and much more here.

 http://www.usps.gov

Thomas Library ★★★★★
This immense site has a great deal of congressional and legislative information.

http://thomas.loc.gov

White House ★★★★
See the First Family or take a tour of the White House.

 http://www.whitehouse.gov

GOVERNMENTS AND INFORMATION ON THE WORLD

Australia ★★★
Find information on the Australian government and its agencies.

 http://gov.info.au

Gateway to Antarctica ★★★★
That's right. The South Pole is on the Internet.

 http://icair.iac.org.nz

NATO ★
North Atlantic Treaty Organization.

 http://www.nato.int

New Zealand ★★★
Learn all there is to know about this country in the Pacific.

http://www.akiko.lm.com/nz

http://www.akiko.lm.com

Saudi Arabia ★★
An intriguing look at the Middle Eastern country.

URL http://imedl.saudi.net

United Kingdom ★★★
The U.K.'s Central Office of Information.

URL http://www.coi.gov.uk/coi

United Nations ★★★★★
Take a tour of the U.N. or keep up-to-date with the latest information.

URL http://WWW.UN.ORG

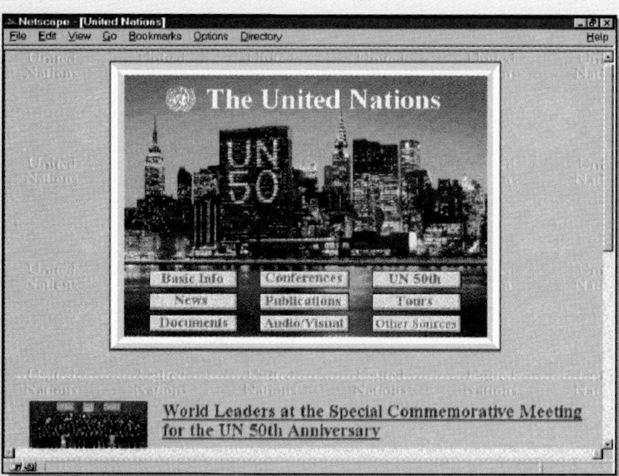

World Bank ★★★★
Find out all about the World Bank here.

URL http://www.worldbank.org

HEALTH

American Medical Association ★★★
You can find medical journals and much more at this site.

URL http://www.ama-assn.org

A B C D E F G H I J K L M N O P Q R S T U V W X Y Z

HEALTH (CONTINUED)

Centers for Disease Control ★★★★★
Learn how to prevent and control many diseases, injuries and disabilities.

 http://www.cdc.gov

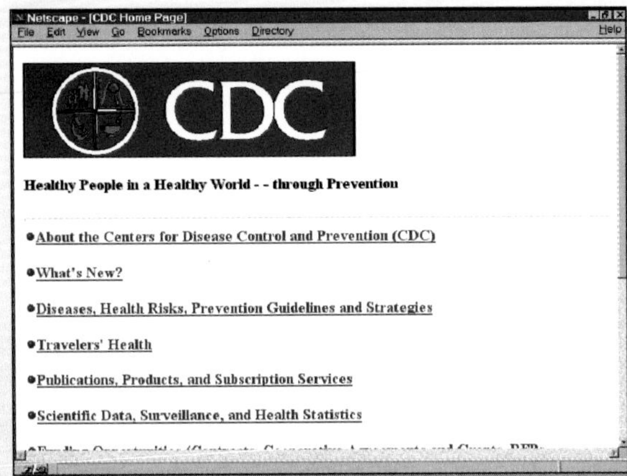

Central Institute for the Deaf ★
This site provides information on the Institute's programs and education for the hearing impaired.

 http://cidmac.wustl.edu

Children With Diabetes ★★★
This is an excellent site for kids and families with juvenile diabetes.

 http://www.castleweb.com:80/diabetes

EKA ★★★
Find disability resources, products and services at this site.

 http://disability.com

Global Health Network ★★
Worldwide resources on various health issues.

 http://www.pitt.edu/HOME/GHNet/GHNet.html

Good Medicine Magazine ★
A magazine to keep you healthy and happy.

 http://www.coolware.com/health/good_med

National Library of Medicine ★★★
Access medical and scientific information from the National Library of Medicine.

 http://www.nlm.nih.gov/welcome.html

Online AA Resources ★★★★
Alcoholics Anonymous online information.

 http://matrix.casti.com:80/aa

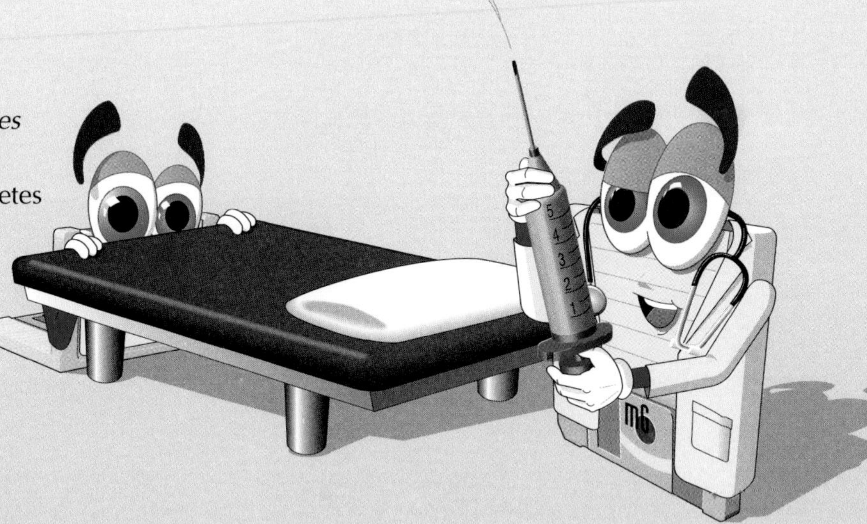

The Heart Preview Gallery ★★★
Everything you wanted to know about your heart.

 http://sln.fi.edu/tfi/preview/heartpreview.html

Virtual Hospital ★★★
Find the latest health information at this site.

 http://indy.radiology.uiowa.edu/VirtualHospital.html

Virtual Medical Center ★★
A large collection of medical information, as well as glossaries and dictionaries.

 http://www-sci.lib.uci.edu/HSG/Medical.html

World Health Organization ★★★★
Find out all about the World Health Organization here.

 http://www.who.ch

HISTORY

1492: An Ongoing Voyage ★★
This exhibit examines how the discovery of America affected nations around the world.

 http://sunsite.unc.edu/expo/1492.exhibit/Intro.html

American Memory ★★★★★
This glorious site will keep an American history buff busy for days.

 http://rs6.loc.gov/amhome.html

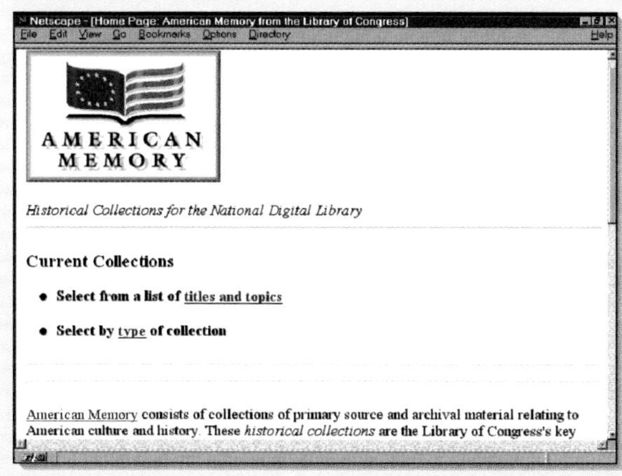

Gateway to World History ★
This site offers a collection of documents and links to many other history-related sites.

 http://neal.ctstateu.edu/history/world_history/world_history.html

HISTORY (CONTINUED)

Genealogy Home Page ★★

A good starting point to trace your family tree.

URL http://ftp.cac.psu.edu/~saw/genealogy.html

History ★

You can quickly find historical information on any part of the world.

URL http://www.arts.cuhk.hk/His.html

Labyrinth ★★★

This site provides access to information on medieval studies around the world.

URL http://www.georgetown.edu/labyrinth/labyrinth-home.html

Mil-Hist ★★

The who, what, where, when and how of military history.

URL http://kuhttp.cc.ukans.edu/history/milhst/index.html

Scrolls From the Dead Sea ★★★

Read ancient scrolls found in the caves surrounding the Dead Sea.

URL http://sunsite.unc.edu/expo/deadsea.scrolls.exhibit/intro.html

Seven Wonders of the Ancient World ★★★★

Can you name all seven?

URL http://ce.ecn.purdue.edu/~ashmawy/7WW

U.S. Civil War Center ★★★

Learn more about the battle between the North and South.

URL http://www.cwc.lsu.edu/civlink.htm

World History Archives ★★

A collection of documents related to world history.

URL http://neal.ctstateu.edu:80/history/world_history/archives/archives.html

HTML (HYPERTEXT MARKUP LANGUAGE)

Background Colors ★★★

A list of background colors available in Netscape and other browsers.

 http://www.infi.net/wwwimages/colorindex.html

Beginner's Guide to HTML ★★

For those who aren't quite sure what HTML is all about.

 http://www.ncsa.uiuc.edu/demoweb/html-primer.html

David Siegel's Home Page ★★

A WWW designer struts his stuff. This site was runner-up for "Cool Site of the Year."

URL http://www.dsiegel.com

HotDog Web Editor ★★★

One of many HTML Editors.

URL http://www.sausage.com

HTML Writers Guild ★★★★★

The cream of the crop of HTML experts.

 http://www.mindspring.com/guild

InterNIC ★

The people who keep track of North American sites on the Internet.

 http://rs.internic.net

HTML (HYPERTEXT MARKUP LANGUAGE) CONTINUED

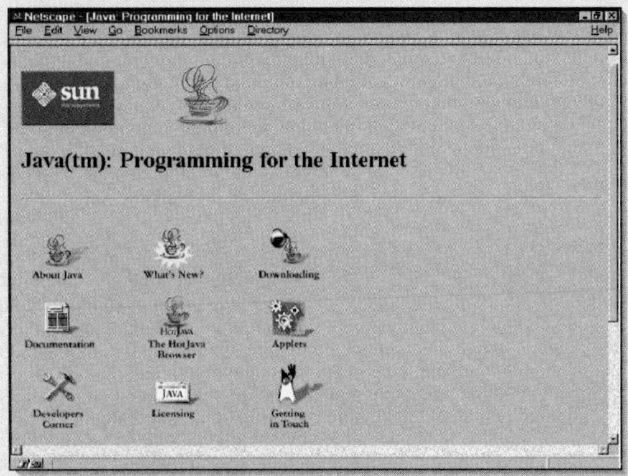

Java ★★★

The latest WWW programming language from Sun Microsystems.

 http://java.sun.com

Mag's Big List of HTML Editors ★★

The name says it all.

 http://union.ncsa.uiuc.edu/HyperNews/get/www/html/editors.html

Netscape's Guide to HTML ★★★★

The mighty Netscape's HTML handbook.

 http://home.netscape.com/assist/net_sites/index.html

Types of Web Page Creators ★

That's right, HTML humor. You knew it was inevitable.

 http://pizza.bgsu.edu/~mhaynes/9types.html

Web Developer's Virtual Library ★★

For the serious WWW page designer.

 http://www.stars.com

Web Tools ★★★

A list of some HTML programmers' favorite utilities.

 http://babylon.dsu.edu/index/tools.html

HUMOR

Comedy Central ★★★

The all-comedy television network has a wacky site on the Web.

 http://www.comcentral.com

Humor Web ★★★

This site is full of laughs.

 http://www.usmcs.maine.edu/~laferrie/humor/humor.html

Jay's Comedy Club ★★★
This site has something for everyone—jokes, stories and much more.

URL http://paul.spu.edu/~zylstra/comedy/index.html

LaughWEB ★★
If the Humor Web is missing something, you can find it here.

URL http://WWW.Misty.com/laughweb

Monty Python WWW Homepage ★★★
Sketches, songs and information on the famous comedy troupe.

URL http://www.iia.org/~rosenr1/python

Stupid Paramedic Questions ★★★★
Strange questions asked of paramedics and other ambulance attendants.

URL http://community.net/~sierra/stupid.htm

Top Ten List Archive ★★★★★
A collection of David Letterman's top ten lists.

URL http://www.cbs.com/lateshow/ttlist.html

Wrecked Humor Collection ★★
Some of the zaniest jokes on the Web.

URL http://www.infi.net/~cashman/humor

TOP TEN REASONS WHY MG
ALWAYS HAS A SMILE ON HIS FACE
1 He copied an exciting flying game from the Internet.
2 He has a new girlfriend.
3 He works with such great people.
4 People always listen to what he says.
5 MG visited the maranGraphics Web site.
MG met a new friend through the Internet.
He thinks that he is a celebrity.
He loves to help people learn about computers.
9 A friend sent him a funny e-mail message
He discovered a Web site

INTERNET: PROGRAMS

Adobe Acrobat ★
A new artist-friendly WWW tool that is becoming more and more popular.

http://www.adobe.com/Acrobat/Acrobat0.html

Eudora ★★★
Snag a copy of Eudora, the most popular e-mail program for Macintosh and Windows users.

http://www.qualcomm.com/quest/QuestMain.html

INTERNET: PROGRAMS (CONTINUED)

HotJava ★★★
Get a copy of HotJava, the new WWW browser created by Sun Microsystems.

 http://java.sun.com

Internet Explorer ★★
Microsoft's new browser for Windows 95.

 http://www.microsoft.com/windows

Internet Phone ★★★
The program that may someday crush the phone companies.

 http://www.vocaltec.com

NCSA Mosaic ★★
The first graphical browser for the WWW, the newest version of NCSA's Mosaic is available here.

 http://www.ncsa.uiuc.edu/SDG/Software/Mosaic/NCSAMosaicHome.html

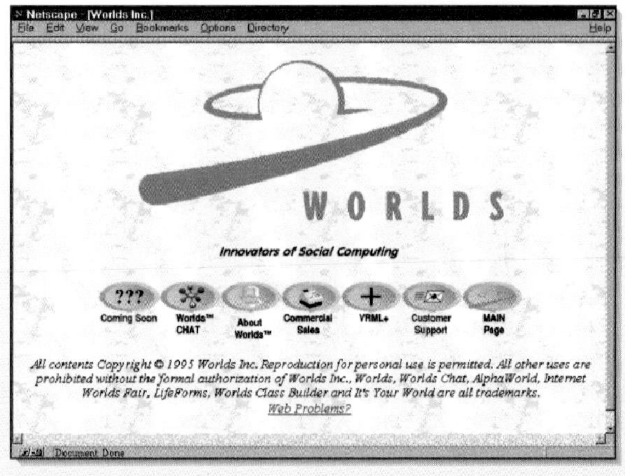

Netscape ★★★★★
The most popular Web browser is available here.

 http://www.netscape.com

RealAudio ★★★★
Get the RealAudio program and hear sound on the Internet live, without a delay.

 http://www.realaudio.com

WebFX ★★★
WebFX was one of the first 3-D browsers for Windows.

 http://www.paperinc.com

WebSpace ★★
Often referred to as the best 3-D browser currently available.

 http://www.cts.com/~template

Worlds Inc. ★★★

The new innovative 3-D Chat program is available here.

 http://www.worlds.net

Xing Technology ★

RealAudio's main competitor, Xing has developed audio and video without a delay.

 http://www.xingtech.com

INTERNET: RESOURCES

A Day in the Life of Cyberspace ★★

The first global portrait of human life in the digital age.

 http://www.1010.org

Blazin' Bookmark ★★

Each week, maranGraphics introduces you to one of the WWW's best sites.

 http://www.maran.com/surf.html

Cool Site of the Day ★★★★★

This popular site lists a new "cool" WWW site every day of the year.

 http://cool.infi.net

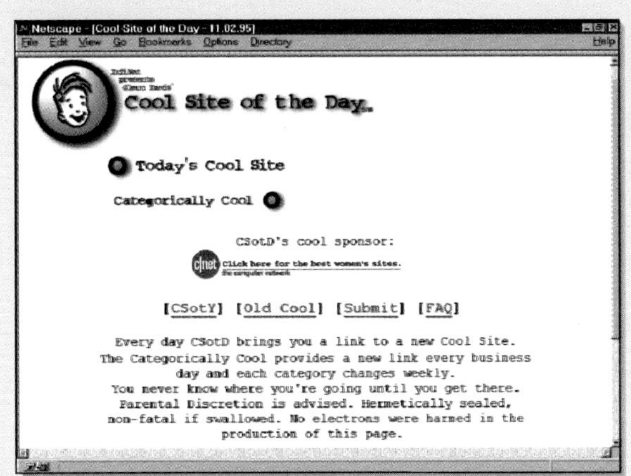

MG'S WEB SITE PICKS

Coolest Hostnames ★

Some of the stranger URLs on the Internet, like 'waiting@busstop.com'.

 http://homepage.seas.upenn.edu/~mengwong/coolhosts.html

Free Range Media ★★★

One of North America's top WWW design companies.

 http://www.freerange.com

Huge List ★

A list of sites in many categories, including shopping, computers and sports.

 http://thehugelist.com

INTERNET: RESOURCES (CONTINUED)

Internet Audit Bureau ★★

The IAB keeps track of the number of people who visit Web sites and provides lists of the most popular sites.

 http://www.internet-audit.com

Internet Town Hall ★

The Internet Town Hall has online radio stations, discussion groups and a place to send faxes over the Internet.

 http://town.hall.org

Mailing Lists ★★★

Browse through the available mailing lists at this WWW site.

 http://www.NeoSoft.com/internet/paml

Mirsky's Worst of the Web ★★★

Mirsky gives you his picks for the worst sites on the Web.

 http://turnpike.net/metro/mirsky/Worst.html

MIT Media Lab ★★★★

Find out where information technology is going.

 http://www.media.mit.edu

Peeping Tom Homepage ★★

Links to cameras that are connected to the Internet.

 http://www.ts.umu.se/~spaceman/camera.html

Point Communications ★★★

This company reviews and rates WWW sites.

http://www.pointcom.com

Spider's Pick of the Day ★★

Spider selects one excellent Web site every day.

 http://miso.wwa.com/~boba/pick2.html

JOBS

America's Job Bank ★

There are thousands of jobs posted here by employment offices across the country.

URL http://www.ajb.dni.us

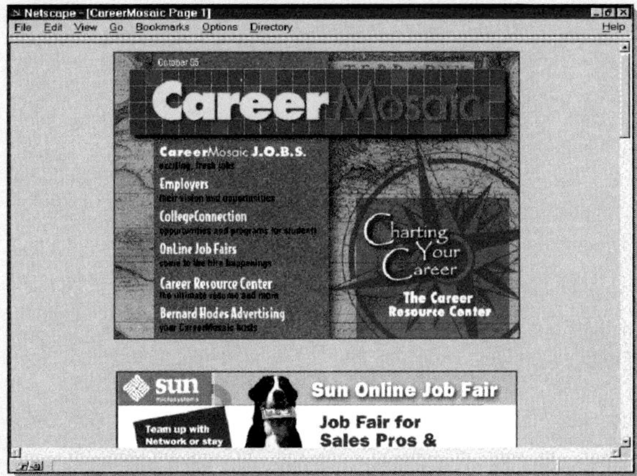

CareerMosaic ★★★★★

A collection of job postings from around the world.

URL http://www.careermosaic.com/cm

Computer Animation Jobs ★★★

Find the job of your dreams working in the cartoon or video game industry.

URL http://www.cinenet.net/GWEB/lists.html

Direct Marketing World Job Center ★★

Search for a job that's right for you.

URL http://mainsail.com/jobs.htm

E-Span Employment Database ★★★

Search for available jobs.

URL http://www.espan.com/cgi-bin/ewais

Heart ★

This site connects employers and job seekers around the world. A unique feature of Heart is virtual interviews.

URL http://www.career.com

Internet Job Information Center ★★

Browse through this collection of job postings.

URL http://tvp.com/vpjic.html

JobHunt ★★★

A list of online employment resources.

URL http://rescomp.stanford.edu/jobs.html

JOBS (CONTINUED)

Microsoft Employment ★★★

Browse through the available positions at Microsoft.

 http://www.microsoft.com/Jobs

NetJobs ★★★★

Add a job or look one up.

 http://www.netjobs.com:8000/index.html

MACINTOSH

Apple ★★★★★

At this site, you can find information on existing and upcoming products.

 http://www.apple.com

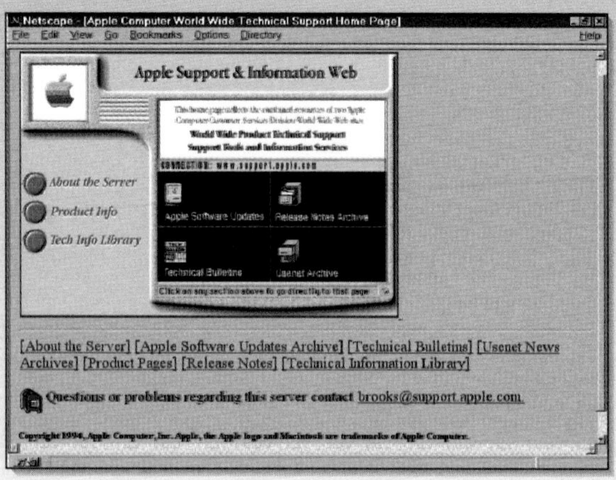

Apple Technical Support ★★

Get the latest Apple software updates here.

 http://www.support.apple.com

Claris ★

One of the best-known creators of Mac software.

 http://www.claris.com

eWorld on the Web ★

This site provides links to many interesting pages on the Web.

 http://www.eworld.com

Info-Mac HyperArchive ★★★

One of the largest collections of Mac files on the Internet.

 http://hyperarchive.lcs.mit.edu/HyperArchive.html

Macworld Online ★★★★

The online version of Macworld magazine.

 http://www.macworld.com

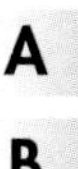

Power Mac Home Page ★★

The official site for information on the Power Macintosh computer.

 http://www.info.apple.com/ppc/ppchome.html

TidBits ★★★

A well-known Macintosh collection.

 http://www.dartmouth.edu/pages/TidBITS/TidBITS.html

Ultimate Mac Page ★★

This site claims to have everything a Mac user could need.

 http://www.freepress.com/myee/ultimate_mac.html

Well Connected Mac ★★★

A site with bits and pieces of everything from periodicals to a list of mailing lists and newsgroups.

 http://www.macfaq.com

MAGAZINES

2600 ★★★

A magazine dedicated to hacking and various other activities.

 http://www.2600.com

Addicted To Noise ★★★★★

One of the best magazines around, this music leader often gets the scoop before Rolling Stone and Vibe.

 http://www.addict.com/ATN

Blue Stocking ★★

The Internet's first feminist magazine.

 http://www.teleport.com/~bluesock

bOING bOING ★★★

This magazine is a blueprint for the flipside of serious culture.

 http://www.zeitgeist.net/Public/Boing-boing

MAGAZINES (CONTINUED)

Buzznet ★★
Buzznet is a "down-to-earth" electronic publication like no other.

 http://www.buzznet.com

URL http://140.174.80.57

Electronic Newsstand ★★★★
This site has excerpts from many popular magazines.

URL http://www.enews.com

E-TexT Listing ★
You can find many electronic magazines at this site.

URL http://www.etext.org/Zines

HotWired ★★★
The online edition of "Wired," the magazine dedicated to media, technology and pop culture.

URL http://www.hotwired.com

International Teletimes ★★★
This magazine run by teenagers in Vancouver, Japan and around the world has articles and links to other sites.

 http://www.wimsey.com/teletimes/teletimes_home_page.html

Internet World ★★★★
The online issues of Internet World magazine often have double the content of the print editions.

 http://www.iw.com

Mother Jones ★★
Mother Jones is a magazine dedicated to free thought and alternative ideas.

 http://www.mojones.com/motherjones.html

Pathfinder ★★★★★
This site includes excerpts from many magazines, including Time, People, Life and many more.

 http://www.pathfinder.com

Urban Desires ★
An interactive magazine of metropolitan passions.

 http://desires.com/issues.html

Word ★★★★
This electronic magazine covers a variety of issues and includes stories, news, graphics and animation.

 http://www.word.com

Ziff-Davis Interactive ★
Read excerpts from many popular computer magazines, including PC Magazine, Computer Shopper and MacUser, to name a few.

 http://www.ziff.com

MOVIES

007 ★
This site is dedicated to James Bond.

 http://www.mcs.net/~klast/www/bond.html

Alfred Hitchcock ★
Fans of "The Birds," "Vertigo" and "Psycho" should check out this site.

 http://nextdch.mty.itesm.mx/~plopezg/Kaplan/Hitchcock.html

Alliance Releasing ★★
The company behind many big movies and television shows.

 http://alliance.idirect.com

Buena Vista Pictures ★★
Check out the latest movies from Disney, Touchstone and Hollywood Pictures.

 http://bvp.wdp.com

MOVIES (CONTINUED)

Early Motion Pictures ★

A collection of some of the earliest films made in North America.

http://lcweb2.loc.gov/papr/mpixhome.html

Film.com ★★★

This site includes reviews of most major movies and videos.

http://www.film.com

Gigaplex ★★★

You will find dozens of interviews with Hollywood stars at this arts and entertainment site.

http://www.directnet.com/wow

Godzilla ★★★★

That's right, a site dedicated to the big green monster.

http://www.ama.caltech.edu/users/mrm/godzilla.html

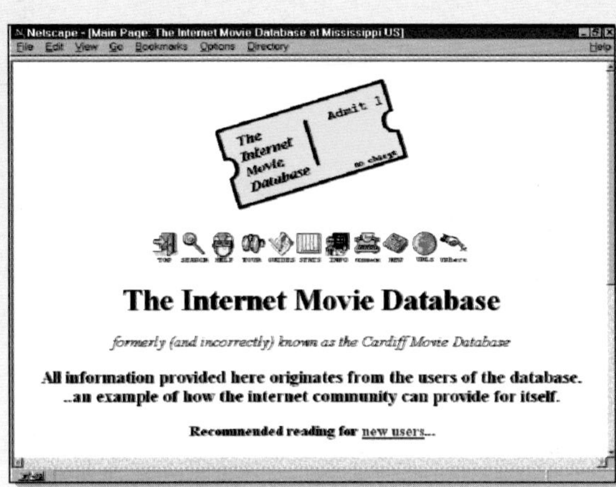

Hollywood Online ★★

A great source for information on the hottest movies and movie stars.

http://hollywood.com

Indiana Jones WWW Page ★★

A site dedicated to the fictional hero and his trusty whip.

http://dialin.ind.net/~msjohnso

Internet Movie Database ★★★★★

This enormous database provides information on all North American movies, big and small.

http://www.msstate.edu/Movies

MCA/Universal ★★★

View clips of several different MCA/Universal movies.

 http://www.mca.com

Movie Clichés List ★★★

A large collection of Hollywood clichés.

 http://www.well.com/user/vertigo/cliches.html

Mr. Showbiz ★★★★

This site provides excellent information on the latest films. This site was nominated "Cool Site of the Year."

 http://web3.starwave.com/showbiz

National Film Board of Canada ★★

This award-winning group has produced many well-known Canadian films.

 http://www.nfb.ca

Paramount ★★

Contains information on Paramount movies and television.

 http://www.paramount.com

Sony Movies ★★★★

Check out the latest films by Sony. You can find reviews, sound, video, photos and much more.

http://www.spe.sony.com/Pictures

Web Wide World of Film Music ★

Whether you create music for films or just enjoy listening to it, this site is for you.

http://www.filmmusic.com

INTERESTING WEB SITES

MUSEUMS

Andy Warhol Museum ★★★
A site dedicated to one of America's most famous artists.

 http://www.warhol.org/warhol

Computer Museum ★★
This museum is opening soon and will include interactive exhibits, a multimedia timeline of the history of computers and much more.

 http://www.net.org

Exploratorium ★★★
A museum of art, science and technology.

http://www.exploratorium.edu

Field Museum ★★
Browse through exhibits, learn about science and more.

http://www.bvis.uic.edu/museum

Internet Arts Museum for Free ★★★
Take a tour of the museum dedicated to art, music and literature.

http://www.rahul.net/iamfree

Leonardo da Vinci Museum ★★★★
This site is dedicated to the famous artist and engineer.

 http://www.leonardo.net/main.html

Live From Antarctica ★★★
This site is designed to show you what it is like to live in one of the coldest places on Earth.

 http://quest.arc.nasa.gov/livefrom/livefrom.html

Natural History Museum ★★
Get a taste of this British museum by previewing a few items online.

http://www.nhm.ac.uk

Ontario Science Centre ★★★
This site provides information on the Science Centre in Toronto, Canada.

http://www.osc.on.ca

Smithsonian ★★★★
You can read about the many exhibits at the Smithsonian Institute.

http://www.si.edu

United States Holocaust Memorial Museum ★★★
A museum dedicated to the Holocaust.

http://www.ushmm.org

Virtual Science Museum ★★
This is an interactive museum where you can take quizzes, listen to sound and watch movies.

http://sln.fi.edu

WebMuseum ★★★★★
The most well-known museum on the Internet.

http://www.emf.net/louvre

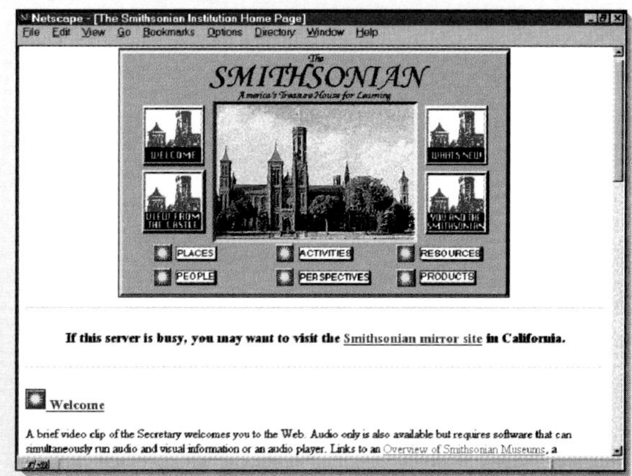

MUSIC

CD Now ★★
You can buy your CDs online at this site.

http://cdnow.com

DefJam ★★★★
One of North America's top hip-hop labels.

http://www.defjam.com/defjam

MUSIC (CONTINUED)

EMI Records ★★★

Find information on the latest artists, listen to unreleased songs and more at this site.

 http://www.rockonline.com/emi

Geffen/DGC Records ★★

This music label is grabbing more and more hot bands.

 http://geffen.com

Global Electronic Music Marketplace ★

A database of musical resources on the Internet.

 http://gemm.com

Guitar Net ★★★

This site offers great resources for guitar enthusiasts.

 http://www.guitar.net

Internet Underground Music Archive ★★★★

This site has become a big hit with experienced Internet users. It offers information on all types of music, from heavy metal to easy listening.

 http://www.iuma.com

Jazz Online ★★★

If you're not into grunge or rock music, Jazz Online offers a fresh alternative.

 http://www.jazzonln.com/JAZZ

Polygram ★★

Find information on your favorite band and even listen to sound clips.

 http://www.polygram.com/polygram

Rock and Roll Hall of Fame ★★★★★

This music museum in Cleveland has an A+ site.

 http://www.rockhall.com

Rocktropolis ★★

You can check out information on the world of rock music at this site.

URL http://underground.net/Rocktropolis

RockWeb ★★★

Information on rock artists and much more.

URL http://www.rock.net

Sony Online ★★★★

Read about Michael Jackson, Mariah Carey, Michael Bolton and lots of other artists.

URL http://www.sony.com

TicketMaster Online ★★★

Find out when your favorite band is coming to town.

URL U.S. http://www.ticketmaster.com

URL Canada http://www.ticketmaster.ca

Ultimate Band List ★★

Can't find the home page for Madonna or Simon & Garfunkel? Try here.

URL http://american.recordings.com/wwwofmusic/ubl/ubl.shtml

Warner Brothers Records ★★★

Like the Sony site, Warner lets you browse through information on your favorite artists.

URL http://www.iuma.com/warner

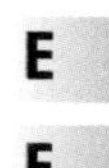

NEWS

ClariNet ★

A popular service that provides news via newsgroups.

URL http://www.clarinet.com

clnet Online ★★★

The online site of clnet, the weekly computer show on cable.

URL http://www.cnet.com

NEWS (CONTINUED)

CNN ★★★★★
CNN is one of the world's most popular all-news television networks. This site is full of articles, updates and video clips.

 http://www.cnn.com

Detroit News ★★★★
A great site for one of Detroit's largest papers. This site is updated daily.

 http://www.detnews.com

Electronic Telegraph ★
News from the UK and around the world.

 http://www.telegraph.co.uk

Nando Times ★
An online newspaper with all of the latest headlines.

 http://www2.nando.net/nt/nando.cgi

National Public Radio ★★
A schedule of news programming on National Public Radio.

URL http://www.npr.org

New York Times Fax ★★★
An online, condensed version of the New York Times.

URL http://nytimesfax.com

NewsPage ★★★★
NewsPage provides you with current, pre-sorted news across a broad array of topics and industries.

URL http://www.newspage.com

Newspaper and Periodical Room ★★
Find out which newspapers and periodicals are currently available at the Library of Congress.

URL http://lcweb.loc.gov/global/ncp/ncp.html

San Diego Source ★★
A newspaper that covers news "from a different perspective."

 http://www.sddt.com

San Jose Mercury News ★★★
The first large newspaper to go online, the Mercury News is still one of the best.

 http://www.sjmercury.com

Top 100 Newspapers ★★★
This great site provides links to the Top 100 newspapers in the country.

 http://www.interest.com/top100.html

United Media Comics ★★
Read comic strips that appear in newspapers nationwide.

 http://www.unitedmedia.com/comics

USA Today ★★★★
This site has all of the latest news and, for now, is offered for free to the public.

 http://www.usatoday.com

Yahoo Headlines ★★★
Up-to-the-minute news, entertainment, sports and much more.

http://www.yahoo.com/headlines/current

ORGANIZATIONS (NON-PROFIT)

America's Charities ★
A guide to charities nationwide.

 http://www.charities.org

Amnesty International ★★★★
An organization dedicated to protecting human rights.

 http://www.io.org/amnesty/overview.html

ORGANIZATIONS (NON-PROFIT) CONTINUED

Electronic Frontier Foundation ★★★
This organization is working to protect your rights online.

URL http://www.eff.org

Greenpeace ★★★★★
The most well-known environmental agency in the world.

URL http://www.greenpeace.org

Internet NonProfit Center ★★★
Provides access to information on non-profit organizations.

URL http://www.human.com:80/inc

KidsPeace ★★
The national center for kids in crisis.

URL http://www.kidspeace.org

Meta-Index for Non-Profit Organizations ★★★
A listing of non-profit organizations with sites on the Web.

URL http://www.duke.edu/~ptavern/Pete.meta-index.html

National Rifle Association ★★★
The NRA is really, really big on guns.

URL http://www.nra.org

Red Cross ★★★
Find out how the Red Cross is helping people around the world.

URL http://www.crossnet.org

Santa Claus and Company ★★★★
A few of Santa's more computer-literate elves have put up a Web site in the North Pole.

URL http://north.pole.org/santa

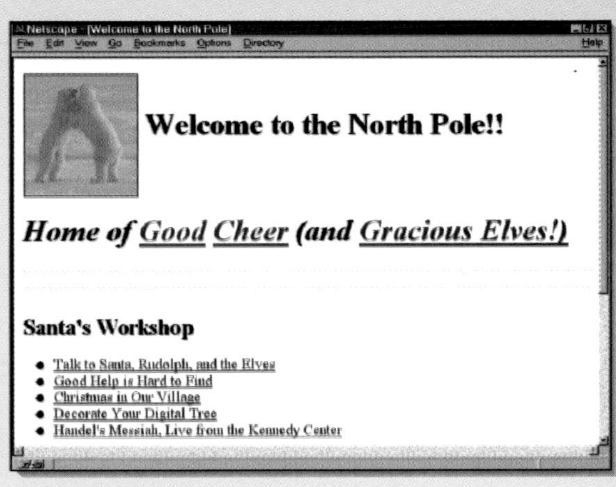

PHILOSOPHY

American Philosophical Association ★★
This site provides reference materials, information on conferences, links to other philosophy sites and more.

URL http://www.oxy.edu/apa/apa.html

EJAP ★★★
The Electronic Journal of Analytic Philosophy.

URL http://www.phil.indiana.edu/ejap/ejap.html

Environmental Ethics ★★★
This site gives you access to resources worldwide that focus on environmental philosophy.

URL http://www.cep.unt.edu

Noam Chomsky Archive ★★★
Information on philosopher Noam Chomsky and his work.

URL http://www.lbbs.org/archive/index.htm

URL http://www.worldmedia.com

Origins of Knowledge ★★
This site is about the evolution and anatomy of knowledge.

URL http://www.hsr.no/~onar/Ess/Origin.html

Philosophy Archive ★★★★★
Another great collection at Carnegie Mellon University.

URL http://english-www.hss.cmu.edu/philosophy.html

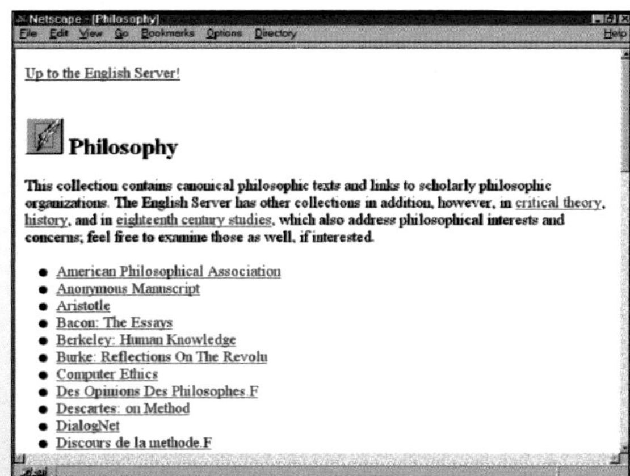

Religion and Philosophy Resources ★★★
A list of philosophy and religion sites on the Web.

URL http://web.bu.edu/LIBRARY/Religion/contents.html

PHYSICS

American Institute of Physics ★★★★★

The AIP is the best source for research information.

 http://www.aip.org

American Physical Society ★★★

Resources to discover what's hot in the world of physics.

 http://aps.org

Center for Astrophysics ★★

A list of astrophysics resources.

 http://cfa-www.harvard.edu

Holography ★★★

Holograms and other related information.

 http://www.holo.com/holo/gram.html

Laser Focus World ★★

A magazine dedicated to lasers—what will they think of next?

 http://www.lfw.com/WWW/home.html

Nuclear Physics Electronic ★

Find information and articles from nuclear physics journals at this site.

 http://www.nucphys.nl/www/pub/nucphys/npe.html

Physicists' Bill of Rights ★★

Humor in its most scientific form.

 http://www.brandonu.ca/~johannes/billorights.html

Physics Internet Resources ★★★★

What more is there to say?

 http://www.het.brown.edu/physics/index.html

Plasma Science and Technology ★★★

This site can help you find information on almost 200 different areas in plasma science and technology.

 http://www-plasma.umd.edu

SEG ★★

Find information on the Society of Exploration Geophysicists.

 http://sepwww.stanford.edu/seg

POETRY

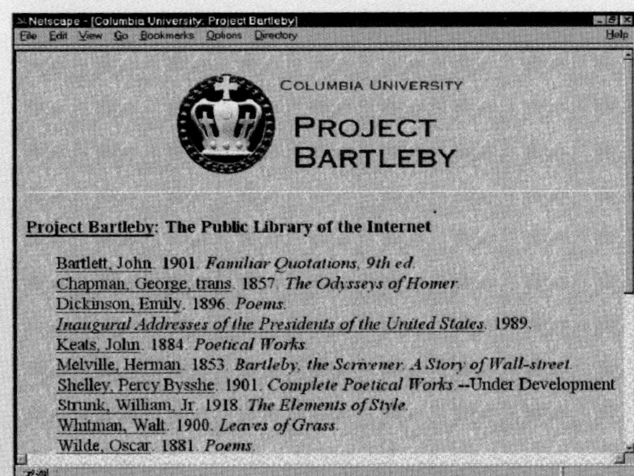

British Poetry ★

A collection of British poetry written between 1780 and 1910.

 http://www.lib.virginia.edu/etext/britpo/britpo.html

Electronic Poetry Center ★★★

A great place to read some poetry.

 http://wings.buffalo.edu/epc

English Poetry Server ★★★★★

Put up your feet, relax and enjoy reading poetry here.

 http://english-server.hss.cmu.edu/Poetry.html

Internet Poetry Archive ★★★

You can read poetry or listen to poets read their work at this site.

 http://sunsite.unc.edu/dykki/poetry/home.html

Poetry Reading Room ★★★

Poems chosen from thousands of submissions.

 http://www.coolsite.com/poetry.html

Poet's Park ★★

Read poems or check out other poetry sites on the Internet.

 http://www.soos.com/poetpark

POETRY (CONTINUED)

Project Bartleby ★★★★

A large collection of online poetry.

 http://www.columbia.edu/~svl2

Voice of the Prisoner ★★

Poetry and other creative works by people behind bars.

 http://clickshop.com/prisoner

RELIGION

Bible Gateway ★★★

Search the Bible in many different languages.

 http://www.gospelcom.net/bible

BuddhaNet ★

This site provides answers to common questions about Buddhism.

 http://www2.hawkesbury.uws.edu.au/BuddhaNet

Christ in the Desert ★★★

A group of monks in the Santa Fe desert have their own Web site.

 http://www.christdesert.org

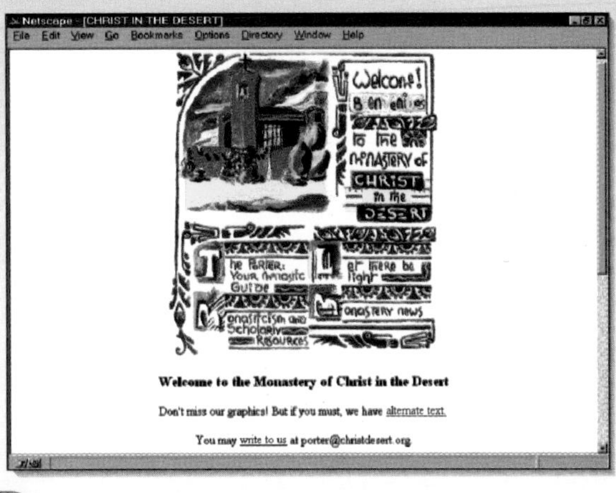

Christus Rex et Redemptor Mundi ★★★★★

A collection of Christian information and writings.

 http://www.christusrex.org

Finding God in Cyberspace ★★

A guide to all types of religious material on the Web.

 http://www.dur.ac.uk/~dth3maf/gresham.html

First Church Of Cyberspace ★★
People who are REALLY into their computers.

URL http://www.freenet.ufl.edu/ht-free/fcoc.html

GHEN ★★★
The Global Hindu Electronic Network provides information on Hindu culture and heritage.

URL http://rbhatnagar.csm.uc.edu:8080/hindu_universe.html

Islamic Resources ★★★
A directory of Islamic sites on the Web.

URL http://www.wam.umd.edu/~ibrahim

Jerusalem Mosaic ★
Take a virtual tour of Jerusalem.

URL http://www1.huji.ac.il/jeru/jerusalem.html

Library of God ★★
Many theological texts are available at this site.

URL http://convex.uky.edu/~rtcrit00/atemple.html

Scrolls From the Dead Sea ★★★★
Browse through an exhibit of ancient scrolls.

URL http://sunsite.unc.edu/expo/deadsea.scrolls.exhibit/intro.html

Secular Web ★★★★
A source of information for atheists.

URL http://freethought.tamu.edu

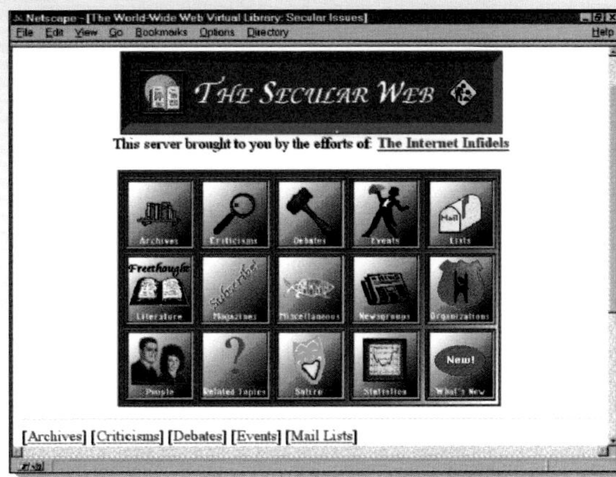

RELIGION (CONTINUED)

Shamash Home Page ★★★
A site dedicated to serving Jewish people on the Internet.

http://shamash.nysernet.org

Sikhism ★★★★
A guide to a popular Eastern religion.

http://www.io.org/~sandeep/sikhism.htm

SEARCH TOOLS

DejaNews ★★
A tool for searching newsgroup articles.

http://www.dejanews.com

Galaxy ★
An Internet directory with a smaller selection of topics than Yahoo.

http://www.einet.net

InfoSeek ★★★★
A commercial Internet search tool that offers free trial accounts.

http://www.infoseek.com

Inktomi ★
This search tool is small, but fast.

http://inktomi.berkeley.edu/query.html

Lycos ★★★★
Located at Carnegie Mellon University, this is one of the top Internet search tools in the world.

http://www.lycos.com

Open Text Index ★★★
A new search tool that uses leading edge technology.

http://www.opentext.com:8080

Point Communications ★★★

You can search through Point's ratings and reviews to find the best Web sites on a specific topic.

 http://www.pointcom.com

SavvySearch ★★

SavvySearch sends your inquiry to many different search tools around the world.

 http://www.cs.colostate.edu/~dreiling/smartform.html

Virtual Library ★★★

A catalog with a wide variety of Web sites.

 http://www.w3.org/hypertext/DataSources/bySubject/Overview.html

W3 Catalog ★★

A tool for searching the resources on the Web.

WebCrawler ★★★★

An Internet search tool sponsored by America Online.

http://www.webcrawler.com

What's New with NCSA Mosaic ★

NCSA lists most of the new sites on the Web and is updated 3 times a week.

http://www.ncsa.uiuc.edu/SDG/Software/Mosaic/Docs/whats-new.html

Whole Internet Catalog ★★

You can use this catalog to find sites that interest you.

http://gnn.com/wic/index.html

World Wide Web Worm ★

This search tool won a Best of the Web '94 award.

http://www.cs.colorado.edu/home/mcbryan/WWWW.html

SEARCH TOOLS (CONTINUED)

Yahoo! ★★★★★
The ever-popular Internet directory.

URL http://www.yahoo.com

Yecch! ★
A parody of Yahoo.

http://www.smartlink.net/~yeeeoww/yecch/yecchhome.html

SPORTS

1996 Olympic Site ★★★★
A great site offering information on every aspect of the 1996 Olympic Games.

http://www.atlanta.olympic.org

Broomball ★
All you ever wanted to know about broomball.

http://www.ozemail.com.au/~kshapley

CFL ★
At this site, you will find statistics, scores, schedules and much more.

URL http://www.cfl.ca

DiveNet ★★
World Wide Divers' Network.

http://divenet.com

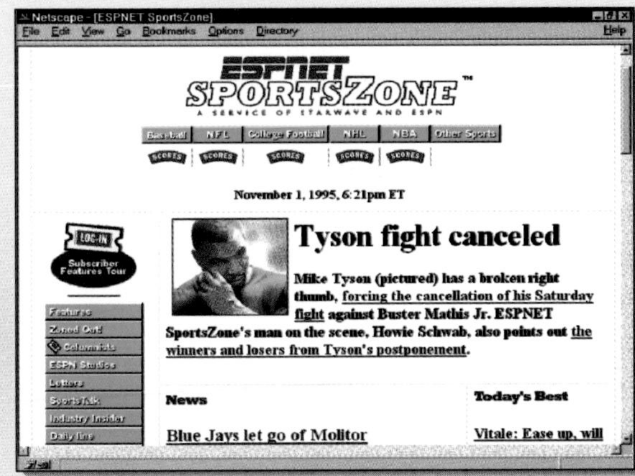

ESPNET SportsZone ★★★★★
This site provides all a sports fan could want: scores, pictures, schedules and more.

http://espnet.sportszone.com

GolfWeb ★★★
A complete golf information service.

http://www.golfweb.com

Michael Jordan Home Page ★★

This site is dedicated to the man who has worn the numbers 45 and 23 like no other.

URL http://gagme.wwa.com/~boba/mj.html

NBA ★

Find information on your favorite teams and players from the NBA.

URL http://www.nba.com

NFL ★★★

You can keep up-to-date on the latest scores while you surf the Net.

URL http://www.nflhome.com

NHL OPEN NET ★★

At this site, you will find schedules, contests and the latest news.

URL http://www.nhl.com

NHLPA ★★★★

The National Hockey League Players' Association provides statistics and information on players.

URL http://www.nhlpa.com

Skydive! ★

Like bungee jumping, but without the bungee.

URL http://www.afn.org/skydive

Sports Illustrated ★★★★

The online version of the famous magazine. And yes, there is an annual online swimsuit issue.

URL http://www.timeinc.com/si

SportSite ★

Several different forums on areas of sports such as cycling, skiing and camping.

URL http://www.sportsite.com

SPORTS (CONTINUED)

SportsLine USA ★★★
SportsLine provides scores and reports for your favorite sports.

URL http://www.sportsline.com

Sumo Information Page ★★
This site is dedicated to the ancient Japanese form of wrestling.

URL http://akebono.stanford.edu/~jerry/sumo

TSN ★★★★
After providing information about yourself, you can get scores and standings for many major sports.

URL http://www.tsn.ca

Ultimate Frisbee ★★
Learn about the new sport that combines basketball, football, soccer and frisbee.

URL http://www.cs.rochester.edu/u/ferguson/ultimate

Volleyball WorldWide ★★
Bump, set, spike, surf.

URL http://www.volleyball.org

World Whiffleball Server ★★
This site promotes the youthful sport of whiffleball.

URL http://conan.bedge.com/whiffleball

TELEVISION

Academy of Television Arts and Sciences ★
The official site of the Emmys.

URL http://www.emmys.org

Amazing Discoveries ★
The infomercials we can't resist.

URL http://www.AmazingDiscoveries.com

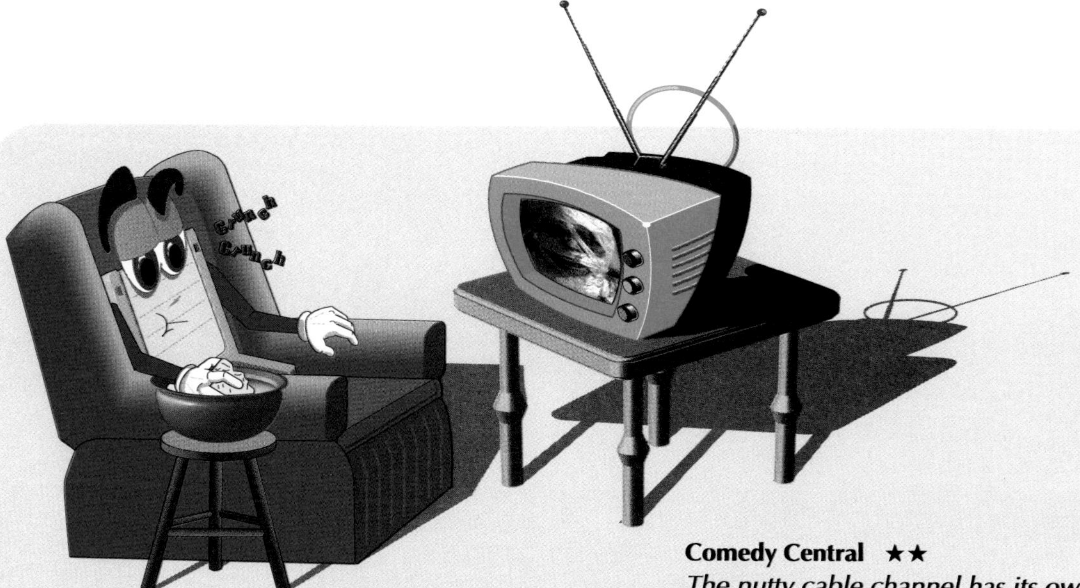

BBC ★★

Find out what the British are watching on TV and listening to on the radio.

URL http://www.bbc.co.uk

Bill Nye the Science Guy ★★

Learn about science the fun way—with Bill Nye.

URL http://www.seanet.com/Vendors/billnye/nyelabs.html

CBC ★★★

Find out what's on Canadian television and radio.

URL http://www.cbc.ca

CBS ★★★

CBS was the first of the three big networks to go online.

URL http://www.cbs.com

CNN ★★★★

CNN is one of the world's most popular all-news television networks. This site is full of articles, updates and video clips.

URL http://www.cnn.com

Comedy Central ★★

The nutty cable channel has its own Web site full of laughs.

URL http://www.comcentral.com

CourtTV ★★

All trials, all the time.

URL http://www.courttv.com

Discovery Channel ★★★

The Canadian and American branches of the Discovery Channel each have their own Web site.

URL U.S. http://www.discovery.com

URL Canada http://www.discovery.ca

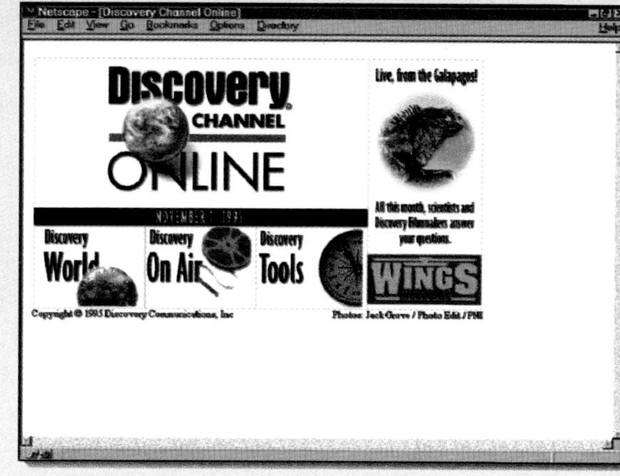

TELEVISION (CONTINUED)

FOX Broadcasting ★★★

This site has information on shows such as The X-Files, Melrose Place and The Simpsons.

URL http://www.foxnetwork.com

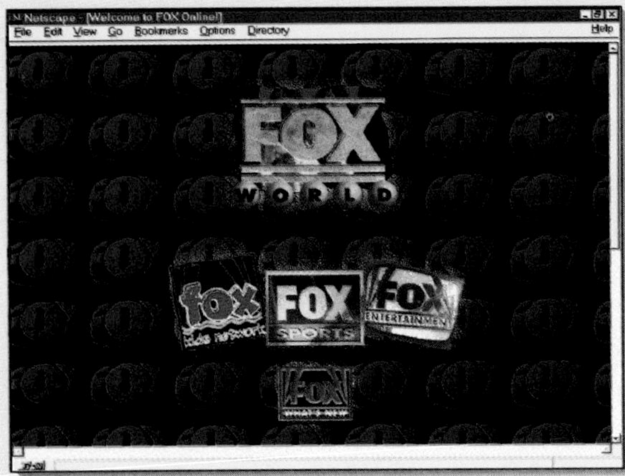

Late Show with David Letterman ★★★★

This site includes a collection of Dave's Top Ten lists.

URL http://www.cbs.com/lateshow

MTV Online ★

MTV's site provides great graphics and a schedule of programs.

URL http://www.mtv.com

MuchMusic ★

Canada's equivalent of MTV.

URL http://www.muchmusic.com/muchmusic.html

NBC ★★ 

Find information on popular NBC shows such as Frasier, Friends, Seinfeld and more.

URL http://www.nbc.com

PBS ★★★

Check out the latest programs, visit the online store and much more at this site.

URL http://www.pbs.org

QVC ★★

The home-shopping channel. QVC features a bus-ride theme with stops to visit the hosts and see the featured products of the week.

URL http://www.qvc.com

Ricki Lake ★

The official site for Ricki Lake's popular talk show.

URL http://www.spe.sony.com/Pictures/tv/rickilake/ricki.html

TV Bytes ★★★

A huge collection of television theme songs.

 http://www.parkhere.com/tvbytes

TV Net ★★★★★

A great site for couch potatoes.

 http://tvnet.com/TVnet.html

Ultimate TV List ★★★

If you are looking for a Web site for a particular program, look no further.

URL http://www.tvnet.com/UTVL

Weather Channel ★★

That's right. You read it correctly. The weather channel.

URL http://www.infi.net/weather

Sci-Fi Channel ★★

Nicknamed "The Dominion," this site has information on the Sci-Fi channel and science-fiction in general.

 http://www.scifi.com

Showtime Online ★★★

Find information, reviews and schedules for this large cable network.

URL http://showtimeonline.com

Simpsons Archive ★★★

Homer, Marge, Bart, Lisa and Maggie.

URL http://www.digimark.net/TheSimpsons/index.html

Star Trek On The Net ★★

A list of Star Trek sites on the Internet.

URL http://Grimmy.cnidr.org/star_trek_resources.html

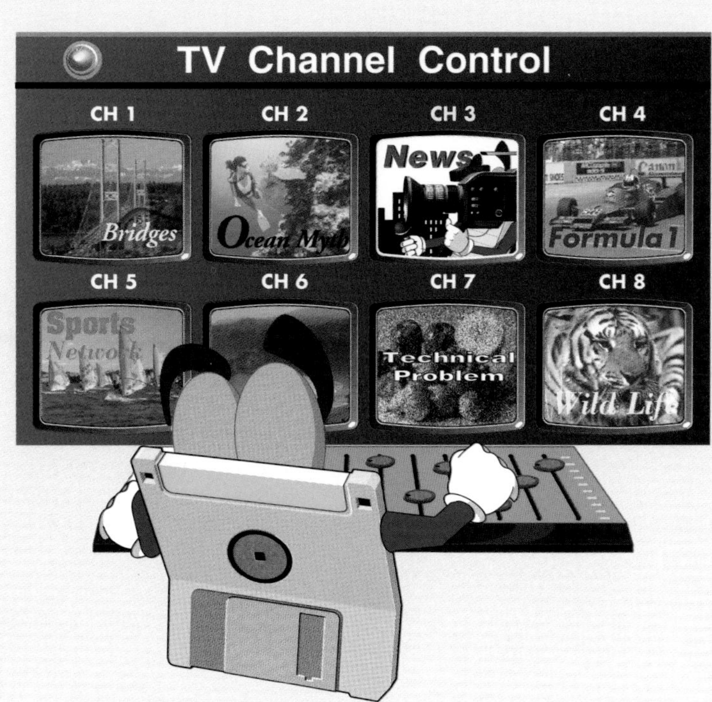

TELEVISION (CONTINUED)

What's on TV Right Now! ★

Find out what you're missing while you're surfing the Internet.

 http://www.star.niu.edu/jeff/tv/tv.cgi

X-Files ★★★

This popular television show has many sites on the Web with pictures, sound and information.

http://www.delphi.com/XFiles

http://www.neosoft.com/sbanks/xfiles/xfiles.html

http://www.rutgers.edu/x-files.html

THEATER

ActNow! ★

An online talent agency.

 http://www.i-corp.com/actnow

Drama Server ★★★

Located at Carnegie Mellon University, this is a great directory of plays, screenplays and discussions.

 http://english-www.hss.cmu.edu/drama.html

Dramatic Exchange ★★★

A place to review the works of playwrights.

http://www.cco.caltech.edu/~rknop/dramex.html

Gilbert & Sullivan Archive ★★★

Find information on musicals like H.M.S. Pinafore.

 http://diamond.idbsu.edu/gas/GaS.html

Les Misérables ★★★

This site has information about the musical based on the famous French novel.

 http://www.ot.com/lesmis

On Broadway ★★

A list of the shows currently playing in the Big Apple.

 http://artsnet.heinz.cmu.edu:80/OnBroadway

Playbill Online ★★★★

A great source of theater news, information and trivia from the company that creates the programs for most Broadway shows.

URL http://www.webcom.com/~broadway

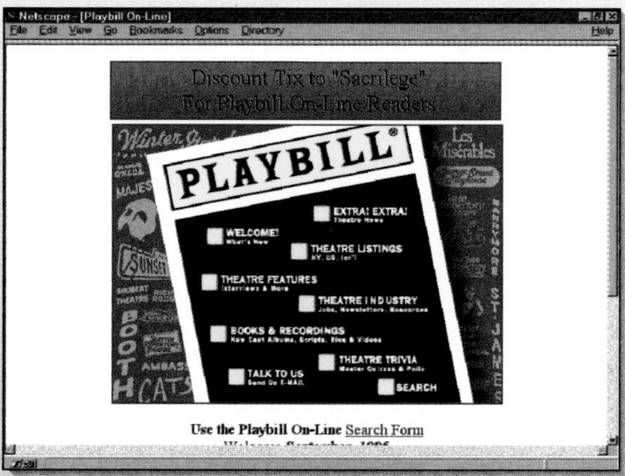

Screenwriters & Playwrights ★★

All kinds of resources for all kinds of writers.

http://www.teleport.com/~cdeemer/scrwriter.html

Shakespeare Web ★★★★

A good place to start if you want to learn more about Shakespeare.

http://www.shakespeare.com

Steven Sondheim Stage ★★★

The man and his music.

http://www.innocence.com/sondheim

Talent Network ★★

An online talent agency.

http://www.talentnet.com

Theatre Central ★★★★★

An up-to-date site dedicated to theatre on the Internet.

http://www.mit.edu:8001/people/quijote/theatre-central.html

TRAVEL

American Airlines ★★

Find flight schedules, information and much more at this site.

http://www.amrcorp.com

Condé Nast Traveler ★★★★★

A guide to trips around the world.

http://www.cntraveler.com

TRAVEL (CONTINUED)

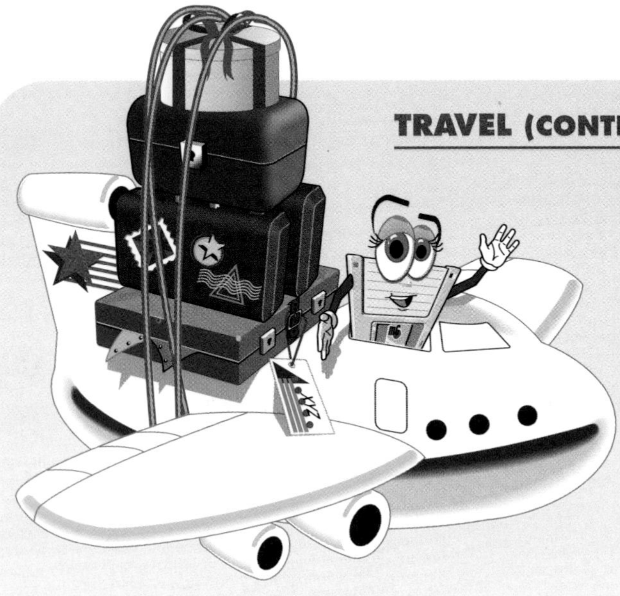

Southwest Airlines ★★
Find information on the cities Southwest flies to, learn how to pack smart and more at this site.

 http://www.iflyswa.com

Subway Navigator ★★★
How to get from A to B via the subway in over 50 cities around the world.

 http://metro.jussieu.fr:10001/bin/cities/english

Switzerland ★★★
Information on the land known for its neutrality.

 http://heiwww.unige.ch/switzerland

Travel Advisories ★★
This site provides travel information for countries around the world. It also lets you know which countries to avoid due to disease, war and natural disasters.

 http://www.stolaf.edu/network/travel-advisories.html

Travel Channel ★★★★
Browse the globe with a click of a button.

 http://www.travelchannel.com

Travel Weekly ★★★
Information on destinations in the U.S. and around the world.

 http://www.traveler.net

TravelEZ ★★
A guide to travel information on the Internet.

 http://www.travelez.com

Web Travel Review ★★
First-hand accounts from people who have travelled to countries around the world.

 http://webtravel.org/webtravel

WWW Travel Guide ★★★★
Find travel information for destinations around the world. This site also features a special guide to the 1996 Olympics.

 http://www.infohub.com

WINDOWS

Consummate Winsock Apps List ★★★★

The place to check out the latest Internet programs for Windows 95.

 http://cwsapps.texas.net/win95.html

Microsoft ★★★★★

The giant company behind Windows.

 http://www.microsoft.com

Microsoft Network ★★★

Information on The Microsoft Network and the Internet.

 http://www.msn.com

Microsoft Windows 95 ★★★

This site has news, support, tips and programs for Windows 95.

 http://www.windows.microsoft.com

Randy's Windows 95 Resource Center ★★

Randy (whoever he is) has some tips and tricks for Windows 95.

URL http://www.cris.com/~randybrg/win95.html

Win 95 Net ★★★

Articles and discussions about Windows 95.

URL http://www.pcix.com/win95/win95home.html

Windows 95 Tech Support ★★

The place to go if you are having problems with Windows 95.

URL http://www.windows.microsoft.com/windows/techsup.htm

Windows Software ★★★

Where to find Windows software on the Internet.

URL http://www.nova.edu/Inter-Links/software/windows.html

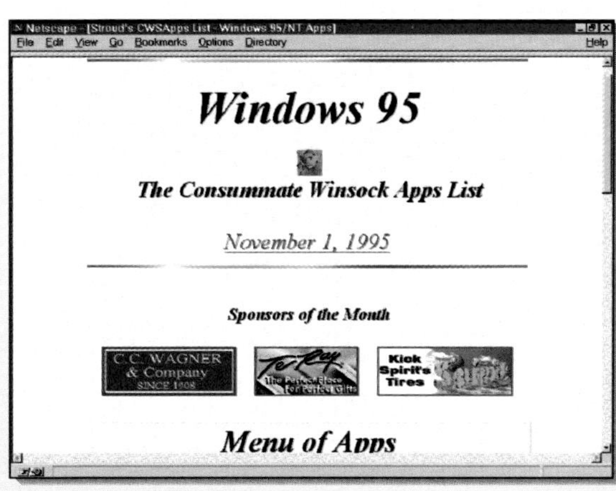

INDEX

INDEX

O

P

Q

R

S

INDEX

Y

The fun & easy way to learn about computers and more!

SUPER STAR

Windows 3.1 For Dummies,™ 2nd Edition
by Andy Rathbone

ISBN: 1-56884-182-5
$16.95 USA/$22.95 Canada

SUPER STAR

MORE Windows For Dummies™
by Andy Rathbone

ISBN: 1-56884-048-9
$19.95 USA/$26.95 Canada

SUPER STAR

DOS For Dummies,® 2nd Edition
by Dan Gookin

ISBN: 1-878058-75-4
$16.95 USA/$22.95 Canada

IX FINALIST Ninth Annual Computer Press Awards 1993

The Internet For Dummies™
by John Levine & Carol Baroudi

ISBN: 1-56884-024-1
$19.95 USA/$26.95 Canada

NATIONAL BESTSELLER!

Personal Finance For Dummies™
by Eric Tyson

ISBN: 1-56884-150-7
$16.95 USA/$22.95 Canada

VIII FINALIST Eighth Annual Computer Press Awards 1992

PCs For Dummies,™ 2nd Edition
by Dan Gookin & Andy Rathbone

ISBN: 1-56884-078-0
$16.95 USA/$22.95 Canada

SUPER STAR

Macs For Dummies,™ 2nd Edition
by David Pogue

ISBN: 1-56884-051-9
$19.95 USA/$26.95 Canada

Here's a complete listing of IDG's...*For Dummies* Titles

Title	Author	ISBN #	Price
DATABASE			
Access 2 For Dummies™	by Scott Palmer	ISBN: 1-56884-090-X	$19.95 USA/$26.95 Canada
Access Programming For Dummies™	by Rob Krumm	ISBN: 1-56884-091-8	$19.95 USA/$26.95 Canada
Approach 3 For Windows For Dummies™	by Doug Lowe	ISBN: 1-56884-233-3	$19.99 USA/$26.99 Canada
dBASE For DOS For Dummies™	by Scott Palmer & Michael Stabler	ISBN: 1-56884-188-4	$19.95 USA/$26.95 Canada
dBASE For Windows For Dummies™	by Scott Palmer	ISBN: 1-56884-179-5	$19.95 USA/$26.95 Canada
dBASE 5 For Windows Programming For Dummies™	by Ted Coombs & Jason Coombs	ISBN: 1-56884-215-5	$19.99 USA/$26.99 Canada
FoxPro 2.6 For Windows For Dummies™	by John Kaufeld	ISBN: 1-56884-187-6	$19.95 USA/$26.95 Canada
Paradox 5 For Windows For Dummies™	by John Kaufeld	ISBN: 1-56884-185-X	$19.95 USA/$26.95 Canada
DESKTOP PUBLISHING/ILLUSTRATION/GRAPHICS			
CorelDRAW! 5 For Dummies™	by Deke McClelland	ISBN: 1-56884-157-4	$19.95 USA/$26.95 Canada
CorelDRAW! For Dummies™	by Deke McClelland	ISBN: 1-56884-042-X	$19.95 USA/$26.95 Canada
Harvard Graphics 2 For Windows For Dummies™	by Roger C. Parker	ISBN: 1-56884-092-6	$19.95 USA/$26.95 Canada
PageMaker 5 For Macs For Dummies™	by Galen Gruman & Deke McClelland	ISBN: 1-56884-178-7	$19.95 USA/$26.95 Canada
PageMaker 5 For Windows For Dummies™	by Deke McClelland & Galen Gruman	ISBN: 1-56884-160-4	$19.95 USA/$26.95 Canada
QuarkXPress 3.3 For Dummies™	by Galen Gruman & Barbara Assadi	ISBN: 1-56884-217-1	$19.99 USA/$26.99 Canada
FINANCE/PERSONAL FINANCE/TEST TAKING REFERENCE			
QuickBooks "X" For Dummies™	by Stephen L. Nelson	ISBN: 1-56884-227-9	$19.99 USA/$26.99 Canada
Quicken "X" For DOS For Dummies™, 2nd Edition	by Stephen L. Nelson	ISBN: 1-56884-210-4	$19.95 USA/$26.95 Canada
Quicken "X" For Macs For Dummies™	by Stephen L. Nelson	ISBN: 1-56884-211-2	$19.95 USA/$26.95 Canada
Quicken "X" For Windows For Dummies™, 2nd Edition	by Stephen L. Nelson	ISBN: 1-56884-209-0	$19.95 USA/$26.95 Canada
The SAT I For Dummies™	by Suzee Vlk	ISBN: 1-56884-213-9	$14.99 USA/$20.99 Canada
TurboTax For Windows For Dummies™	by Gail A. Perry, CPA	ISBN: 1-56884-228-7	$19.99 USA/$26.99 Canada
GROUPWARE/INTEGRATED			
Lotus Notes 3.0/3.1 For Dummies™	by Paul Freeland & Stephen Londergan	ISBN: 1-56884-212-0	$19.95 USA/$26.95 Canada
Microsoft Office 4 For Windows For Dummies™	by Roger C. Parker	ISBN: 1-56884-183-3	$19.95 USA/$26.95 Canada
Microsoft Works For Windows 3 For Dummies™	by David C. Kay	ISBN: 1-56884-214-7	$19.99 USA/$26.99 Canada

FOR MORE INFO OR TO ORDER, PLEASE CALL ▸ 800 . 762 . 2974 For volume discounts & special orders please call Tony Real, Special Sales, at 415. 312. 0644

DUMMIES PRESS

Title	Author	ISBN #	Price
INTERNET/COMMUNICATIONS/NETWORKING			
CompuServe For Dummies™	by Wallace Wang	ISBN: 1-56884-181-7	$19.95 USA/$26.95 Canada
Modems For Dummies™, 2nd Edition	by Tina Rathbone	ISBN: 1-56884-223-6	$19.99 USA/$26.99 Canada
Modems For Dummies™	by Tina Rathbone	ISBN: 1-56884-001-2	$19.95 USA/$26.95 Canada
MORE Internet For Dummies™	by John Levine & Margaret Levine Young	ISBN: 1-56884-164-7	$19.95 USA/$26.95 Canada
NetWare For Dummies™	by Ed Tittel & Deni Connor	ISBN: 1-56884-003-9	$19.95 USA/$26.95 Canada
Networking For Dummies™	by Doug Lowe	ISBN: 1-56884-079-9	$19.95 USA/$26.95 Canada
ProComm Plus 2 For Windows For Dummies™	by Wallace Wang	ISBN: 1-56884-219-8	$19.99 USA/$26.99 Canada
The Internet Help Desk For Dummies™	by John Kaufeld	ISBN: 1-56884-238-4	$16.99 USA/$22.99 Canada
The3 Internet For Dummies™, 2nd Edition	by John Levine & Carol Baroudi	ISBN: 1-56884-222-8	$19.99 USA/$26.99 Canada
The Internet For Macs For Dummies™	by Charles Seiter	ISBN: 1-56884-184-1	$19.95 USA/$26.95 Canada
MACINTOSH			
Mac Programming For Dummies™	by Dan Parks Sydow	ISBN: 1-56884-173-6	$19.95 USA/$26.95 Canada
Macintosh System 7.5 For Dummies™	by Bob LeVitus	ISBN: 1-56884-197-3	$19.95 USA/$26.95 Canada
MORE Macs For Dummies™	by David Pogue	ISBN: 1-56884-087-X	$19.95 USA/$26.95 Canada
PageMaker 5 For Macs For Dummies™	by Galen Gruman & Deke McClelland	ISBN: 1-56884-178-7	$19.95 USA/$26.95 Canada
QuarkXPress 3.3 For Dummies™	by Galen Gruman & Barbara Assadi	ISBN: 1-56884-217-1	$19.99 USA/$26.99 Canada
Upgrading and Fixing Macs For Dummies™	by Kearney Rietmann & Frank Higgins	ISBN: 1-56884-189-2	$19.95 USA/$26.95 Canada
MULTIMEDIA			
Multimedia & CD-ROMs For Dummies™, Interactive Multimedia Value Pack	by Andy Rathbone	ISBN: 1-56884-225-2	$29.95 USA/$39.95 Canada
Multimedia & CD-ROMs For Dummies™	by Andy Rathbone	ISBN: 1-56884-089-6	$19.95 USA/$26.95 Canada
OPERATING SYSTEMS/DOS			
MORE DOS For Dummies™	by Dan Gookin	ISBN: 1-56884-046-2	$19.95 USA/$26.95 Canada
S.O.S. For DOS™	by Katherine Murray	ISBN: 1-56884-043-8	$12.95 USA/$16.95 Canada
OS/2 For Dummies™	by Andy Rathbone	ISBN: 1-878058-76-2	$19.95 USA/$26.95 Canada
UNIX			
UNIX For Dummies™	by John Levine & Margaret Levine Young	ISBN: 1-878058-58-4	$19.95 USA/$26.95 Canada
WINDOWS			
S.O.S. For Windows™	by Katherine Murray	ISBN: 1-56884-045-4	$12.95 USA/$16.95 Canada
Windows "X" For Dummies™, 3rd Edition	by Andy Rathbone	ISBN: 1-56884-240-6	$19.99 USA/$26.99 Canada
PCS/HARDWARE			
Illustrated Computer Dictionary For Dummies™	by Dan Gookin, Wally Wang, & Chris Van Buren	ISBN: 1-56884-004-7	$12.95 USA/$16.95 Canada
Upgrading and Fixing PCs For Dummies™	by Andy Rathbone	ISBN: 1-56884-002-0	$19.95 USA/$26.95 Canada
PRESENTATION/AUTOCAD			
AutoCAD For Dummies™	by Bud Smith	ISBN: 1-56884-191-4	$19.95 USA/$26.95 Canada
PowerPoint 4 For Windows For Dummies™	by Doug Lowe	ISBN: 1-56884-161-2	$16.95 USA/$22.95 Canada
PROGRAMMING			
Borland C++ For Dummies™	by Michael Hyman	ISBN: 1-56884-162-0	$19.95 USA/$26.95 Canada
"Borland's New Language Product" For Dummies™	by Neil Rubenking	ISBN: 1-56884-200-7	$19.95 USA/$26.95 Canada
C For Dummies™	by Dan Gookin	ISBN: 1-878058-78-9	$19.95 USA/$26.95 Canada
C++ For Dummies™	by S. Randy Davis	ISBN: 1-56884-163-9	$19.95 USA/$26.95 Canada
Mac Programming For Dummies™	by Dan Parks Sydow	ISBN: 1-56884-173-6	$19.95 USA/$26.95 Canada
QBasic Programming For Dummies™	by Douglas Hergert	ISBN: 1-56884-093-4	$19.95 USA/$26.95 Canada
Visual Basic "X" For Dummies™, 2nd Edition	by Wallace Wang	ISBN: 1-56884-230-9	$19.99 USA/$26.99 Canada
Visual Basic 3 For Dummies™	by Wallace Wang	ISBN: 1-56884-076-4	$19.95 USA/$26.95 Canada
SPREADSHEET			
1-2-3 For Dummies™	by Greg Harvey	ISBN: 1-878058-60-6	$16.95 USA/$22.95 Canada
1-2-3 For Windows 5 For Dummies™, 2nd Edition	by John Walkenbach	ISBN: 1-56884-216-3	$16.95 USA/$22.95 Canada
1-2-3 For Windows For Dummies™	by John Walkenbach	ISBN: 1-56884-052-7	$16.95 USA/$22.95 Canada
Excel 5 For Macs For Dummies™	by Greg Harvey	ISBN: 1-56884-186-8	$19.95 USA/$26.95 Canada
Excel For Dummies™, 2nd Edition	by Greg Harvey	ISBN: 1-56884-050-0	$16.95 USA/$22.95 Canada
MORE Excel 5 For Windows For Dummies™	by Greg Harvey	ISBN: 1-56884-207-4	$19.95 USA/$26.95 Canada
Quattro Pro 6 For Windows For Dummies™	by John Walkenbach	ISBN: 1-56884-174-4	$19.95 USA/$26.95 Canada
Quattro Pro For DOS For Dummies™	by John Walkenbach	ISBN: 1-56884-023-3	$16.95 USA/$22.95 Canada
UTILITIES			
Norton Utilities 8 For Dummies™	by Beth Slick	ISBN: 1-56884-166-3	$19.95 USA/$26.95 Canada
VCRS/CAMCORDERS			
VCRs & Camcorders For Dummies™	by Andy Rathbone & Gordon McComb	ISBN: 1-56884-229-5	$14.99 USA/$20.99 Canada
WORD PROCESSING			
Ami Pro For Dummies™	by Jim Meade	ISBN: 1-56884-049-7	$19.95 USA/$26.95 Canada
More Word For Windows 6 For Dummies™	by Doug Lowe	ISBN: 1-56884-165-5	$19.95 USA/$26.95 Canada
MORE WordPerfect 6 For Windows For Dummies™	by Margaret Levine Young & David C. Kay	ISBN: 1-56884-206-6	$19.95 USA/$26.95 Canada
MORE WordPerfect 6 For DOS For Dummies™	by Wallace Wang, edited by Dan Gookin	ISBN: 1-56884-047-0	$19.95 USA/$26.95 Canada
S.O.S. For WordPerfect™	by Katherine Murray	ISBN: 1-56884-053-5	$12.95 USA/$16.95 Canada
Word 6 For Macs For Dummies™	by Dan Gookin	ISBN: 1-56884-190-6	$19.95 USA/$26.95 Canada
Word For Windows 6 For Dummies™	by Dan Gookin	ISBN: 1-56884-075-6	$16.95 USA/$22.95 Canada
Word For Windows 2 For Dummies™	by Dan Gookin	ISBN: 1-878058-86-X	$16.95 USA/$22.95 Canada
WordPerfect 6 For Dummies™	by Dan Gookin	ISBN: 1-878058-77-0	$16.95 USA/$22.95 Canada
WordPerfect For Dummies™	by Dan Gookin	ISBN: 1-878058-52-5	$16.95 USA/$22.95 Canada
WordPerfect For Windows For Dummies™	by Margaret Levine Young & David C. Kay	ISBN: 1-56884-032-2	$16.95 USA/$22.95 Canada

FOR MORE INFO OR TO ORDER, PLEASE CALL ▸ 800 . 762 . 2974 For volume discounts & special orders please call Tony Real, Special Sales, at 415. 312. 0644

The Proven 3-D Visual Approach to Learning Computers In A Handy NEW Pocket Size

Windows 95 Visual PocketGuide

ISBN 1-56884-661-4
$14.99 USA/£13.99 UK

Windows 3.1 Visual PocketGuide

ISBN 1-56884-650-9
$14.99 USA/£13.99 UK

Excel 5 For Windows Visual PocketGuide

ISBN 1-56884-667-3
$14.99 USA/£13.99 UK

Word 6 For Windows Visual PocketGuide

ISBN 1-56884-666-5
$14.99 USA/£13.99 UK

WordPerfect 6.1 For Windows Visual PocketGuide

ISBN 1-56884-668-1
$14.99 USA/£13.99 UK

Lotus 1-2-3 R5 For Windows Visual PocketGuide

ISBN 1-56884-671-1
$14.99 USA/£13.99 UK

This is what reviewers are saying about our books...

"We recommend them for any novice 10-90 and for school use, too."
—Franklynn Peterson & Judi K-Turkel, *The Business Computer® Syndicated Column*

"It's the easiest book on computers I've ever used."
—M.L. Podolsky, *BUYLine*

"Your book is the FIRST one I can understand and easily follow along."
—Jim Davis, *Satisfied User #899,043*

FOR 3-D VISUAL CORPORATE ORDERS, PLEASE CALL: 800 469 6616 ext. 206

ORDER FORM

TRADE & INDIVIDUAL ORDERS

Phone: **(800) 762-2974**
or **(317) 895-5200**
(8 a.m.–6 p.m., CST, weekdays)
FAX : **(317) 895-5298**

EDUCATIONAL ORDERS & DISCOUNTS

Phone: **(800) 434-2086**
(8:30 a.m.–5:00 p.m., CST, weekdays)
FAX : **(817) 251-8174**

CORPORATE ORDERS FOR 3-D VISUAL™ SERIES

Phone: **(800) 469-6616** *ext.* **206**
(8 a.m.–5 p.m., EST, weekdays)
FAX : **(905) 890-9434**

Qty	ISBN	Title	Price	Total

Shipping & Handling Charges

	Description	First book	Each add'l. book	Total
Domestic	Normal	$4.50	$1.50	$
	Two Day Air	$8.50	$2.50	$
	Overnight	$18.00	$3.00	$
International	Surface	$8.00	$8.00	$
	Airmail	$16.00	$16.00	$
	DHL Air	$17.00	$17.00	$

Subtotal ______________

CA residents add applicable sales tax ______________

IN, MA and MD residents add 5% sales tax ______________

IL residents add 6.25% sales tax ______________

RI residents add 7% sales tax ______________

TX residents add 8.25% sales tax ______________

Shipping ______________

Total ______________

Ship to:

Name ______________________________

Address ______________________________

Company ______________________________

City/State/Zip ______________________________

Daytime Phone ______________________________

Payment: ☐ Check to IDG Books (US Funds Only)
☐ Visa ☐ Mastercard ☐ American Express

Card # ______________ Exp. ________ Signature ______________________

IDG BOOKS WORLDWIDE REGISTRATION CARD

RETURN THIS
REGISTRATION CARD
FOR FREE CATALOG

Title of this book: Internet and the World Wide Web Simplified

My overall rating of this book: ❑ Very good [1] ❑ Good [2] ❑ Satisfactory [3] ❑ Fair [4] ❑ Poor [5]

How I first heard about this book:

❑ Found in bookstore; name: [6] ______ ❑ Book review: [7] ______

❑ Advertisement: [8] ______ ❑ Catalog: [9] ______

❑ Word of mouth; heard about book from friend, co-worker, etc.: [10] ______ ❑ Other: [11] ______

What I liked most about this book: ______

What I would change, add, delete, etc., in future editions of this book: ______

Other comments: ______

Number of computer books I purchase in a year: ❑ 1 [12] ❑ 2-5 [13] ❑ 6-10 [14] ❑ More than 10 [15]

I would characterize my computer skills as: ❑ Beginner [16] ❑ Intermediate [17] ❑ Advanced [18] ❑ Professional [19]

I use ❑ DOS [20] ❑ Windows [21] ❑ OS/2 [22] ❑ Unix [23] ❑ Macintosh [24] ❑ Other: [25] ______ (please specify)

I would be interested in new books on the following subjects:
(please check all that apply, and use the spaces provided to identify specific software)

❑ Word processing: [26] ______ ❑ Spreadsheets: [27] ______

❑ Data bases: [28] ______ ❑ Desktop publishing: [29] ______

❑ File Utilities: [30] ______ ❑ Money management: [31] ______

❑ Networking: [32] ______ ❑ Programming languages: [33] ______

❑ Other: [34] ______

I use a PC at (please check all that apply): ❑ home [35] ❑ work [36] ❑ school [37] ❑ other: [38] ______

The disks I prefer to use are ❑ 5.25 [39] ❑ 3.5 [40] ❑ other: [41] ______

I have a CD ROM: ❑ yes [42] ❑ no [43]

I plan to buy or upgrade computer hardware this year: ❑ yes [44] ❑ no [45]

I plan to buy or upgrade computer software this year: ❑ yes [46] ❑ no [47]

Name: ______ Business title: [48] ______ Type of Business: [49] ______

Address (❑ home [50] ❑ work [51]/Company name: ______)

Street/Suite# ______

City [52]/State [53]/Zipcode [54]: ______ Country [55] ______

❑ **I liked this book!** You may quote me by name in future IDG Books Worldwide promotional materials.

My daytime phone number is ______

IDG BOOKS
THE WORLD OF COMPUTER KNOWLEDGE

❑ YES!

Please keep me informed about IDG's World of Computer Knowledge.
Send me the latest IDG Books catalog.

BUSINESS REPLY MAIL

FIRST CLASS MAIL PERMIT NO. 2605 FOSTER CITY, CALIFORNIA

IDG Books Worldwide
919 E Hillsdale Blvd, STE 400
Foster City, CA 94404-9691